*Our Lady
of the Lost
and
Found*

Also by Diane Schoemperlen

Forms of Devotion

In the Language of Love

Hockey Night in Canada and Other Stories

The Man of My Dreams

Hockey Night in Canada

Frogs and Other Stories

Double Exposures

Red Plaid Shirt

DIANE SCHOEMPERLEN

Our Lady of the Lost and Found

A Novel

A Phyllis Bruce Book
HarperPerennialCanada
HarperCollinsPublishersLtd

Our Lady of the Lost and Found

Copyright © 2001 by Diane Schoemperlen.

For information address:
HarperCollins Publishers Ltd.,
55 Avenue Road, Suite 2900,
Toronto, Ontario, Canada M5R 3L2

www.harpercanada.com

HarperCollins books may be purchased for
educational, business, or sales promotional use.
For information please write:
Special Markets Department,
HarperCollins Canada,
55 Avenue Road, Suite 2900,
Toronto, Ontario, Canada M5R 3L2

First PerennialCanada edition

Canadian Cataloguing in Publication Data

Schoemperlen, Diane
Our lady of the lost and found : a novel

"A Phyllis Bruce book".
ISBN 0-00-648585-5

I. Title.

PS8587.C4578O97 2002   C813'.54
C2002-900530-2
PR9199.3.S34O87 2002

RRD 9 8 7 6 5 4 3 2 1

Printed and bound in the United States

For Merilyn

She [is] in a class by herself. It is not often that someone comes along who is a true friend and a good writer.

—E. B. White, *Charlotte's Web*

Then I saw the Virgin Mary. I didn't know it was her at first, because she was dressed not in the usual blue or white and gold, but in black. She didn't have a crown. Her head was bowed, her face in shadow, her hands held out open at the sides. Around her feet were stubs of candles, and all over her black dress were pinned what I thought at first were stars, but which were instead little brass or tin arms, legs, hands, sheep, donkeys, chickens, and hearts.

I could see what these were for: she was a Virgin of lost things, one who restored what was lost. She was the only one of these wood or marble or plaster Virgins who had ever seemed at all real to me. There could be some point in praying to her, kneeling down, lighting a candle. But I didn't do it, because I didn't know what to pray for. What was lost, what I could pin on her dress.

I paint the Virgin Mary descending to the earth, which is covered with snow and slush. She is wearing a winter coat over her blue robe, and has a purse slung over her shoulder. She's carrying two brown paper bags full of groceries. Several things have fallen from the bags: an egg, an onion, an apple. She looks tired.

—Margaret Atwood, *Cat's Eye*

The irony of writing about such an experience in the modern era is such that, if I say to people, "This really happened," not unreasonably, they will be inclined to doubt me. They might suspect me of boasting, or assume that I have lost my mind. If I say, "I imagined it, I made it up, it's fiction"—only then are they free to believe it.

— Kathleen Norris, *Amazing Grace*

Ultimately, I have found it is meaningless to hold the yardstick of fact against the complexities of the human heart. Reality simply isn't large enough to hold us.

— A. Manette Ansay, *River Angel*

Contents

This is a work of fiction.

*Our Lady
of the Lost
and
Found*

Signs

*L*ooking back on it now, I can see there were signs. In the week before it happened, there was a string of unusual events that I noticed but did not recognize. Seemingly trivial, apparently unconnected, they were not even events really, so much as odd occurrences, whimsical coincidences, amusing quirks of nature or fate. It is only now, in retrospect, that I can see them for what they were: eclectic clues, humble omens, whispered heralds of the approach of the miraculous.

These were nothing like the signs so often reported by other people who have had similar experiences. The sun did not pulsate, spin, dance, or radiate all the colors of the rainbow. There were no rainbows. There were no claps of thunder and no bolts, balls, or sheets of lightning. There were no clouds filled with gold and silver stars. The moon did not split in two, the earth did not tremble, and the rivers did not flow backward. A million rose petals did not fall from the sky and ten thousand blue butterflies did not flock around my head. There were no doves. There were no advance armies of angels. There was not even one angel, unless you care to count the squirrel.

* * *

Three mornings in a row a fat black squirrel with one white ear came and balanced on the flower box at my kitchen window. It was the middle of April. There was nothing in the box but last year's dirt, hard-packed and dense with the ingrown roots of flowers long-gone to the compost pile. It would soon be time to refill them with fresh soil and plant the annuals: impatiens, lobelia, some hanging vines.

The squirrel appeared on Monday, Tuesday, and Wednesday, each morning at seven o'clock. I sat at the kitchen table in my nightgown and housecoat, drinking coffee and reading *The House of the Spirits* by Isabel Allende for the second time. I had read it when it first came out a dozen years before, and had picked it off the shelf again on impulse, without wondering why it suddenly seemed important to read it again. I was enjoying it even more the second time around. The squirrel sat on the edge of the window box nibbling on something that looked suspiciously like a tulip bulb from the flower bed below.

I realize there is nothing intrinsically unusual about a squirrel on a window box eating a tulip bulb. What piqued my interest was that white ear. The squirrel looked in at me with its head cocked as if listening hard with its white right ear. We stared at each other. The squirrel kept eating and listening. Even when I leaned closer to the window and made ferocious faces and carnivorous sounds, the squirrel stayed put, twitching its fluffy tail like a flag.

On each of those three mornings, the squirrel sat at my window for exactly half an hour and then it scampered away.

On the fourth morning, I got up early, got dressed, and waited. I am no more sure now than I was then of what I intended to do if and when the squirrel appeared. Feed it, kill it, or tame it and keep it for a pet? Chase it away with the broom, invite it in for coffee, or simply sit and stare into its beady eyes some more?

I waited and waited but the squirrel never came. I went outside and repaired the damage to my flower bed. I came back inside and began my day again just as if nothing had happened. Because, of course, nothing had.

That day, Thursday, turned out to be what I now think of as The Day of Mechanical Miracles.

The kitchen faucet, which had been dripping for a year and half, stopped.

The toaster, which for a month had been refusing to spit out the toast (thereby necessitating its extraction by means of a dangerous operation with a fork), repented. That morning the toast popped up so perky and golden, it fairly leaped onto my plate.

The grandfather clock in the living room, which I had bought on impulse at an auction six years before and which had not kept good time since, became accurate and articulate, tolling out the hours with melodious precision.

The answering machine, which had been recording my callers as if they were gargling underwater or bellowing into a high wind, recovered its equanimity and broadcast my new messages into the room in cheerful, dulcet tones.

I, of course, marveled extensively at these small miracles but had no reason to suspect they were anything but fortuitous gifts meant perhaps to finally prove my theory that if you just leave things alone and let them rest, they will eventually fix themselves. I had no reason to suspect that these incidents of spontaneous repair might be products or premonitions of the divine. These self-generated mechanical healings were just as likely, I thought, to be the ultimate and inevitable culmination of such modern innovations as self-cleaning ovens, self-defrosting refrigerators, self-sealing fuel tanks, and self-rising bread.

The next day, Friday, I had several errands to run. I was hardly surprised to discover that my car, which had lately been suffering from some mysterious malady that caused it to buck and wheeze whenever I shifted into second gear, had quietly healed itself during the night, and it now carried me clear across town without complaint. There were parking spaces everywhere I needed them, some with time still on the meter.

At the bank, I got the friendliest, most efficient teller after a wait of less than five minutes. On a Friday afternoon, no less. While I waited, I noticed that all three of the women in line in front of me were wearing navy blue trench coats and white running shoes.

At the library, all the books I wanted were in and shelved in their proper places.

At the bakery, I got the last loaf of cheese bread.

At the drugstore, all the things I needed—toothpaste, shampoo, bubble bath, and vitamins—were on sale.

On the way home, I stopped at the corner store for a quart of milk and a chocolate bar. The clerk behind the cash register was new, a young woman with long brown hair and dark dreamy eyes. She was sipping coffee out of a Styrofoam cup and reading *The House of the Spirits* by Isabel Allende. The clerk who was usually there at this time of day would have been doing her nails and reading the *National Enquirer*. There was no one else in the store. There was no one choosing a dollar's worth of penny candy one candy at a time; no one trying to cash a check; no one buying forty-seven Scratch-and-Win tickets and then feeling obliged to scratch them all right there. Feeling gregarious in my good fortune, I asked the clerk how she was enjoying the book. She said it was wonderful. I agreed wholeheartedly and mentioned that by coincidence I was reading it too. She said that was amazing.

At home I put away my purchases, ate my chocolate bar, and thanked my lucky stars. Still it did not occur to me that there might be anything more going on here than a random bout of serendipity at work in my life. We have all had weeks where everything went wrong. So why not a week where everything went right? As far as I was concerned, I deserved a day or two of smooth sailing through the hazardous waters of daily life. Undoubtedly this was my just reward for having so often weathered the more familiar barrage of everyday ordeals.

I thought of all those times I had finally reached a cranky, incompetent bank teller after waiting in line for half an hour wedged between a crying baby and an unwashed man who had recently eaten a large clove of garlic, only to have her put up her NEXT TELLER sign or inform me that my checking account was overdrawn by $2,486.99. And what about all those times when every book I wanted to borrow from the library was either already out, lost, or stolen? How many times had the bakery run out of cheese bread three minutes before I got there? How many times had I searched that same drugstore for my favorite health and hygiene products only to find that they were temporarily out of stock, permanently discontinued, or twice as expensive as they had been six weeks ago? How many times had the only available parking spot within a four-block radius been whisked right out from under my wheels by a more aggressive (and remorseless) driver in a hulking black minivan? And how many times had I been so overjoyed to finally find a parking spot that I had walked away without putting money in the meter and so got ticketed the minute my back was turned?

Obviously I deserved a good day and I was not about to question either its meaning or its message.

On Saturday morning, I did my regular rounds of vacuuming, dusting, dishes, and laundry. In the afternoon, I got groceries. Then I decided to clean out my bedroom closet. It was spring, after all, and some extra cleaning seemed appropriate. Once a year I sort the contents of my closet into three piles: Keep, Give Away, and Back Bedroom, the closet in the back bedroom being the way station between Keep and Give Away, the place where I put all those things that I know I will never wear again but that I'm not quite ready to part with either. After a respectable period of time in Back Bedroom limbo, these items, too, eventually find their way out the door. This time the Back Bedroom pile included a pair of flowered cotton drawstring pants that made me look fat, an expensive olive green blouse that made me look sallow, a short purple skirt that made me look ridiculous, and a chocolate brown cardigan that made me feel dowdy and depressed every time I looked at it.

As I hung these items in the otherwise empty back bedroom closet, I caught sight of a small cardboard box wedged into the far right corner of the top shelf. I could not imagine what it contained. I couldn't reach it, so I dragged a chair in from the kitchen, climbed up on it, and lifted down the box. On the top was a yellowed mailing label, addressed in my mother's handwriting to an apartment I had lived in nineteen years ago. The label and several lengths of brittle cellophane tape came off in my hands. I thought briefly of Pandora's box, all those eager evils let loose upon the unsuspecting world.

Inside the box was another box, of a color somewhere between robin's egg and sky blue, with a gold insignia embossed on the lid. Inside the blue box, in a nest of cotton batting, was my old charm bracelet.

I had begged for and got this bracelet from my parents on my fifteenth birthday. It came with one silver charm already soldered on: a round *Happy Birthday* with my name and the date engraved in italic script on the back. Over the following years, the charms accumulated one by one. Most were gifts from my parents, on Christmas, other birthdays, Valentine's Day, high school graduation. There was a Christmas tree studded with tiny red and green stones and, from another year, a miniature Christmas stocking with multicolored gems the size of pinheads bursting out the top. There were charms that said *Sweet Sixteen*, *Always Eighteen*, *Congratulations*, and *Good Luck*. There was a diploma, a typewriter, and a bicycle.

By the end of high school, all my friends sported similar bracelets heavy with charms. We jingled through the high school hallways, laughing, gossiping, and watching for handsome football players out of the eagle-eyed corners of our eyes. As we pulled lunch bags, gym shoes, and battered textbooks from our lockers, the charms sometimes caught in our sweaters, our nylons, or each other's hair. They were the amulets of all our hopes and dreams, the untarnished talismans of our promising futures, our expectant selves.

Looking at them now, I found a few that seemed to have nothing to do with me: an airplane, a horse, a treble clef, a tiny ball of wool pierced by two crossed needles. As if the charms from someone else's bracelet had somehow detached themselves and migrated to mine. Or maybe it was just that at the time anything was possible. I might fly to Mexico, France, or Kathmandu. I might learn to ride a horse. I might learn to play the harp, the trumpet, the mandolin. I might compose a symphony. I might knit up the raveled sleeve of care.

When I moved away from home at the age of twenty-one, I left the bracelet behind on purpose, having decided in my fledgling maturity that it was childish, tacky, and cheap. My mother, discovering it still there in my jewelry box after I'd left, assumed I'd forgotten it by mistake, and promptly mailed it to me.

I had given the bracelet up for lost a long time ago. Having mellowed somewhat over the years, no longer feeling the need to guard so vigilantly against the seductions of nostalgia or regret, I had looked for it several times but without success. I figured it had been accidentally left behind somewhere in one of the many moves I'd made since that first one.

But now here it was in my hands. How had I not seen that little box on the top shelf all the other times I had used this closet? Why did I not remember putting it up there in the first place?

I could not answer either of these questions. I am not a careless person. I never forget appointments, birthdays, letters to be answered, or phone calls to be returned. I have never lost my keys, my wallet, or my gloves. I once left my favorite scarf on a train but that was an aberration brought on by my own travel anxiety. Until this day, I would have sworn that I could close my eyes and conjure up the contents of every single closet in my house, also the junk drawer, the spice cabinet, and the laundry hamper.

At first, my discovery made me uneasy but then I began to feel exhilarated, wondering what other unexpected treasures might show up, what other mislaid pieces of my self might eventually be unearthed and reclaimed.

I put on the bracelet and wore it for the rest of the day. At bedtime, I put it back in the blue box. Then I put the box in my top dresser drawer beside my socks and underwear where I would not lose track of it again.

* * *

On Sunday, after six days of bright spring weather, it rained, just the kind of gentle, steady rain you want in April, the kind of rain you know really will bring those alleged May flowers.

We were enjoying an early spring that year. Since Easter, which had also been early, falling at the end of March, the temperature had been steadily rising and the snow had long since melted away. Other years in April, there were still gray patches of it under trees and in shady corners, and we were still being warned by the weather forecasters to expect one more big storm before winter was done with us. But that year, April was not the cruelest month, the forsythia and the crocuses were blooming, the tulips were in bud, and we had put away our shovels with confidence and relief. I had already raked the lawns and cleaned out the flower beds, delighted to be digging in the dirt once again.

The day passed quietly. Nothing unusual happened until later in the evening. I had put on my nightgown and housecoat and curled up on the couch to watch the ten o'clock news. The anchorwoman, in a smart red suit and a frilly white blouse, told of an earthquake, a civil war, a military coup, a car bombing, a hostage-taking, and a missing child whose clothes had been found in a Dumpster behind a fast-food restaurant five hundred miles from her home. There was video footage of each of these stories and a series of still shots from various angles of a well-dressed man lying in the street while all the blood ran out of his head.

Then they cut to a commercial for a new improved brand of sanitary napkins with wings. A pair of graceful female hands caressed the wings, then slowly poured a blue liquid over the napkin, and spoke in a soothing voice while it was neatly absorbed.

As if we all bleed blue blood once a month. As if all we really need is a new pair of wings. Then one hand caressed the napkin and its manicured fingers came away clean and dry. This was followed by a commercial for furniture polish, which was being lovingly applied by apparently the same pair of hands.

Just then I heard a strange sound. It seemed to be coming from near or behind the potted fig tree in the corner to the left of the television set. It was the soft sound of a sigh, a breath inhaled deeply through the mouth, held for a second, and then let go slowly. Once, twice, a third time. These were not sighs of exasperation or impatience, but simply the sighs of fatigue, tinged with a shadow of resignation or regret.

I thought maybe a branch of the fir tree outside was brushing against the corner of the house in the wind. I went to the window and pushed the drapes aside. The rain had stopped but the pavement was still wet, glistening in the glow of the street-lights. The grass in my front yard looked lush and moist, visibly green even in the darkness. I thought I could smell it right through the glass. The air was perfectly still.

I looked behind the fig tree. I saw a dust bunny, a dime, and three dead leaves the vacuum cleaner had missed. I turned off the television. I listened. I heard the grandfather clock ticking, a car passing, the fridge humming in the kitchen.

I decided the sighing must have been my imagination, the way sometimes in the street you think you hear someone calling your name but when you stop and turn, there is not a familiar face in sight and the crowd on the sidewalk parts impatiently around you, then regroups and charges on.

I locked the doors, turned off the lights, and went to bed.

That night I slept soundly and deeply, undisturbed by dreams, desire, or any prescient inkling of what was going to happen next.

Facts

Name. Address. Age. Sex. Height. Weight. Hair. Eyes. Marital Status. Education. Occupation. Income. Religion.

I will tell you what I can.

I am in my mid-forties. I have brown eyes and short brown hair that is just beginning to go gray. I am of average height and weight. I use makeup only sparingly: mascara always, and a little lipstick when I think of it. I save the foundation, the blusher, and the eye shadow (brown only, never blue, green, or mauve with sparkles) for special occasions. I do not pluck my eyebrows or wax my upper lip. Having been a chronic nail-biter since the age of five, I am proud to say that I recently conquered that bad habit and have now entered the wonderful world of nail polish.

If you passed me on the street, you wouldn't notice me. This does not especially bother me. I have outgrown the need to draw attention to myself and have no particular desire to stand out in a crowd. Anonymity, I have found, has its own rewards.

I dress in a style I like to think of as casual but chic, favoring outfits that subtly reflect my artistic inclinations. I do not wear polyester, plastic, or fur. I have never owned a cape or a beret. I am not extravagant in my sartorial spending. I take extreme pleasure in finding great clothes on sale cheap.

I am myopic. I have worn glasses since I was nine years old. I have never worn contact lenses because I don't like the thought of sticking them in my eyes. The glasses I wear now are bifocals. My optometrist was amused when I asked for them at my last visit. He said most people are reluctant to take this step. He said most people get depressed when they have to make this first concession to aging. Not me. My bifocals are the type without that visible line across the middle of each lens. They don't look like bifocals, yet I often feel compelled to tell people that they are.

I do not long to be young again, nor am I especially afraid of growing old. These days I am looking at the lines in other women's faces and finding them beautiful.

I am in consistently good health. The sickest I have ever been was when I succumbed to a particularly virulent strain of the flu five years ago and was laid low for a whole month. On my doctor's recommendation, I've had a flu shot every fall since and have never been sick like that again.

I have never been married. I live alone. I own my own home. For reasons which will become clear soon enough, I cannot tell you my name.

Nor can I tell you the name of the city in which I live. Suffice it to say that it is a medium-sized city in the western hemisphere on the northern shore of a large lake. I have lived here for fifteen years. I fully expect to die here. I cannot imagine a reason good enough to make me want to leave.

After finishing high school, I left my hometown to attend university in a different city, not this one, a larger city two hundred miles to the west. My major was English Literature, my minor, Philosophy. I filled out my program with an eclectic assortment of other courses. After graduation (with honors) three years later, I knew three things for sure: I did not want to do postgraduate studies, I wanted to stay in the city, and I wanted to be a writer when I grew up.

During the ten years I lived there, I held down a variety of jobs, some full-time, some part-time, for all of which I was more or less overqualified. I worked as a secretary in a real estate office, a clerk in a bookstore, a tutor for reluctant readers, a typesetter for a weekly newspaper, a bank teller, and, for one disastrous week, a waitress. I did whatever I had to to keep food in the fridge and a roof over my head. The rest of the time I wrote. Short stories mostly, the odd poem, some book reviews. Then I started a novel.

While living in that city, I moved eight times, from one small apartment to another in all parts of town. I lived on top floors, main floors, and in basements both damp and dry. I had roommates, both male and female, good and bad, and when I could afford it, I occasionally lived alone, an arrangement which I much preferred.

After ten years, I was tired of packing and unpacking boxes and sending out change-of-address cards. Things had happened that I did not understand. For months I wallowed in a welter of depression and uncertainty. The only thing I knew for sure was that I was ripe for a change.

So I decided to move to this city, a much smaller one. I had been here several times on long weekends just to visit and I liked it. I was thirty years old and I was ready to begin my life again. I gave notice to my latest landlord and my current employer (I had been doing typing and filing at a small law office for the previous six months) and began to make some serious preparations for moving. A week later, my maternal grandfather died and left me some money. Of course I was sorry to see him go, but I thought of the inheritance as a stroke of luck, a happy coincidence, a soupçon of serendipity. Now I am more inclined to think of it as grace.

With that money I put a sizable down payment on this house. Located on the northern edge of the south side of the city, it is a three-bedroom, red-brick bungalow. According to the real estate agent, it was built in 1950. Although it looks rather small and unremarkable from the outside, inside the rooms are spacious and bright, the casement windows are large, the ceilings are high, and the hardwood floors are immaculate.

At the front facing the street are the living room on one side and the large, sunny kitchen on the other. A long hallway runs down the center of the house. Behind the living room is my bedroom. Behind that is the back bedroom, used for guests, sewing, and miscellaneous arts-and-crafts projects. The bathroom is behind the kitchen and behind that is what was once the master bedroom and is now my study. There is a wooden deck at the back and the whole backyard is tastefully fenced. I have a vegetable garden, many flower beds, and several large trees and bushes both front and back. Modest by some standards, all this feels quite luxurious to me.

Shortly after I bought the house, I got a job teaching two writing courses at the local community college. But I did not think of myself as a teacher. I thought of myself as a writer. I had already published a dozen short stories in magazines and anthologies. I had been interviewed once on national radio and twice on local cable television. My first novel had just been accepted by a major publishing house and was due out the following spring.

When my book was published, it received considerable critical acclaim. The reviewers bandied about words like *honest, wise, unflinching,* and *insightful.* One even said it was *a tour de force.* Admittedly, this outpouring of adulation was tempered by those other reviewers who used words and phrases like *mundane, neurotic, no plot, no villain, no reason to read this book.* Perhaps worst of all was the one who dismissed it as *light but pleasant reading.* I was favorably compared to a number of famous writers. This was flattering but, as is often the case when you're told that you look like someone else, I mostly could not see the resemblance. Still, all the praise was more than I had dared hope for and it provided me with more than enough encouragement to go on. The truth is, I would have gone on anyway, but the positive response to my novel boosted both my confidence and my determination. I could now call myself a writer, even on my income tax form, without feeling like a pompous little liar.

Since then I have published a collection of short stories and two more novels, each garnering a little more praise and making a little more money than the last. After the publication of my second novel, I decided to quit teaching and write full-time. This was considered a wildly risky (and/or ridiculous) move by most of the people I knew, including my parents. Now that I am doing quite well, all of these dissenters are quick to assure me that they had faith in me right from the beginning, that they always knew I could make a go of it.

Although my name is not exactly a household word and you will probably never find my books for sale in supermarkets or drugstores, still I am reasonably successful, both on this continent and abroad. I am now published in translation in several foreign countries.

My fiction is of the sort called *serious* (which means that although it is frequently humorous, it is not meant to be purely entertaining and it may or may not have a happy ending) or *literary* (which means that it is not of a genre like romance, horror, fantasy, mystery, or science fiction, and it seeks to shed some light on the larger truths of human nature and experience) or *domestic* (a word which means it is often about women and many of the scenes take place in kitchens, bedrooms, and shopping malls) or *postmodern* (a word which nobody really knows what it means).

Generally speaking, I write about the lives of ordinary people, both male and female, about lives which, upon closer examination, turn out to be not so ordinary after all. My stories are frequently ironic and I like to tell them in unusual ways. I am not especially attracted to the traditional beginning-middle-end approach to narrative.

People often ask me how much of my fiction is autobiographical, how much of what I am writing is actually the real story of my own life. I freely admit that some parts of each book are true but I am not about to say which parts or how true.

I try not to be cranky about these questions. I try not to say that it is nobody's business. I try not to say that all of it and none of it is true. I try not to bring up the issue of what do we really mean when we say "real" and what are we truly looking for when we say "true"? Instead, I like to quote the American author Jayne Anne Phillips who wrote, in the disclaimer to her short story collection, *Black Tickets*:

> *Characters and voices in these stories began in what is real, but became, in fact, dreams. They bear no relation to living persons, except that love or loss lends a reality to what is imagined.*

I cannot tell you the titles of my books because then you would be able to figure out who I am.

* * *

I am the middle child of three. I have an older brother and a younger sister. My brother is a civil servant with a lovely wife and three adolescent children, two boys and a girl. My sister and her husband recently opened their own restaurant. They have one young daughter. My siblings and their families all still live in the city where we were born and raised. I go there once or twice a year to visit and we always spend Christmas together.

I had a reasonably happy childhood and my adolescence was no more or less angst-ridden than necessary. In my final year of high school, I graduated at the top of my class. Asked to contribute a bit of biographical information or a morsel of pithy wisdom to accompany my picture in the yearbook, I, with adolescent bravado and pretention, wrote: *Embrace the absurdity of life.*

My parents are old now but alive and well, minding their own business in a retirement community in the sunny south. They go golfing and swimming every day. They belong to a bridge club, a book club, and a gourmet cooking club. Their lives are busy and full. We write and phone regularly. We see each other for a week every summer. Either I go there or they come here. They are healthy and happy. We all act as if they will live forever. Maybe they will.

We are an ordinary middle-class family with the usual share of joys and triumphs, problems and disappointments.

I would also like to mention that there is no history of insanity in either my immediate or my extended family.

Although I visit my family regularly and must make frequent trips to give readings and lectures, I do not like traveling.

I have learned the hard way that it is not advisable to say this out loud in certain circles. People who love traveling can be a rather zealous bunch, a touch self-righteous, and easily offended by my failure to appreciate their point of view. They tell me over and over again that traveling is exciting, interesting, educational, that it will expand my mind and broaden my horizons. They are persistent in their attempts to convert me, convinced that if only they can get me to listen to the voice of reason, I will finally see the error of my parochial ways and head for the nearest travel agent.

But I am not convinced. Myself, I truly believe that home is where the heart is. There is no place that I would rather be. This means that I do not spend a lot of money on frequent lavish vacations to exotic locales. In fact, I do not spend a lot of money on anything except books. I do not think of myself as a cheapskate but the habit of careful budgeting is long ingrained and it serves me well. I live frugally and quietly. Like many writers, I am a solitary person by nature and my lifestyle reflects that.

I like gardening and sewing, and I have been told that I have a flair for interior decorating. I have also been told that I am a good cook. At one time I could have dazzled you with dishes like Chicken Cacciatore, Beef Stroganoff, and Roast Pork Stuffed with Sauerkraut. But lately, having reached an age at which you finally realize that you are not immortal and that if you take better care of your body, it will last longer, I have nearly cut meat out of my diet altogether. These days I would be more likely to tempt you with Zucchini and Barley Casserole, Marinated Cauliflower à la Greque, or Lentil Soup Creole. I am not a good baker, however. My cookies burn, my cakes fall, and my puddings always curdle.

I don't like playing cards, checkers, backgammon, or chess. I like word games, crossword puzzles, and Trivial Pursuit. I began collecting stamps when I was ten years old and, although philately has long since gone out of fashion, I still enjoy it occasionally, especially in the winter when the evenings are so long and dark.

I am not athletically or musically inclined. I don't know how to swim, ski, skate, or play any game involving a ball. Although they say you never forget how to ride a bicycle, I suspect I probably have. I do not know how to play the piano, the guitar, the tuba, or the violin. In fact, the last time I played either a sport or a musical instrument was back in high school when I had to.

I am not religiously inclined either. The last time I was in a church was for my sister's wedding twelve years ago. The time before that was for my grandfather's funeral.

Both these ceremonies took place in the same church back in my hometown, Saint Matthew's United, where my brother and sister and I were baptized and where we attended Sunday school as children. My mother was an Anglican and my father was a Methodist. They did not attend either church. We children were sent to Saint Matthew's United because it was close to our house and we could walk there by ourselves while our parents stayed home Sunday mornings and had a long breakfast or went back to bed. They apparently had no strong feelings about religion and even then I suspected that we were sent to Sunday school mostly so they could have some time to themselves. And yet, when my cousin Sarah married a Catholic man and converted, they were upset for reasons I did not understand. One Sunday morning a few years later, Sarah, her husband, and their young daughter were involved in a car accident on their way home from mass. Thankfully, no one was injured. It was the other driver's fault. This accident seemed to prove my parents right about something and, in the next few weeks, they referred to it frequently with a kind of smug satisfaction, as if their reservations about Sarah's conversion had been thus confirmed.

I have not dabbled in the New Age spiritual stuff that has become so popular in recent years. I've had little or no acquaintance with crystals, prisms, angels, and the like. Like most people, I read my daily horoscope in the newspaper but believe it only when it tells me something I would like to hear. I have never been attracted to such trappings of the occult as tarot cards, palm reading, or runes. I did have a brief flirtation with the Ouija board the summer I turned fourteen. The only questions I really wanted to ask were what was the name of the man I would marry and how many children would we have. Every time I asked, the Ouija would indeed spring to life and move mysteriously around the board. But every time I asked, the answers were different: Andrew, Robert, David, John, four, three, two, none. I soon lost interest, and the Ouija board went to the attic.

As for some of my other personal habits . . . I probably watch too much television. I read two or three books a week, mostly fiction. I figure these two facts balance each other out. I keep track of my reading in a list on my computer. Last year I read 133 books. I do not keep track of how many hours I spend in front of the television.

I prefer baths to showers. My favorite color is blue. My favorite season is spring. My favorite time of day is morning and my favorite day of the week is Monday. I like coffee. I like Beethoven and Bach. I like a quiet rain. I am afraid of subways, snakes, and young people with blue hair and rings in their tongues.

I do not know if I take myself too seriously or not seriously enough. Sometimes one, sometimes the other, sometimes both at once. Engaged, as I seem to be, in a never-ending conversation with myself, there have been many times when I wished I could stop thinking so much, when I wished I could just shut myself up and get on with my life. Now that I am in my forties, I like to think I am doing just that. We all have our issues and I like to believe that I have dealt more or less successfully with mine.

People are always telling me how lucky I am. Most often they say it while shaking their heads, sighing, and rolling their eyes. I suppose they have a point, and yet their insistence upon my luckiness makes me uncomfortable. They do not say it in a kind way.

Much as these people like to think of me as lucky, they also like to dislike me for it. They want to remind me that somehow I don't deserve it. They want me to feel guilty, as if my living a happy life somehow takes away from their chances of ever doing the same. Any admiration they may harbor for me is offered only grudgingly, with reluctance, suspicion, or downright envy. Then they dismiss me with a wave of the hand and go on to enumerate the long sad list of their own miseries, their bad breaks, their bitter grievances against God and the world. I do not count these people among my true friends. What exactly are they accusing me of?

It's not that I don't believe in luck. At various times in my life I, too, have carried a pink rabbit's foot in my pocket, a four-leaf clover in my purse. I have put my faith in a lucky sweater, a lucky jacket, and a lucky teddy bear. I once bought a pair of earrings shaped like horseshoes. I still pick up pennies in the street.

I can think of many examples of good luck, none of which have anything to do with me and my life.

Imagine a tornado striking your street and yours is the only house left standing. Imagine winning the lottery the first time you ever buy a ticket. Imagine that you are finally going to Paris for the vacation you have been dreaming of all your life. Imagine missing your flight because of a traffic jam on the way to the airport. Imagine the plane you were supposed to be on crashing into the middle of the Atlantic Ocean. Imagine the seat cushions, the suitcases, the bodies floating on the cold black waves.

Or imagine going to your friendly neighborhood bank on a Tuesday afternoon. Imagine depositing a birthday check from your aunt, wiring money to your brother who has fallen on hard times, or withdrawing your last thirty dollars, which you are either going to spend sensibly on a quart of milk, a loaf of bread, a dozen eggs, and a bag of apples, or else you're going to blow it on that fat new novel you've been just dying to read. Imagine that five minutes after you have left the bank, a man with a gun takes the tellers and all the customers hostage. Imagine him making them lie facedown on the floor and then shooting them one by one in the back of the head. Imagine yourself at home eating an apple when the story comes on the six o'clock news. Imagine your mouth falling open, the sweet juice running down your chin, the half-eaten apple rolling around the room.

I also believe in bad luck and take appropriate measures to guard against it. I do not walk under ladders. I do not open my umbrella in the house. If I happen to spill the salt, I always toss a pinch over my left shoulder. I watch out for any errant black cats who might be considering crossing my path. I am careful around mirrors. I frequently knock on wood.

But much as I may be as superstitious as the next person, I seldom think of myself as lucky. I do consider myself extraordinarily privileged to be able to make a living doing what I love the most. I realize that few people can say the same. But I do not like to think that the course of my life has been determined solely by luck. I like to think it all depends on what you do with what you are given. I think of myself as having made a series of decisions and then worked hard to end up here.

Good luck is something you cannot take credit for. Good luck is also something that most people just naturally assume they deserve (whereas other people frequently, in their estimations, do not). Bad luck is something that happens to you through no fault of your own and which you do not deserve (but which other people, on occasion, do). Either way, luck is beyond your control. It engenders neither credit nor blame. It has nothing to do with volition, desire, effort, or will. I try to explain this to the people who harp on my luckiness but they don't listen. They think I have always been blessed.

Whenever I hear the word *lucky,* I think of the dog that lived next door to us when I was a baby. Lucky was a young border collie, so named because he was the seventh puppy of the litter. In those days, in the warm months, babies were often put outside in their carriages to sleep in the shade. Every afternoon when my mother put me out for my nap, Lucky would amble over from his yard to ours and flop down on the grass beside the carriage. In those days, there were no fences. I, of course, was too young to remember this, but there are pictures in the family album of Lucky stationed beside my carriage with his chin resting on his crossed black paws. That swaddled bundle inside is me. My mother tells me Lucky guarded me like that every afternoon for as long as I slept and would not let anyone into the yard, including my father once, on a day when he came home from work early.

For a while, Lucky did live up to his name, surviving many canine calamities over the years. There was a fight with a German shepherd, a battle with a barbed wire fence, a taste of poisoned meat, and a brush with the lawn mower. At various times, Lucky swallowed, without serious ill effect, a live bumblebee, a warm charcoal briquette, a whole candy cane, a blue crayon, a pink mitten, and a foam rubber duck.

When I was seven, Lucky chased a cat into the street where he was hit and killed by a truck. The cat ran on, oblivious. I think it was a beer truck, I think the cat was black, but I could be wrong. It was a long time ago.

So these are the facts, some of them anyway.

I am telling you all this now because I want you to know from the outset that I am a normal, rational, well-educated, well-adjusted woman not given to delusions, hallucinations, or hysterical flights of fancy. I do not drink or do drugs. The only voice I hear in my head is my own.

I want you to know from the outset that I am not a psychotic, an eccentric, a fanatic, or a mystic.

I want you to know that I am not a lunatic.

Arrival

It began on Monday, the day after the sighing in the corner. I got up at six o'clock, my usual time, feeling well rested and clearheaded. I made the coffee and brought in the newspaper. I skimmed the front page in case there were any earthshaking events I should know about. There was nothing catastrophic so I read my horoscope and then put the paper aside, planning, as usual, to give it a more thorough reading later on. I made my to-do list for the day and then spent a quiet hour at the kitchen table drinking coffee and continuing my second reading of *The House of the Spirits*. The radio played at low volume in the corner, broadcasting muffled music, sports scores, weather and traffic reports into the room. The sky was clear but there were scattered showers in the forecast. The radio announcer predicted an unsettled afternoon with great panache, as if he had just peered into his crystal ball and seen the future.

Two black squirrels chased each other up and down the telephone pole across the street, then back and forth along the line between my house and the pole. The smaller squirrel lost its balance briefly and hung for a breathless minute by its front paws, its back feet scrabbling frantically in midair. It managed, by a series of splendid acrobatic contortions, to heave itself back onto the line and the game continued.

I wondered if they ever fell off. I imagined furry bodies plummeting from the sky and thudding onto the concrete sidewalk below.

But this time the squirrels came safely back down to earth, raced up my driveway, and disappeared. All four of their ears were black.

I had breakfast: a bowl of yogurt, a slice of cantaloupe, a piece of toast, more coffee. I tidied the kitchen. Then I had a long bubble bath and, while I soaked in the water till my skin was all wrinkled, I thought about painting the bathroom green. I got dressed and went into my study.

A square, spacious room, it is large enough to accommodate several bookcases, two filing cabinets, a stationery cabinet, and three desks: a white one for my computer, a plain wooden work table in front of the window, and an oak rolltop which was my gift to myself when I sold my third book. The room also contains a chair on wheels for navigating from desk to desk, a large armchair for reading, and all the smaller accoutrements of a home office.

I turned on my computer and checked my e-mail. I sent a few replies and then made some phone calls. There were travel arrangements to be made for a reading I was to give the following month. There were, as always, papers to be filed, books to be shelved, and bills to be paid. I also spent half an hour reorganizing my stationery cabinet.

My mornings are not usually so leisurely. When fully immersed in working on a book, I keep a regular (some would say "rigid") daily routine. But when the events I am about to tell you took place, I was between books. My last manuscript was in the hands of my editor and I was just beginning to think about my next book. It was in the very earliest stages of creation and so still far too fragile to be discussed with anyone. I was jotting down my ideas in a crisp, new spiral-bound notebook with a red cover. What I had so far were pages and pages of unconnected images and free-floating snatches of dialogue that were swirling through my mind like the high- and low-pressure systems churning across the continent on a television weather map:

A woman stands at a window. The early morning light is soft and forgiving. Her eyes are locked in the middle distance. Her thoughts, for the moment, are stalled in space. Not wishing or remembering, worrying, waiting, hoping, or regretting, the woman, for now, is neither happy nor unhappy. She is not thinking about herself. She begins to hum tunelessly. The sunlight is warm on the window. The new day begins to gather momentum.

In the dream about the valley, there were buttercups and clover, a man and a woman making love on a green blanket in a green pasture, their legs entwined like vines, and the cumulus clouds floated above them. But it was only a dream.

I said that I loved him.
He said that he loved me.
What it all boils down to is this: who said it first? Therein lies the story.

The pink flowers, called alstroemeria, are still alive but the white ones, freesia, which he said would last longer, have already died.

I am sleeping better lately but the weather remains unseasonably warm.

Sometimes the woman at the window is me.

On the last page of the red notebook, I had started a list of possible titles for the book:

Absolute Truths.
Beginning, Middle, End.
Definitions of Happiness.
The History Ahead of Us.
Victims, Villains, and Excess.

This first stage of writing a book involves a lot of thinking time which, to the uninitiated, appears to be a lot of time wasted doing nothing more than looking out the window. I sat at my work table and did some of that.

From the window of my study I can see my own backyard and portions of the backyards of three adjoining lots. That morning, I tried to decode the laundry hanging on the clothesline in one of those other yards. Studying laundry on a line strikes me as a suburban version of reading palms, tea leaves, or tarot cards, a method of divination useful in determining not so much the past or the future but the present, which, to my way of thinking, is a state every bit as occult and enigmatic as the other two, requiring, but seldom accorded, equal measures of interpretation and exegesis.

The neighbors whose laundry I attempted to decipher that morning had just moved in at the beginning of the month. I had not actually met them yet, but the family appeared to include a man, a woman, and two young children, hardly an unusual arrangement. That morning their clothesline was full. I wondered if they had heard there was rain in the forecast. I looked closely at the items on display. Such nosiness, I tell myself (but I call it curiosity), is a necessary attribute for a writer.

In addition to a conventional assemblage of towels, pillow-cases, and socks of several sizes, there were five identical shirts: short-sleeved, with blue and white vertical stripes, buttons down the front. Next to the last shirt was a large white teeshirt printed with the face of Jesus in vivid deep colors. The five shirts and the teeshirt, all man-sized, were hung by their tails so that Jesus' face was upside down, smiling in a friendly way while flapping gently in the breeze.

I meditated on this configuration of shirts and came up with nothing. But I made a note of it, certain that it was something I would use someday.

I heard the mailman and went to see what he had brought. All writers have intense relationships with their mailmen, whether their mailmen know it or not. There were the usual pizza flyers, credit card bills, and letters from charitable founda-tions requesting donations. There were catalogs from a computer warehouse and an outdoor clothing manufacturer. There was a letter from a former student asking me to write her a grant rec-ommendation and one from a graduate student who wanted to know why I had used the word *apparently* forty-one times in my last book. There were no checks.

I ground some more coffee beans and made another pot, decaf this time. I bundled last week's newspapers and put them in the recycling box in the basement. I filled up the salt and pep-per shakers. I cleaned out the fridge. I turned up the radio and listened to an interview with a ninety-year-old blind man who carved duck decoys. I tried to think about my next book and not think about it at the same time. Proceeding in a gingerly fash-ion, I tried to sneak up on the ideas that had been nudging at me without scaring them away.

The grandfather clock tolled twelve and I thought about lunch. Should I have cream of asparagus soup or a toasted tomato sandwich? While trying to decide, I watered the plants in the kitchen. Then I refilled the watering can and went into the living room.

There was a woman standing in front of the fig tree.

She was wearing a navy blue trench coat and white running shoes. She had a white shawl draped over her hair like a hood. Over her right shoulder she carried a large leather purse. In her left hand she held the extended metal handle of a small suitcase on wheels that rested on an angle slightly behind her like an obedient dog.

—Fear not, she said.

I was too stunned to be scared. I put the watering can down on the coffee table and stared at her.

—It's me, Mary, she said. Mother of God.

I must have looked blank. She went on, smiling.

—You know. Mary. Lamb of the Redeemer. Queen of Heaven. Pilgrim of Peace. Daughter of Zion. Ark of the Covenant. Fount of Beauty. Summit of Virtue. Sublime Peak of Human Intellect.

She paused. I could not speak. Her eyes twinkled. She went on:

—Mother of the Mystical Body. Unplowed Field of Heaven's Bread. Cloud of Rain That Offers Drink to the Souls of the Saints. Virgin Most Venerable. Virgin Most Powerful. Virgin Most Merciful. More Holy Than the Cherubim, the Seraphim, and the Entire Angelic Hosts.

—Hello, I said.

She put down her purse and then set her suitcase upright

beside it. She pushed a red button and the handle retracted. She slid back the shawl, and her fine hair, which was dark brown streaked with silver, fell in tangled waves around her shoulders. She rummaged in her coat pocket, pulled out an elastic band, gathered her hair in her hands, and tied it back at her neck.

Recovering my manners, I said:

—Come in, do come in.

—It would appear that I am already in, she said.

—Yes, indeed, I stammered. Well then, may I take your coat?

—Thank you, yes, she said.

She took off her trench coat, then the shawl, folded them over her arm, and stepped toward me where I still stood in the same spot, my feet apparently frozen to the floor. She handed me the coat and the shawl.

Close up, I could see her face more clearly. She looked to be about my age, perhaps a few years older. Her skin was very smooth, golden brown as if she had been spending time in the southern sun. Her eyes were deep brown and the skin below them was a little crepey and thin-looking. There were fine friendly lines around her mouth.

She was wearing a long black dress. Between her breasts there was an embroidered red heart with pink rosebuds encircling it and yellow flames shooting from the top. The heart was pierced by a golden sword. Her skirt at first appeared to be decorated with heavy silver embroidery. But when she reached down to straighten its folds, this embellishment proved to be hundreds of tiny metal objects somehow fastened to the cloth. They jingled a bit and glinted in the sunlight streaming through the front window.

Of all the things I might have said at that moment, of all the questions I might have asked, what came out of my mouth was:

—I was just thinking about making some lunch. Are you hungry?

—Oh yes, she said. I'm famished. And may I use the washroom, please? It has been such a long journey. I'd like to freshen up and change my clothes.

She spoke softly and slowly, with a slight accent that I could not place. There was something of Europe in it, Latin America too. France, Spain, Italy, Mexico? I couldn't tell. Listening to her was like reading a book in translation, where the cadences and inflections of the original language hang like a memory just behind the words.

With me still carrying her coat and shawl in my arms and her carrying her purse and her suitcase, I showed her to the bathroom. I hung up her things in the front closet. I watered the fig tree as had been my original intention when I first went into the living room.

Then I went back to the kitchen and got out the bread, the milk, two tomatoes, and a can of soup. I thought we should have both soup and sandwiches. She'd said she was famished and I suddenly realized that I was too.

I opened the can of soup and emptied it into a pot on the stove. I added a can of milk and stirred it in with the silver whisk. I remember hoping that she liked asparagus, worrying in case she might be lactose-intolerant.

In fact, I remember every single thing I did and thought while the Virgin Mary freshened up in my bathroom and I made lunch. Those fifteen minutes and all that came after are indelibly engraved in my mind, each moment like a single frame from a movie, one frame after another fixed in my brain, isolated and illuminated, set impeccably apart from everything that has happened to me before or since.

I cannot explain why the thought never crossed my mind, not then and not since, that this person might well have been a delusional and possibly dangerous fanatic who had somehow broken into my home and was now about to either murder me or regale me with religious ravings and condemn me to eternal damnation unless I promised to repent. It strikes me now as the ultimate testament to the power of her presence that I had not a doubt in my mind about her reality, not then and not since. I knew from the very beginning that it was really her: Mary, Mother of God, Queen of Heaven, Our Lady of the Angels.

She was not a vision or an apparition, at least not in the usual sense of these words. She was not a vision any more than seeing the fir tree in my front yard could be said to constitute having a *vision* of a fir tree. She was not an apparition any more than running into a neighbor at the grocery store by accident would lead me to say I'd seen an *apparition* of my neighbor at the A&P. She was not a fantastical specter or a figment of my feverish imagination. She was as solid and sturdy as either my neighbor at the grocery store with a cart full of food and the kids clinging to her legs or the fir tree in the front yard dropping needles and cones all over the grass.

As I wiped off the kitchen table, I tried to remember Plato's theory of idealism that I had studied at university, the one where he said that the table we see in our everyday reality is simply a form, a shadow of the ideal table which exists somewhere else, on a higher plane of reality to which we mere mortals do not have access. This seemed no more likely to me now than it had then. If there was a place filled with perfect furniture, surely we, who had traveled to the moon and back, would have figured out how to get there by now. I tried to puzzle out how Plato's theory could be applied to an appearance of the Mother of God.

As I put the real or not real place mats on the real or not real table, I heard the real or not real toilet flush.

I could not imagine what Plato would have had to say about this.

By the time Mary came out of the bathroom, I had toasted and buttered the bread, sliced the tomatoes, and put some black olives in a bowl. The soup was steaming and I was filling two tall glasses with cranberry juice.

Now Mary was wearing a deep blue cotton shirt with the sleeves rolled up and a pair of black cotton pants, soft and slightly faded from many washings. Her hair was still tied back and damp dark curls framed her freshly scrubbed face. She wore silver hoop earrings and a silver and turquoise necklace. She was in her bare feet, with her runners in her hand. Her feet, I noticed, were very small.

—I'll just leave these here for now, she said, setting her shoes, her purse, and her suitcase down near the kitchen doorway.

I was taking plates and bowls from the cupboard, cutlery from the drawer.

—Here, let me do that, she said, and took them from me.

As she set them on the table, I could smell her perfume, a mix of lavender and musk.

—That's a lovely fragrance you're wearing, I said, bringing the pot of soup to the table and filling the bowls.

—Yes, it's new, she said. Everyone expects me to smell like roses all the time but quite frankly, I get a little tired of it. Left to my own devices, I like a change once in a while.

—These dishes are lovely, she said, patting a plate.

The dishes were new too. For years I had made do with mismatched bits and pieces: traditional floral gold-rimmed dinner plates donated by my mother when I left home, chunky yellow bread and butter plates, striped pink and green soup bowls, and miscellaneous saucers, cups, and mugs picked up at flea markets and garage sales along the way. When I received the advance for my latest book, I splurged and bought myself these new dishes, four matching place settings in a pattern called Mexican Blue. Each piece is white in the middle with a wide border of intense cobalt blue. I especially like the bowls, which are of the new larger, more shallow style. I think they are more attractive than regular bowls.

I garnished the soup with cubes of sharp cheddar cheese and put the sandwiches on the plates. The green soup, the orange cheese, the brown bread, the red cranberry juice, the blue and white dishes: it all looked good enough to paint. I wished I had a bouquet of fresh flowers to put in the center of the table.

We sat down. Mary bowed her head and said what I assumed was a small grace, a quick prayer of thanksgiving. I could see her lips moving but I could not hear the words.

We made small talk while we ate.

First we talked about food, nutrition, how complicated it was these days, always striving for more fiber, less fat, how frustrating it was when every week there was something else they had decided was bad for you, usually something you loved. We laughed about how we were always making, and then breaking, resolutions to eat more salad, less salt, more fruit, less sugar, and no more potato chips, doughnuts, or French fries ever again. Not surprisingly, she said she did not smoke or drink, except for a tiny glass of red wine now and again.

She admired the kitchen which I had repainted and redecorated in the fall when I took a month off between drafts of my new novel. I needed to put some distance between myself and my words before I could go back to the manuscript with a fresh and objective eye for the final draft. I had painted the kitchen walls a soft buttery yellow with white trim. I had sewn new curtains for the front and side windows, also matching place mats and pot holders. The pots and pans, previously stashed any which way in a lower cupboard, now hung from a cast-iron rack on the wall beside the stove. Much as I loved the look of this new arrangement, it meant I had to dust them regularly, something I had not done in a while.

—If I had known you were coming, I would have cleaned those pots, I said.

—No need, Mary said. Don't worry. Everything looks wonderful to me.

—I'm glad you like it, I said.

Then she asked after my family. She said she was happy to hear that my brother had received another promotion, that my sister and her husband were enjoying their new restaurant venture, that my oldest nephew was doing so well in his last year of high school. She was glad that my parents were making the most of their retirement and that the problem my father had had with his prostate turned out to be a false alarm.

Then she congratulated me on the recent completion and sale of my latest book. She said she was sure it would be my best yet, even better than the others which, by the way, she had absolutely loved. I was so flattered I blushed.

She did not volunteer any information about herself and I did not ask many questions beyond those directly involving lunch.

—Would you like some more soup? I asked when her bowl was nearly empty.

—Are you not fond of black olives? I asked when I offered them and she declined.

—No, she said regretfully. I'm afraid black olives are one of those things I've just never acquired a taste for.

Having been interviewed ineptly a few times myself, I am not one to interrogate another. I have been asked all kinds of questions for which I have no answers. Once, an earnest doe-eyed young woman writing an article for her university newspaper asked me, in all sincerity and with innocent expectation of a coherent answer: What is the meaning of life?

At which point I guffawed in a most unintelligent manner and spewed my mouthful of coffee all over her, embarrassing us both and bringing the interview to an abrupt end.

As far as less ponderous inquiries go, it has been my experience that if you ask people too many questions too soon, they have a tendency to clam up and say nothing. But if you just let them talk, eventually they will tell you everything you want or need to know.

—Would you like fruit salad or some chocolate wafers for dessert? I asked Mary now.

But we both decided we were too full to eat another bite. I pushed back my chair and stood up to clear the table. As I reached across for Mary's empty plate, she put her hand on my wrist.

—Never mind that just now, she said. I'll do it. You sit down and relax. I'll wash up these dishes and make us some coffee. Then we need to talk some more. I think it's time I got to the point. I think it's time I told you what I want from you.

Both her hand and her voice were warm but firm.

I did as I was told.

I sat back down and I waited.

Images

$\mathcal{B}$efore that Monday in April when the Virgin Mary turned up in my living room and stayed for lunch, I knew no more or less about her, I presume, than the average person living in a largely Christian country in the western world during the last part of the twentieth century. Much of what I knew (or thought I knew) about Mary was a kind of *a priori* knowledge, an image of her that I seemed to have always had, a picture I had acquired through no concrete or conscious means, as if it were contained in the very air I breathed, the water I drank.

My scant factual knowledge of Mary began with what I remembered from Sunday school at Saint Matthew's United. This was mostly Christmas and Easter stories, carols and hymns.

I knew that Mary and her husband Joseph had traveled from Nazareth to Bethlehem to be counted and taxed by the Roman emperor, Caesar Augustus. Being very pregnant at the time, Mary made the journey riding on a donkey. I knew that Joseph was not the baby's father, that it was God who had made Mary pregnant. In those days, I did not know or even wonder exactly how this had been accomplished. I knew that an angel named Gabriel had appeared to Mary back in Nazareth. *And the angel*

said unto her, Fear not, Mary: for thou hast found favour with God. . . .
The Holy Ghost shall come upon thee, and the power of the Highest shall
overshadow thee: therefore also that holy thing which shall be born of
thee shall be called the Son of God. In those days, I had never heard
the phrase "Immaculate Conception."

When Joseph and Mary finally got to Bethlehem, there
was no room at the inn so they had to stay in a stable with the
cows. There Mary gave birth to the baby Jesus on a bed of straw.
Because they had no cradle, they had to put him in the manger,
which was actually a feeding trough for the animals.

Meanwhile, some shepherds tending their flocks in a field
near Bethlehem were visited by an angel. *Fear not: for, behold, I*
bring you good tidings of great joy, which shall be to all people. For unto
you is born this day in the city of David a Saviour, which is Christ the
Lord. So the shepherds went to the stable and looked with wonder upon Jesus in the manger.

Three wise men, who had been guided by a brilliant star in
the sky, also traveled to the stable, riding on camels, bringing
the new baby gifts of gold, frankincense, and myrrh. I was never
told exactly what myrrh and frankincense were, and I could not
imagine why a baby would want them.

Then Joseph had a dream in which God warned him that
King Herod was looking for the baby in order to kill him. So
they fled to Egypt and stayed there until King Herod died and it
was safe to return home to Nazareth.

After that we heard all about the life of Jesus, his parables,
his miracles, his disciples, but not much more about his mother.
There was the time when twelve-year-old Jesus was missing in
Jerusalem for three days and was then finally found by Joseph
and Mary, talking in the temple with the learned men. Mary
knew then that her son was different. There was the Marriage at

Cana when Jesus, then about thirty years old, performed his first miracle. At Mary's suggestion but apparently with some reluctance, he turned six pots of water into wine.

Mary appeared again when Jesus was nailed to the cross at Calvary, a word I always got mixed up with *cavalry*. The Roman governor, Pontius Pilate, giving in to the demands of an angry mob, had sentenced Jesus to death by crucifixion for proclaiming himself the Messiah, Son of God. Three crosses were erected at Calvary that day. Jesus, wearing a crown of thorns, was on the middle one with a convicted thief on either side. Iron spikes were driven through Jesus' hands and feet. Over his head a sign was hung that said INRI, an abbreviation of the Latin words for Jesus of Nazareth, King of the Jews. Mary was there crying at the foot of the cross while her son suffered and died.

And it was about the sixth hour, and there was a darkness over all the earth until the ninth hour. And the sun was darkened, and the veil of the temple was rent in the midst. And when Jesus had cried with a loud voice, he said, Father, into thy hands I commend my spirit: and having said thus, he gave up the ghost.

I did not understand why this day was called Good Friday. It did not seem very good to me.

There were many pictures of Jesus and Mary in the Bible storybooks we read in Sunday school and more on the walls of the basement room where we met while the grown-ups listened to the sermon upstairs.

Jesus was portrayed either as a very sweet baby or as a tall, slender man with long brown hair, dark eyes, and a brown beard. Sometimes his hair was wavy and thick, sometimes stringy and limp. Sometimes his cheeks were rosy, sometimes pale. In all of these pictures, his face was noble and kind. He was often surrounded by small children and he always looked to be about thirty years old.

All the images of Mary involved the Nativity. She was shown in various poses beside the manger, always in blue, always pale and beautiful, always smiling calmly down at her precious newborn son sleeping on his bed of straw. In these scenes there was also always Joseph looking proud, the shepherds and the wise men looking amazed, the barnyard animals looking unconcerned, and the wondrous star glowing jubilantly in the high night sky.

At Saint Matthew's United we never prayed to Mary, but only directly to God himself:

Our Father, who art in heaven, hallowèd be thy name. Thy kingdom come, thy will be done on earth as it is in heaven. Give us this day our daily bread, and forgive us our trespasses as we forgive those who trespass against us. And lead us not into temptation, but deliver us from evil. For thine is the kingdom, the power, and the glory, forever and ever. Amen.

I did not know much about sin in those days. I thought trespassing was when you went onto somebody else's property when you weren't supposed to and so I was very careful never to do that.

The summer that I turned eight, the whole Sunday school class memorized the Twenty-third Psalm: *The Lord is my shepherd; I shall not want. He maketh me to lie down in green pastures: he leadeth me beside the still waters.* We memorized one verse a week so that after six weeks we could recite the whole thing in unison: *Surely goodness and mercy shall follow me all the days of my life: and I will dwell in the house of the Lord for ever.* Mary did not figure into this exercise.

On the Christmas card we received each year from my converted cousin, Sarah, there was always a picture of Mary holding
the baby Jesus. The one I remember most clearly had a pale blue
background with a fancy gold border. In the middle was a drawing of Mary wearing a blue shawl and a bright pink dress. She
seemed to be wearing mascara and lipstick. She cradled the baby
in her arms, gazing sweetly down upon him. He was wrapped in
a green receiving blanket and looked just like the Gerber baby.
Below the picture, in gold script, it said: *Behold, thou shalt bring
forth a son.* Inside it said: *Wishing you a blessèd Christmas and a holy
New Year.*

All the other cards we got had reindeer and elves, puppies
and birds, snowmen and tin soldiers, old-fashioned winter scenes
with bridges and horses. And Santa Claus, of course, in all his
traditional incarnations: making his list and checking it twice,
filling his sack, flying through the sky in his big red sleigh, tumbling down the chimney, filling up the stockings, sitting in his
undershirt and suspenders having hot chocolate and cookies with
plump Mrs. Claus. The Virgin Mary was nowhere in sight.

After a few years, the pictures of Mary and Jesus on my
cousin's cards were replaced by color photographs of Sarah and
her husband and their growing family, all of them dressed in
their best clothes, standing stiffly in front of a shiny silver tree
with a twinkling red star on top.

When I was in university I had several Catholic friends.
From them I pieced together more information about Mary,
information which confirmed my impression that she played a
far more important role in Catholicism than she ever had at Saint
Matthew's United.

Some of the Catholic girls had laminated holy cards propped

up on their night tables or taped to the wall above their beds and desks. Many of these cards featured images of Mary with long brown hair, parted in the middle, hanging straight to her shoulders where it rested in gentle waves. In these pictures, her flawless skin was very pale and luminous, her nose was dainty, her eyes were dark, and her lips were full and pink. Sometimes she was smiling faintly. Sometimes she looked very sad, as if she knew too much, as if she already knew what was going to happen in the end. She wore a white shawl over her hair and either a floor-length, long-sleeved flowing blue dress or a long blue cloak worn like a kimono over a plain white gown. Her small feet were bare. Her delicate hands were drawn in various expressive poses: pressed together in prayer, or outstretched at her sides, open and expectant, or with the right hand held palm up at her side and the left resting on her chest over her heart. Sometimes she was holding the baby Jesus in her arms. As in the images of Jesus that I remembered from Sunday school, in these pictures Mary, too, always looked young, forever no more than thirty years old.

I learned about the Immaculate Conception which I knew was celebrated on December 8 because it was marked on the calendar I'd hung on my wall. I learned that it doesn't refer to the conception of Jesus at all but to Mary herself having been conceived exempt from original sin. This cleared up the question of how the Conception could be celebrated only seventeen days before the birth of Jesus.

There was one girl who always wore a slightly tarnished medal on a silver chain. When I asked her about it, she told me how in 1830 the Virgin Mary had appeared to a young nun, Catherine Labouré, in the chapel of the Daughters of Charity convent in Paris. Mary was standing on a globe with a green serpent twined around her feet. Her hands were outstretched at her sides, emitting brilliant rays of light. Then an oval frame appeared around her. Written on it were the words *O Mary, conceived without sin, pray for us who have recourse to you.* Then Catherine saw a large letter *M* on the reverse side surrounded by twelve stars. On top of it was a large cross and below were two hearts, one pierced by a sword and the other circled with thorns. Mary told Catherine to have a medal struck bearing these images. Catherine did as she was told. In 1832, 1,500 medals were cast and sold. Now mass-produced by the millions, this is called the Miraculous Medal.

The girl who told me this story had been to Paris with her parents when she was a child. She had visited the chapel where Catherine Labouré's body is displayed in a glass casket near the altar. She had seen Catherine's brilliant blue eyes looking straight into her own and she had worn her medal ever since.

I learned about the rosary which had been a gift from Mary to Saint Dominic in 1208. She had appeared to him while he was praying to her in the chapel of Notre Dame in Prouille, France. She gave Dominic the rosary and asked him to go forth and teach people how to use it in prayer. I learned about the fifteen decades of the rosary, how each commemorates a miraculous event in the lives of Mary and Jesus: the Five Joyful Mysteries, the Five Sorrowful Mysteries, and the Five Glorious Mysteries.

The rosaries and the medals were most noticeably in evidence during pregnancy scares and final exams. During such times of extreme stress, I frequently came upon one or another of my Catholic friends crossing themselves, fingering their medals, or mumbling under their breath and fiddling with their rosary beads. Like many twenty-year-olds, I was working on the perfection of my own brand of cynicism and, in that frame of mind, these religious objects sometimes struck me as being akin to the lucky rabbit's feet or four-leaf clovers the rest of us relied on.

Although the faith of my Catholic classmates was rather

erratic, essentially they believed that Mary, in her role as media-
trix, would intervene on their behalf and relay their messages to
her son who, hopefully, could not refuse his blessèd mother
anything. Over and over again, they whispered their prayers of
petition:

Hail Mary, full of grace: The Lord is with thee. Blessèd art thou
among women, and blessèd is the fruit of thy womb, Jesus. Holy Mary,
Mother of God, pray for us sinners, now and at the hour of our death.
Amen.

Sometimes their prayers were answered.

In my third year of university I took a course in Medieval
and Renaissance Art. Many of the painters we studied had taken
biblical, especially New Testament, events and characters as their
subjects. I still have the textbook. In it, Mary is everywhere. Few
of these richly dramatic renderings bear much, if any, resemblance to those milky clichéd images of Mary as passive vessel
that I had seen back in Sunday school. Each of these artists had
conjured her and the narrative of her life according to his own
personal vision. Most had outfitted her with the clothing and
accessories of their own eras, translating her forward in time, filling the canvas around her with objects and symbolic details
sometimes verging on the bizarre.

The Annunciation by Fra Angelico. A young blond Mary
dressed in a soft pink dress and a deep blue robe sits inside an
arched portico. The vaulted ceiling is blue dotted with gold and
the floor is a swirling wave of color. Mary has been surprised at

her reading by the arrival of the angel Gabriel. Her book is open upon her right knee, her hands are crossed against her breasts. Gabriel, resplendent in pink and gold and carefully balancing his large feathered wings, bows humbly before her and delivers the big news. A beam of golden light bearing a white dove shines down upon Mary, poured from a pair of hands inside the sun. To the left of the portico is a lush green forest out of which Adam and Eve are being firmly ushered by Michael the Archangel. Everyone in this painting is pale and blond and the haloes of Mary and Gabriel are as big as plates.

Virgin and Child by Jean Fouquet. An apparently bald Mary wears a large gold crown studded with rubies and pearls. Her white skin is tinged with green, so shiny and smooth she looks like an alien. Her tight-fitting, low-cut blue gown has burst open at the laces in the middle and her left breast has popped out. It is also greenish white, looking as round and hard as a billiard ball, with a tiny white nipple in the center. This bulbous breast hovers above the head of a plump baby Jesus resting naked on a pale gray sheet. He has red hair and colorless eyes, rolls of fat under his chin and around his elbows, wrists, ankles, and thighs. Both his left index finger and his fat little penis are pointing to the right at something beyond the frame. There are circles under his eyes and a single tear on his left cheek.

Glorification of the Virgin by Geertgen tot Sint Jans. Another Mary with long, thin red hair and a large forehead wears a bejeweled red and white crown. Her dress and cloak are both bright red. Beneath them she is wearing what appears to be a black leotard, the kind you would wear to aerobics class. She is apparently legless, poised on a golden half-circle with a nasty-looking lizard curled around it. The lizard has sharp claws and fangs and is spitting either its thin red tongue or a stream of blood up at Mary. She is holding the baby Jesus against her right shoulder. His arms and legs are gangly and thin. He is kicking his feet and holding in his hands two hollow silver globes that could be either Christmas tree ornaments or a pair of gaudy earrings. Mary and Jesus are contained in an oval of orange light which fades to black toward the frame. Both these light and dark areas are filled with hundreds of tiny naked angels so scrawny they look like skeletons.

Mater Dolorosa by El Greco. The sorrowful mother. This Mary wears a gray scarf over her dark brown hair, a black cloak against a black background. Her thin face is very small, her black eyes very large. Her hands are clasped in prayer at her breast and her head is tilted slightly to the left. Any minute now she is going to cry and cry and never stop.

Hail, Holy Queen, Mother of mercy! Hail, our life, our sweetness, and our hope! To you do we cry, poor banished children of Eve. To you do we send up our sighs, mourning and weeping in this valley of tears. Turn then, most gracious advocate, your eyes of mercy toward us; and after this, our exile, show unto us the blessed fruit of your womb, Jesus. O clement, O loving, O sweet Virgin Mary! Amen.

I do not mean to imply that I have carried these images of Mary in the front of my mind for all these years since. The truth is, I seldom gave her more than a passing thought, even when she did occasionally pop into view. There were those two old

Beatles songs, "Lady Madonna" and "Let It Be,"and there were several houses around town with small shrines set up in their front yards like lawn ornaments.

These featured blue and white plaster or concrete statues of Mary in various sizes. Some were installed in plastic grottoes, others in bathtubs. Many were decorated seasonally, with real or plastic lilies and strings of Christmas lights. I never witnessed anyone actually worshipping at or tending to one of these shrines. It was as if the decorations appeared and disappeared miraculously, by way of divine, rather than human, intervention. I did not give these installations any more serious thought than I gave to the pink flamingos or plastic dwarves that graced the adjoining front yards.

Day after day, week after week, year after year, I went on with my life in the usual secular way: making meals, making beds, making books, making promises, decisions, and mistakes, making my own dogged way in the world, with all of these divine images stowed away somewhere in the intricate folds of my brain. They were like dream images, those ones that are so vivid when you first wake in the morning, and then within minutes they begin to fade until, by the time you get the coffee made, they have disappeared completely and you are left with nothing more than an uneasy sense of having lost something but you cannot say what.

Maybe Mary is one of those archetypes that swim in the pool of the collective unconscious that Carl Jung wrote about, a part of that common symbolic inheritance of all humanity. Maybe everyone has some image of Mary in the back of their minds, an image that, like matter, can be neither created nor destroyed.

I thought about Mary only when she made the news. This

happened more often than you might expect of a woman who had been dead for almost two thousand years.

As the new millennium closed in upon us all, reports of sightings of Mary seemed to increase. News of these phenomena were usually relegated to the back pages of the daily paper. Mary had a habit of popping up in unexpected and unlikely places. At various times, she was said to have appeared in a yucca tree, a privet hedge, and a muddy field of cabbages and onions. In various locations around the world, icons of Mary were changing color, moving around, and weeping blood, tears, oil, or milk. She frequently spoke to the visionaries, delivering messages, warnings, and instructions. She asked them to pray, to fast, to spread the word, to have churches or shrines built in her honor on the sites where she had revealed herself to them. Her image was photographed in the large tinted windows of a finance company in Clearwater, Florida, and on the concrete floor of an auto parts store in Progreso, Texas. And then there was the Holy Camaro— Mary's likeness spotted by a sharp-eyed mechanic in the dents and rust spots on the bumper of a late-model Camaro in Elsa, Texas.

There were numerous sightings of Jesus too. His face was seen in the X ray of the spine of a man whose neck was broken in a car accident, in the wound on a maple tree where a limb had been lopped off, on the side of a soybean oil storage tank, in the scorch marks on a burnt tortilla, on the brick wall of a Tim Hortons donut shop in Bras D'Or, Nova Scotia, and in a plate of spaghetti on a Pizza Hut billboard in Stone Mountain, Georgia.

I read these reports with an ironic postmodern eye. But I tried to be open-minded too. If, for the sake of argument, I managed to overcome my own skepticism and could convince myself that those who claimed to have seen Jesus and Mary were not simply the spiritually inclined equivalent of those who claimed to have seen Elvis or aliens or both, if I could actually accept these divine apparitions as plausible fact, then I had to wonder why Jesus and Mary were choosing to reveal themselves in such ludicrous ways. Why were they so foolishly leaving themselves and the visionaries wide open to ridicule? Was it a test, a test of faith? Were they saying to the faithful: If you can believe this, then you can believe anything?

Or were they simply trying to show the world that even the Almighty has a sense of humor?

How else was I to interpret the newspaper story of several evangelical Christians who claimed that God had implanted gold fillings in their mouths after they prayed for dental healing? (Having had a lifelong aversion to dentists myself, I have to admit that the idea of divine dentistry appeals to me. I assume it would be painless and silent and would not involve being held helpless in a chair for an hour or two while a large man and his assistant stick their hands and an assortment of ghoulish instruments into your mouth.)

God as dentist? Jesus' face in a plate of spaghetti? The Virgin Mary on the bumper of a Camaro? These manifestations struck me as akin to subliminal advertising, the way they used to embed pictures of popcorn between movie frames or images of naked copulating couples in the ice cubes of liquor ads. Buy popcorn. Get drunk, get lucky. Believe in me.

But even while these reservations were going through my rational mind, I found myself deeply moved by the unflinching faith of those who truly believed.

Whenever I was asked (or asked myself) if I believed in God, I always said yes. I guess I was what you might call "a small *c*

Christian." Although I had stopped going to Sunday school as soon as my parents would let me and had seldom set foot in a church since, I, like most people, whether they go to church or not, did pray sometimes, mostly out of sheer desperation, mostly for an easy way out. I prayed in the regular way, begging God, not Mary, for favors, forgiveness, money, or peace of mind. I, too, at certain junctures of anger and despair, had thrown up my arms, glared at the heavens, and wailed:

—Why me, God? Why me?

And sometimes, sweating and sleepless in the middle of a long hot night, I, too, with the humid darkness pressing down upon my mouth like a hand, had whispered:

—Forgive me, God. Please forgive me.

I did not think of myself as a particularly religious or spiritual person. I guess I was what has been called a neoagnostic. My trust in intellectual reasoning as the most important avenue to knowledge and understanding left me feeling skeptical about traditional organized religion. And yet, I did believe in *something,* some higher metaphysical power in operation beyond the merely human, some omnipresent force administering rewards and punishments according to some incomprehensible plan. Perhaps it was simply for want of a better word that I called this power God. My confidence in this supreme being waxed and waned according to my own circumstances and to how hard done by I did or did not feel in any given situation.

Like most people, I was always hoping and praying for something, and I did not know for sure the difference between the two. I could always find something to feel guilty about and so I assumed that punishment could not be far behind. It never occurred to me that some of the things I perceived as punishment might just be coincidences. Like most people, I did not understand that not everything was about me.

I had not worked out the details of this whole arrangement. If anyone challenged my beliefs, I found myself quickly floundering out of my depth. I had always taken God more or less for granted, but I had no more proof of his existence than the next person, no more reasonable explanation as to why there was so much suffering and tragedy in the world if indeed there were actually someone in charge. I did not understand evil either.

For want of a better explanation, I often fell back on the notion of poetic justice. I clung to this idea in a split-brain kind of way: much as I could see little or no consistent evidence of good people being justly and richly rewarded, still I kept insisting that bad people would surely get what they deserved in the end. This was like believing my daily horoscope in the newspaper when it promised riches, romance, and good news from an unexpected source, while dismissing astrology as the trivial construct of simple-minded fools when my horoscope predicted failure, sickness, and betrayal.

As for the matter of poets and justice, I have since read the story of Saints Theodore and Theophanes, two Greek brothers who were tortured in the ninth century for their outspoken belief that images of Mary, Jesus, and the saints were suitable objects for worship and devotion. In an effort to silence them, the iconoclastic emperor, Theophilus, had them bound and tied to a bench. Then twelve lines of poetry were carved into their foreheads.

Although I was mostly of two minds about the whole issue of God, I had to admit that, in my heart of hearts, I wanted very much to believe. Not surprisingly, I was also of two minds on that Monday in April when I first met the Virgin Mary. On the one hand, I figured there was a reasonably good chance that I had lost my mind altogether. On the other hand, I felt as if I had known her all my life. And in many ways, I had.

Of all the images of Mary that had entered my life over the years, the one that came most clearly to mind that day was, not surprisingly, the most recent.

About six weeks earlier, I had happened to turn on the late-night news just as they were showing video footage of the disastrous floods taking place several hundred miles to the southwest. While we were enjoying a pleasant early spring here, it was proving to be a dangerous season in many other areas of the continent. This was the first of many such floods brought on by heavy rains and the run-off from unusually high snowfalls that winter. The camera panned whole towns submerged. The brown water reached to the tops of stop signs in some places, to the second floors of houses and stores in others. Floating in the water were pots and planks, mattresses and kitchen chairs, books, pictures, children's toys, dead dogs and cats, an overturned canoe. More rain was predicted and still the level of the river had not peaked.

This story ended with a shot of a life-sized statue of Mary completely surrounded by water up to the middle of her chest. Her face was battered, her cheekbones chipped, her forehead gouged, and her nose was half broken off. While the water rose around her, she stood there alone in her blue dress, and still the rain continued to fall.

And God said unto Noah . . . behold, I, even I, do bring a flood of waters upon the earth, to destroy all flesh, wherein is the breath of life, from under heaven; and every thing that is in the earth shall die . . . and I will cause it to rain upon the earth forty days and forty nights; and every living substance that I have made will I destroy from off the face of the earth.

They cut then from the statue of Mary to a commercial for a new cold remedy. A cherubic red-haired boy in a shiny yellow slicker couldn't find his other boot. His mother, who had a terrible cold but you'd never know it because she'd taken this amazing new product, helped him look. In seconds, she was standing in the doorway with a smile on her face and a little yellow rainboot in her hand. She helped her son on with his boot, kissed him on the top of the head, and sent him on his merry, puddle-jumping way. Then she enthusiastically explained that these new cold pills made her feel so good that she could once again happily assume her rightful motherly role as the finder of all lost things.

Secrets

$\mathcal{M}$ary found the coffee filters, ground the beans, rinsed out the pot, filled it with cold fresh water, and then poured it slowly into the coffeemaker. I sat at the kitchen table. I watched her and I worried. What *did* she want from me? I thought about those brief newspaper reports I had read and the many requests she had made of those other people over the years. Did she want me to pray, to fast, to go to the bishop and tell him to build a church here on this very spot where my cozy kitchen now stood?

I recalled having seen the movie *Song of Bernadette* on television several months before. It was shown after the late news on a night when I couldn't sleep anyway, so I had stayed up and watched the whole thing. It was either that or the Home Shopping Network.

A raven-haired, dewy-eyed Jennifer Jones had won an Academy Award for her 1943 portrayal of Bernadette Soubirous, the sickly, illiterate, poverty-stricken fourteen-year-old girl to whom Mary had appeared eighteen times in 1858 in a grotto named Massabielle just outside the town of Lourdes in southern France. The movie was based on a novel which was, in turn, based on actual documented events. After the opening credits, the following words appeared in elegant script on the screen: *For those who believe in God, no explanation is necessary. For those who do not believe in God, no explanation is possible.*

At first no one believed Bernadette's story of the beautiful lady in the grotto, not even her own family who berated and abused her for her idiotic imaginings. Even the dean of Lourdes did not believe her. But as word of Bernadette's visions quickly spread, people began following her to the grotto in ever-increasing numbers. The dean told Bernadette to ask for a small miracle to prove the divine identity of her lady. He wanted this lady to make the wild rosebush in the grotto bloom right then, in the last week of February. The rosebush did not bloom. Instead, on the lady's instruction, Bernadette fell to her knees, dug in the dirt, smeared it on her hands and face, and then ate some. The crowd hollered with derision and declared her insane. But later that day, a spring began to flow at that very spot. A blind man was healed. A dying baby was saved. And so began the legacy of the miracles at Lourdes.

I remembered all that had befallen poor Bernadette in the aftermath of her visions, the price she had paid for the privilege of having been so chosen. She was tormented, ridiculed, and humiliated for her ecstasies, endlessly harassed, intimidated, and interrogated by medical, government, and religious authorities.

I remembered Mary saying to Bernadette:

—I cannot promise to make you happy in this world but only in the next.

Eight years after her meetings with Mary, Bernadette was counseled by the dean of Lourdes to enter the convent of the Sisters of Charity at Nevers. He warned her that there was no corner of the world where she could hide and lead a normal life. He said she must now assume the responsibility of having been chosen and so dedicate her life henceforth to God. Bernadette did not want to be a nun but, at the age of twenty-two, she entered the convent. Although it was not supposed to be a prison, she lived there in a small bare cell and spent her days scrubbing pots and washing stone floors. Even there she was scorned and shunned by many of the nuns who could not conquer their own envy and resentment, their own failures of faith.

Bernadette's health steadily declined and she died in the convent on April 16, 1879, at the age of thirty-five. Many years later her body was exhumed and found to be incorrupt, untouched by the normal processes of decomposition and decay. On June 14, 1925, Bernadette was beatified by the Roman Catholic Church, and in 1933, on December 8, the feast day of the Immaculate Conception, she was canonized. It was said that Mary had given Bernadette three sacred secrets but these were never revealed.

Today about 4 million visitors pass through Lourdes each year and 27,000 gallons of water flow from the miraculous spring each day.

Now here I was with the Virgin Mary in my kitchen. I did not want to be so chosen. I was not Catholic and I did not want to become a nun. I did not want to be ridiculed, humiliated, or interrogated. I did not want people to follow me around expecting miracles. I did not want happiness only in the next world. I wanted it *now.*

I did not want to be privy to her secrets. I knew enough about secrets already: how hard it is to keep them, how impossible it is to forget them, how they grow in your heart when you're not looking, busily multiplying like feverish rabbits, silently mutating like malignant cells.

Tell me no secrets, I'll tell you no lies.

* * *

While the coffee brewed, Mary dropped the uneaten black olives back into the jar and put them in the fridge. Then she washed the dishes and stacked them in the rack to dry. She was humming a spritely tune I did not recognize. My silence did not seem to bother her. She wiped the table with the damp dishcloth and did not look at me. I was starting to wonder if she might be drawing this out on purpose, giving me plenty of time to imagine the worst. Faint tweaks of annoyance began to flit through my growing consternation.

She rummaged in the bottom cupboard beside the stove and came up with a black lacquered tray I had not used in years. On it she arranged two mugs, two spoons, a jar of honey, and a small pitcher of milk. I thought these ordinary objects that I handled every day without really looking at them might take on an unearthly radiance in her hands. But they remained unchanged: the cheap glass pitcher with a chip on its spout, the sticky plastic jar with the honey inside half-crystallized and flecked with toast crumbs. In her graceful hands these objects were just what they had always been: inanimate, imperfect, unmoved; certain, silent, and above reproach.

She poured the coffee into the mugs, brought the tray to the table, and sat down. She was silent while I added milk and stirred in a teaspoon of honey. Apparently she preferred her coffee black. She took a sip and made a small appreciative sound in the back of her throat.

Finally she looked at me.

—I need a place to stay for a week, she said.

—Here? I croaked. You want to stay here?

—Yes, she said. I am so tired. I need a break.

She brushed the stray curls back from her forehead and sighed, the same sighing I'd heard the night before in the living room in the corner by the fig tree. Her face faltered in the sunlight and I could see it then around her eyes, in the lines on her forehead and on either side of her mouth. I could see that fatigue all women of a certain age are prone to, that bone-deep weariness that can only be caused by life itself. By all those hours of smiling and frowning, laughing and crying. By all those days of explaining and regretting, hoping and housework. By all those nights of yearning and longing, searching and praying. By all those weeks of loving and caring, worrying and waiting. By all those months of wondering where does the time go. By all those years of aging and changing and staying the same.

By all those years of keeping the faith.

I know full well how it wears you down, like water dripping on a rock. How it puts gray in your hair, wrinkles in your brow, a knot in your stomach, a slump in your shoulders, an ache in your throat, and a stone in your heart.

I could not imagine how it must feel to have been living a life for two thousand years.

—I can certainly understand that, I said.

She looked relieved.

—I need to rest up before next month, she said.

I must have looked puzzled.

—The month of May, she explained, was dedicated to me hundreds of years ago. Around the world people will be honoring me in special ways. A lot will be expected of me and I must not let them down.

—Of course not, I said.

—I know I could go and stay anywhere, she said. I could check into a fancy hotel and order all my meals up from room service. I could go to a seaside resort or take a cruise and spend whole days just dozing in the sun. But that's not what I want, that's not what I need. I am tired of having no fixed address. I've been hungering for a home, a *real* home, if only for a little while. I want to stay here with you.

—Why here? I asked. Why me? I'm not even Catholic.

—Ah yes, the proverbial question, she said, laughing wryly. Well, you have a comfortable home with an extra bedroom. You are a fine writer. I've always been a great lover of books.

I recalled that, in my Medieval and Renaissance Art course back in university, we had indeed looked at several paintings in which she was pictured with a book in her hand or her lap. Most of these were paintings of the Annunciation. When the angel Gabriel appeared to make his big announcement, he had apparently come upon her while she was reading. There were also several depictions of Mary as a child with her mother, Saint Anne, and they had a book open between them, Anne teaching her daughter to read.

—And you're between books right now, Mary continued, so I figured I wouldn't be coming at a bad time. Besides, you're a great cook and I've been just dying for a home-cooked meal.

I had no idea how seriously I was supposed to be taking all of this. She went on.

—And you are quiet, she said. I looked into some other homes before coming here but they were all so crowded and chaotic. There were crying babies always demanding to be fed or changed, surly adolescents playing loud obnoxious music and slamming doors, big smelly dogs galloping up and down hallways, crabby-faced adults arguing, worrying, always rushing around. I want peace. I want quiet. The people of your country have a reputation for being quiet, polite, decent, and rather reserved. I haven't been to this country nearly as often as I've been to some of the others. I thought I was long overdue for another visit. So . . . why you? Why not?

—Besides, she went on, I knew if I came here, I would indeed get some rest. You are not going through a crisis right now—a crisis of faith or anything else. You are not contemplating suicide or murder. You are not suffering from a terminal illness. You are not blind, deaf, mute, lame, or simple-minded. You are strong, you are healthy, you are talented. You don't need me at all right now. And besides, you are not afraid of me.

—Well, maybe a little bit, I had to admit. This is a lot to take in.

—I'm sure it is. But I did try to warn you, Mary said. There were signs that I was coming. But I didn't want to make as grand an entrance as I have been known to in the past.

—Signs? I asked.

And then suddenly some of those unusual incidents of the previous week began to make sense. The squirrel, the mechanical healings, the day all my errands were completed without a single frisson of frustration. And that sighing last night in the corner—which had apparently not been a figment of my imagination after all.

—I'm sorry, I said. I didn't know they were signs. I thought I was just having a good week.

—I was trying to be discreet, Mary explained. This time I didn't want the whole world to know I was about to put in an appearance.

Much as, in retrospect, I could read the signs, still I knew that nothing could have really prepared me for this.

Mary got up and refilled her coffee. I had barely touched mine. I was well beyond my coffee quota for the day and my stomach was queasy—for that and any number of other reasons, no doubt.

When she sat back down, she looked at me sternly and said:

—There is only one thing about you that troubles me.

While listening to all that she had just said, my mind had been racing with reservations, protestations, excuses, and reluctance. I had been piling up all the reasons why I did not want her here. Besides thinking about how I did not want to be chosen, how I was not willing to risk the havoc it was bound to wreak on my quiet life, I had also been thinking of how I do not much like having houseguests, divine or otherwise. I had been thinking of how they always interfere with my routines, they want clean towels and regular meals, they want to help, they want to talk, they want to engage me every time I turn around, and the more unobtrusive they try to be, the more they just get in the way.

But now I was stung to hear that she might have some reservations about me. This was like being hurt when you're not invited to a party you didn't want to go to anyway.

I had to admit that I desperately wanted her to like me. I wanted so much to please her. With all my heart, I wanted to be worthy.

—What is it? I asked with trepidation.

—I am not entirely sure that you'll be able to keep my visit a secret, she said. Will you be able to resist the temptation to go and write a book about it afterwards?

—Probably not, I admitted.

Obviously there was no question of trying to lie to her.

—Then you must make me a promise, she said. You must promise me that you will use a pseudonym and you will call it a novel. When that book comes out, I want to see in big letters that disclaimer on the copyright page: *This is a work of fiction.*

—Yes, I said quickly. I promise.

She leaned closer to me and the look on her formerly friendly face was almost threatening.

—Do you know what will happen if you break this promise?

I could just imagine. I thought about Lot's wife turned into a pillar of salt. I thought about the ten plagues of Egypt: water made blood, frogs, gnats, flies, death to herds and flocks, boils and sores, thunder and hail, a plague of locusts, three days of darkness, the firstborn slain throughout the land. I thought about the Great Flood. I thought about Adam and Eve banished forever from the Garden. I thought about the trials of Job. I thought about being struck down in the prime of life, now when everything was going so well, now when all my dreams were finally coming true.

—Divine wrath, I muttered.

—If you break this promise, divine wrath will be the least of your problems, Mary said. Divine wrath will not even be necessary. If people find out that I have been here, that I have talked to you, eaten with you, and slept in your house, they will descend upon you in droves. They will make a plague of locusts look like a minor inconvenience.

She took a deep breath and her voice became that of a fire-and-brimstone preacher hectoring his flock. Clearly, this was nothing like the casual conversation she had made over lunch.

—They will come to your house by the thousands, she said. They will come by the busload, the curious and the faithful both. Some will even come on their knees. There will be traffic jams, parking problems. The neighbors will complain. The police will come. Every newspaper, magazine, and talk show in the world will cover it. You will be featured on the front page of the *National Enquirer* for months. You will be ridiculed and revered throughout the land. After a while, you will not know which is worse.

Her dark eyes were nearly shooting off sparks as she warmed to her topic.

—You will be worshipped and reviled. You will be called visionary, angel, prophet, saint, and divine messenger of God.

You will also be called charlatan, crackpot, heretic, blasphemer, witch, and vile whore of Satan. Some will say you should be beatified, canonized. Others will say you should be burned at the stake. Most will just shake their heads and say you should be locked up.

She sat perfectly still while she spoke, with her hands folded together on the table in front of her.

—Fast-food stands will spring up, she said. They will sell hamburgers, hot dogs, popcorn, ice cream, and cotton candy in your front yard. There will be a gift shop in the driveway. They will sell souvenir bumper stickers, teeshirts, posters, pencils, fridge magnets, and holy trading cards. They will camp in your yard, both front and back. There will be Porta Potties. They will dig up your garden searching for a miraculous spring. If they don't find one, they will declare the water that comes from your garden hose holy. They will bottle it and sell it by mail-order. They will drink it, bathe in it, and wash their cars with it.

Fully transported now by her own vision of hell on earth, Mary continued. I could do nothing but listen. It was as if the kitchen around us had receded and all I could see was her face.

I remembered watching a television program about a woman in New Mexico who had seen the face of Jesus in the scorch marks on a flour tortilla she was frying for her husband's breakfast. I remembered that more than eleven thousand people had since trooped through their kitchen to have a good look.

—They will follow you everywhere, Mary said. They will touch your skirt, your legs, your shoulders, your hair. They will fall on their knees before you in the supermarket, in your favorite restaurant, even in the dentist's waiting room. They will beg you for miracles. They will cling to your ankles and wash your feet with their tears. They will go through your garbage and your recycling box. They will steal your underwear off the clothesline, peel the paint from your walls, pull the plants out of your flower beds, and worship all these things as holy relics.

I could see that, given the right topic, she had a definite tendency to pontificate. This, I suppose, was to be expected. I also noticed that, the longer she spoke, the fainter her accent became, until, by this point, it had disappeared altogether.

—They will heap so many offerings on your front step that you will not be able to open the door. You will be barricaded inside your own home by the mighty force of their adulation. They will fill up your mailbox with letters, more letters, thousands of letters, just like the letters they write to me.

She closed her eyes and quoted a long litany of desperation.

—Please cure my mother's breast cancer. Please cure my father's bad heart. Please cure my cousin's varicose veins. Please cure my son's brain tumor. Please cure my acne which is making me very ugly and unhappy.

—Please let my baby be born healthy. Please let me pass my Science test on Tuesday. Please let me win the lottery so I can buy a new car.

—Please make my husband stop drinking and fooling around. Please make my husband stop beating me. Please make me stop loving him anyway.

—Please forgive me for lying to my mother. Please forgive me for hitting my dog. Please forgive me for sleeping with my best friend's wife. Please forgive me for ending up in jail again.

—Please help me find a good job. Please help me find a good man. Please help me find my cat. Please help me find my daughter who ran away from home two years ago. Please help me lose twenty pounds by next Saturday. Please help me. Please help me. Please help me.

She bowed her head and her voice dropped to a whisper.

—When you go to bed at night, still you will hear their

voices, like music in the next room, a waterfall in the distance, leaves in the wind, like your own blood coursing through your veins. You will never be able to get them out of your head. Their prayers and promises, their nightmares and dreams. Their pain. Their hope. Their faith. Their innocent faith will break your heart.

She stopped and opened her eyes.

—If you break this promise to keep my visit a secret, your life will never be the same. Do I make myself clear?

—Yes, I whispered.

—Do you understand?

—Yes, I understand.

She looked into my eyes.

—May I stay?

I knew that I was already in over my head. She was already here. She had already talked to me, eaten with me, used my bathroom. I knew there could be no turning back now. I knew there was nothing else I could do.

—Yes, I said. Yes, of course you can stay.

Visitor

—Thank you, Mary said, smiling and patting my hand. I knew I could count on you. I would like to say that you won't regret it, but that, I suppose, remains to be seen.

I nodded and smiled back, limply, not sure whether she was teasing or not. I could not immediately think of what to do next. Mary glanced discreetly at her purse, suitcase, and running shoes where they still sat innocently enough on the kitchen floor near the doorway. I looked at them too.

Both the purse and the suitcase were black. The purse was large, made of smooth leather with zippered pockets front and back. Her suitcase, like a million others, was made of nylon fabric, hard-sided, with pockets, handles, wheels, and feet. There was neither a name tag nor one of those coded destination tickets they stick on at the airport when you check in. The tabs of two zippers met at the top, secured by a tiny gold-colored lock. A rectangular silver badge on the front proclaimed the brand name in stylized black letters: JAGUAR. Whether meant to be evocative of the sleek luxury car or the fierce big cat, either way this name was a lot for a suitcase to live up to.

The running shoes were white, a well-worn pair of Nikes. Most people who wear this brand do not know that Nike was the goddess of victory and constant companion of Zeus. She was one of a family of abstractions who were the offspring of the Titan Pallas and the goddess of the River Styx. Nike's brothers were Cratus (Strength), Zelus (Emulation), and Bia (Violence). Whether or not Mary knew the genesis of their name, the backs of her runners were broken and the left lace was knotted and frayed.

Despite their mythological, animalian, and/or automotive allusions, these objects, like most when taken at face value, told me nothing. Or maybe it was just that what they told me was not at all what I was expecting to hear.

Mary cleared her throat and stood up.

—Maybe I should unpack now? she suggested.

—Yes, yes, I said, relieved to have been given this gentle nudge in the right direction. Let me show you to your room.

Mary picked up her purse and I took the suitcase. We left the running shoes where they were. I led the way down the hall, wondering if the back bedroom was more or less presentable. Generally speaking, I am a passable housekeeper, as long as you don't look too closely. I tend to concentrate on the visible, leaving that which is hidden to its own devices (which, I suspect, include a predisposition toward a form of parthenogenesis that enables both dirt and clutter to spontaneously reproduce themselves). My housekeeping mantra is: Out of sight, out of mind.

Usually when visitors are imminent, I have a little cleaning fit. This is a reflex impressed upon me long ago by my mother, no doubt, for whom the words *company* and *cleaning* are synonymous. It also arises from my recognition of the fact that other people, even your own flesh and blood, are not likely to be as oblivious to or complaisant about your dirt as you are. But since this visitor had not been announced in advance (or, at least, since I had not recognized the announcement), I had not given the room any special attention beyond the usual Saturday vacuuming.

I did not actually expect that Mary would perform a full-scale inspection, get down on her knees and scout out the dust bunnies under the bed, or run her fingers along the windowsill checking for dust. But still I was worried. After all, you know what they say about cleanliness being next to godliness.

It had only been three weeks since I last had visitors. My sister, her husband, and their daughter had been here for the Easter weekend at the end of March. I distinctly remembered making up the bed with fresh sheets and blankets the day after they left. It had not been slept in since. I'd last had the sewing machine out to do some mending a few weeks before, and I had no arts-and-crafts projects in progress at the moment. Other than the few rejected items I had hung up on Saturday, the closet was empty and there were plenty of hangers.

I flicked on the light and tried to see the room through Mary's eyes. I was relieved: it was indeed tidy, and that which was hidden had remained hidden. It is a comfortable room, furnished with odds and ends accumulated over the years. Besides the bed, which is a queen-size with solid wooden head- and foot-boards, there is a night table, an old oak dresser with four drawers and a large mirror, a small bookcase, a wicker armchair, and a wicker trunk in which I store extra blankets and pillows. Everything was in order, if perhaps in need of a thorough dusting.

I set the suitcase down beside the bed and opened the curtains. As forecast, the sky had clouded over and there were spots of rain on the window.

—Lovely, Mary said. The room is just lovely. I'm sure I will be perfectly comfortable here.

—I hope you'll make yourself at home, I said.

Still holding her purse, she sat down on the edge of the bed and I could see it again, the fatigue around her eyes and her mouth. It was there in the way she relaxed her neck and shoulders and in the way she let go of her purse, briefly patted the blue duvet cover, and then let her hands fall limp at her sides.

The room was not large but with Mary in it, it seemed bigger. I had noticed back in the kitchen that she was, not surprisingly, the kind of person whose presence filled up a room. I know from experience that this is not always a good thing. I once briefly dated a man who so filled up a room that whenever I was with him, I felt crowded, squashed, backed into a corner. I suspected that, with him, this would have been the case even if we were in an empty ballroom with twenty-foot ceilings and windows on all sides. I soon realized this was not really an effect of his presence, not even of his personality, but of his ego, which was massive to begin with and possessed of an instant and relentless capacity for expanding to fill the space available. But with Mary, it was the opposite. The room itself seemed to have expanded to accommodate her. And the slightly shabby furniture had acquired a quiescent beauty that I had never noticed before.

She was silent while I fussed around for a few minutes straightening the afghan folded at the foot of the bed and making sure there was room in the dresser and the night table for her things. I could not help but think that if this were a hotel room, there would have been a Gideon Bible in the night table drawer. While traveling to promote my books, I have stayed in many hotel rooms, some lovely, some not, and although I have never actually read one of those bedside Bibles, still I have always been comforted by finding it there.

But here in the night table drawer, there was a yellow flashlight, a ball made entirely of rubber bands, a box of colored paper clips, a broken stapler, and an envelope of photographs I had been meaning to send to my parents for months. I pushed all of these to the back of the drawer. Then I pointed out to Mary what she could see perfectly well with her own two eyes: that there was a telephone on the night table and also a good reading lamp.

Mary reached for her purse, rummaged in the zippered pocket, and took out a set of keys.

Keys to what? I wondered silently. The seven heavens perhaps? Or the twelve pearly gates of the holy city, the post-apocalyptic New Jerusalem?

She held them up so I could see the tag, which was a picture of her encased in clear plastic. There was a blue globe at her feet and fluffy white clouds all around. Her dress was pink, her robe was blue. Above her hovered a circle of blond angels, about to place a golden crown upon her haloed head.

—It was a gift, she said, grinning.

She lifted her suitcase onto the bed and separated a tiny gold key from the rest on the ring. As she inserted the key into the lock on the suitcase, I involuntarily took a step back. I thought again of Pandora's box. In a variation on the theme this time, I imagined not a teeming swarm of evils let loose upon the world but a veritable stampede of angels tumbling over each other to get out. Having been cooped up in there for God knows how long, they would, I imagined, come bursting out, stretching and muttering, unfurling and flexing their white-feathered wings. Or perhaps they would be more graceful, wafting out like the genie from Aladdin's lamp or unfolding one at a time like flowers blossoming on fast-action film.

Barring an entourage of angels, I expected that there would at least be a beam or blaze of light, probably accompanied by harp music and the smell of flowers. Or maybe now was the time for the ten thousand blue butterflies or the million rose petals or the flock of doves to be released into the room.

I held my breath.

Mary unzipped the suitcase and lifted the lid.

Nothing happened: no angels, no music, no fragrance, no special effects whatsoever. I was, I must admit, a little disappointed.

The inside of her suitcase was at first glance as unremarkable as the outside. There was the usual compacted and flattened jumble of clothing, accessories, and toiletries. It looked to be as true for Mary as for anyone else that no matter how carefully you have packed in the first place, by the time you reach your destination, the contents of your suitcase will have been stirred, scrambled, and utterly rearranged while in transit.

Mary began to extract the items from the suitcase one by one, spreading them out neatly on the bed: balls of socks, rolled shirts, folded pants, a pale green nightgown, a brown cardigan much like the one I had just rejected as dowdy, the long black dress she had been wearing when she arrived.

She continued to pull things out of the suitcase, a great many more things than you would expect it to be able to hold. It was as if the suitcase were bottomless and bewitched, as if the more she took out of it, the more it filled up. I was reminded of the familiar cartoon sequence in which a tiny car comes tearing down the road, screeches to a stop, then all the doors are flung open, and dozens of large people get out. I also thought of a souvenir my young niece had brought back from Disneyland the previous summer. It was about the size of a checker to begin with, but when she soaked it in warm water as per the instructions, it slowly turned into a full-sized facecloth with a picture of Mickey Mouse on it.

The bed was nearly covered now, with more shirts, more pants, two pairs of shoes, a blow-dryer, two matching cosmetic bags, a jewelry case, a spiral notebook, and a small pile of books with a black gilt-edged Bible on top (making Gideon in the night table unnecessary after all).

—Obviously, Mary said, I still haven't quite mastered the fine art of traveling light.

I had to admit that I suffered from the same problem. Much as I may sometimes fantasize about setting off on a journey with nothing but a toothbrush, a notebook, and a change of underwear, in actual fact, I know I will never manage it. For me, packing, even for just an overnight stay, is a painful process fraught with anxiety and indecision. I know full well that this is the result of my need to control every little thing (including the weather), to predict and prepare for every possible eventuality, to try to take as much of home with me as I can wherever I may go. When packing, I have to keep reminding myself that I am not trekking off into the tundra, that I am going to a perfectly well-appointed city where anything that I have inadvertently left behind can be quite handily replaced. Still I never leave home without my travel iron.

I also like to bring along a good selection of reading material. I cannot bear the thought of finding myself trapped with the wrong book on an airplane or a train or in a hotel room with no bookstore in sight. I need to take a choice of fiction because how can I know in advance what I'll be in the mood for when the time comes? I usually also pack two or three weighty academic or philosophical volumes that I need to read for research but that I've been saving for months in optimistic anticipation of some future interval in which I will find myself suddenly smarter than usual. I always think that once I am away from home, I will finally be able to muster the focus and acuity of mind needed to make sense of these tomes. This almost never happens and so I cart these books back home again, unopened and still unread.

As I was craning my neck to get a look at the titles of Mary's books, the telephone rang. Automatically I reached to answer it, then stopped myself and looked at her, my left hand still hovering in midair.

—Maybe you should let that go for now, she said.

My hand fell back down to my side and I stood staring at the ringing telephone. Three, four, five rings and then the sound of the answering machine clicking on in my study across the hall, a female voice murmuring into the ostensibly empty house. I could not quite make out the message or identify the speaker but I thought it might be my agent. The voice rambled on and then the machine clicked off. I could picture its little red light flashing doggedly into the room.

—I guess there are still a few details that need to be worked out, Mary said.

—Yes, I agreed. I do have some questions. What should I tell people? How can I explain this without lying or giving the secret away?

The other questions I wanted to ask seemed childish even to me: Could other people see her, could they hear her, was she as real to them as she was to me?

—Of course there must be no lying, Mary said.

—Of course not.

—There is a Catholic doctrine, she said, called *mental reservation.* This means that when speaking or writing, a person can add certain modifications to solve the dilemma of how to keep a secret without actually lying.

To me, this practice sounded more like a common character-istic of human nature than a point of theology. How many times have you exercised mental reservation to avoid hurting someone else's feelings? How many times have you told a friend her new dress was beautiful while thinking: But not on you?

—Although this doctrine is not taught as often as it used to be, Mary said, I think it would serve you well in this particular situation. You could just tell people that you've had an unex-pected visitor, someone from the past, she said with a smile. That much is true.

—Yes, true, quite true.

—I am indeed someone from the past, she said, if not exactly someone from *your* past. But you don't have to tell people that. Probably the best strategy is not to go into too much detail. Perhaps you could just warn people that you'll be tied up for the week with an unexpected houseguest.

This would not be difficult. My friends, knowing that I work at home, are not prone to showing up at my door unannounced. As for my neighbors, we are friendly enough but not especially curious about each other's lives, and we seldom visit back and forth. Besides, no one would find it odd if I were more reclusive than usual for a while. As I have said, I am a very solitary person by nature.

—If more complicated situations come up, Mary said, I'm sure you'll be able to handle them.

—I hope so, I said doubtfully.

—Don't worry, she said. I have faith in you, probably more faith in you than you have in yourself. Or in me, for that matter. And I know you will be able to tell the truth. If not the whole truth, still nothing but the truth.

—I hope so, I said again. I certainly did not want to disappoint her.

As it turned out, none of my friends called or came by all week. I had no more calls from my agent, nor any from my editor or my family. Even the telemarketers fell mostly silent for the week. Solitary though I may be, this almost total lack of contact was unusual, a convenient coincidence in which I suspected Mary herself had a hand.

Now she had piled her books on the night table and started putting her clothes away in the closet and the dresser.

—When I'm finished here, she said, I wouldn't mind having a little nap.

—That sounds like a good idea, I said, checking my watch.

It had been quite the day already and it was only two o'clock.

—I've come directly from Mexico, Mary said, where the siesta, of course, is a national custom. I found it a very easy habit to acquire.

This confirmed my original impression that she had recently been spending time in the southern sun, her skin so brown and golden at a time of the year when we in the north were just emerging pale and grublike from another long dark winter.

—Yes, I said, I've always thought it was a custom that should be adopted here too.

The truth was that even if I had been alone at home having a regular day, I might at that point have been thinking about a nap. I consider being able to have a rest in the afternoon one of the great advantages of working at home.

—And there's the matter of jet lag too, Mary said, leaving me to speculate as to exactly how she got here anyway.

—I'll leave you alone then, I said. My room is right next door if you need anything.

—Thank you, she said. Have a good rest.

—You too.

—I will.

I turned to close the door behind me.

—Try not to worry, Mary said. Everything will be all right. Try to remember what Blessed Julian of Norwich said: *All shall be well and all shall be well and all manner of thing shall be well.*

I closed the door of her room and went into my study. I listened to the message that had been left earlier. It was indeed my agent, calling to tell me that a finer point of negotiation in one of my foreign contracts had been resolved to everyone's satisfaction.

—No need to call me back, she said. So I didn't.

I went into my bedroom, closed the door, and then the curtains. Furnished and arranged in much the same manner as the back bedroom, mine is somewhat larger, with two windows instead of one and enough space for a wicker loveseat. But in my bedroom, the color scheme is shades of white, off-white, and natural wood, with subtle beige and pale gray accents. The walls are eggshell, the curtains are ecru, and the loveseat is white with an oyster-colored cushion. The duvet cover is white eyelet cotton and the afghan folded at the foot of the bed is pearl gray. On top of the dresser I keep an assortment of fragrant white candles of varying sizes.

All of this is thanks in part to a spread I once saw in a home decorating magazine, which stressed the calming effect of this stylistic approach to interiors. But mostly it is the product of a persistent image I had of myself retiring each night to just such an oasis, hungering for peace, sanctuary, and sustenance. After drinking in its refreshment and redemption while I slept, I imagined that I would open my eyes each morning to discover myself reborn, strong again, safe, serene, nigh unto beatific.

That afternoon, the white room, as it was meant to, came as a great relief. I took off my glasses and my watch and set them on the night table. I lay down on the bed and pulled up the afghan to cover myself. Flat on my back, I inhaled the scent of lavender and orange that filled the room. This fragrance did not emanate from some divine mysterious source but from a porcelain dish of potpourri on the night table. I read once in an article about aromatherapy that a combination of these two scents can be soothing, comforting, and conducive to a good night's sleep.

Who among us is not occasionally in need of comfort, even when our lives are apparently going very well? Who among us is immune to the occasional bout of insomnia? Who among us has not suffered through what the French call *une nuit blanche,* a white night? Who among us has not recognized that the person we are during those bleached and febrile sleepless hours bears little or no resemblance to the person we become over and over again in the sensible, multicolored light of day?

I breathed deeply and folded my hands on my chest. I could hear Mary moving around in the next room. I could hear the dresser drawers being opened and closed, the hangers scraping on the metal rod, and then the closet door being shut. I could hear the bed sighing as Mary lay down on it and then there was silence except for the sound of the rain on the roof.

I tried to gather my thoughts, which were, understandably, ricocheting off each other in all directions at once. I read in a self-help book years ago that it is not possible to have more than one thought in your head at any given moment. This is an interesting theory that might prove useful in any number of ways, but in practice, everyone knows it is not true.

First I thought about what we would have for dinner. I did a mental inventory of the fridge and the cupboards and decided that we would have Zucchini and Barley Casserole and a tossed green salad with pine nuts and mandarin orange slices.

But even while thinking about practical matters like zucchini, lettuce, and pine nuts, I had other things hovering in the back of my mind, weightier things like the fact that the Virgin Mary was now napping in the next room and what was I supposed to make of that?

I intended to think about this as soon as I finished thinking about dinner. But once I had decided on the menu, I fell fast asleep.

Milagros

I was roused from my nap by the sound of water running. For a split second I was disoriented and alarmed. But quickly enough I identified the sound as not the basement flooding, the roof leaking, or the whole city being submerged as had those unfortunate cities to the southwest not so long ago. I recognized it as the sound of the shower running. It was Mary, making herself at home just as I had hoped she would.

I squinted at the red numbers on the clock on the dresser and was surprised to discover that the afternoon was almost gone. I had been asleep for nearly three hours.

I got up, folded the afghan, and opened the curtains. From the bathroom, I could hear the sound of Mary's blow-dryer. I went into the kitchen, got out my recipe box, and started the barley for the dinner casserole. It had to cook for an hour before the other ingredients could be added.

Mary emerged looking much refreshed. She thanked me for the use of the facilities, said she hoped I didn't mind that she had used the peach-colored towels on the shelf beside the window and also some of my shampoo as it seemed she had forgotten to pack her own. Her dark hair was loose again, full and fragrant.

She had changed into a pair of khaki pants, a crisp white cotton shirt, and her chocolate brown cardigan. She was still wearing the silver hoop earrings but not the silver and turquoise necklace. She had put on a bit of mascara and some lipstick.

I, too, felt remarkably rested and rejuvenated. We agreed that our naps had done us a world of good. She peeked into the pot on the stove in which the barley was bubbling and then skimmed the recipe on the card I had pulled from the box and left on the counter.

—This sounds delicious, Mary said. I love zucchini.

Together we made dinner. I chopped the zucchini, a small onion, a green pepper, and a large apple. I mixed them with a can of crushed tomatoes, some oregano, and lots of garlic, put all the ingredients together with the cooled barley in a casserole dish, and popped it in the oven with some grated cheese on top. Mary made the salad and set the table while the kitchen quickly filled with the mouth-watering aroma of the casserole cooking.

We were hungry and ate happily, chatting easily about inconsequential things. Mary liked the casserole very much and was impressed when I told her it was my own original recipe. She admitted that, much as she loved to eat, she was not much of a cook herself, having so seldom had time to actually do it.

After we had eaten our fill, Mary insisted, as she had at lunchtime, that I just sit and relax while she washed the dishes and tidied up. So I sat at the kitchen table and read the newspaper just as I would have any other evening. I went back to the front-page stories I had skimmed in the morning and read them properly. I checked the obituaries just in case, puzzling as usual over the coded phrases used to describe each person's demise: *Suddenly, After a long illness,* and *Suddenly after a long illness.* I read the names of the charities and associations cited at the end of each, looking for clues. When my time comes, I want the cause of my death to be spelled out clearly so nobody will have to wonder.

I reread my horoscope for this day now mostly passed: *Cancer. Beware of impulse buying. You must get your financial house in order before making any large purchases. Avoid conflict with coworkers and children.* No hint there as to the fact that this would be the day on which the Virgin Mary appeared in my living room.

—When is your birthday? I asked her.

—September the eighth, she said. I'm a Virgo.

Well, of course she was.

I read aloud: *Virgo. You are in a period of great energy and ambition in your life. There's no time like the present to make your dreams come true. Be careful around ladders.*

—Would that be Jacob's ladder, do you suppose? Mary asked. Or just your run-of-the-mill regular ladder?

We were laughing when the telephone rang and this time I answered it without thinking. With scripted enthusiasm, a woman tried to convince me to schedule a carpet-cleaning for every room in my house. I told her, truthfully, that I had no carpets, just hardwood floors throughout. Undeterred, she said they would come and clean my furniture instead.

—I have no furniture, I said. Practicing the fine art of mental reservation, I silently added: That needs to be cleaned, stretching the technical definition a little.

Flustered, the woman apologized for having bothered me, obviously convinced that I had far greater problems than a good cleaning could possibly solve. She hung up in my ear. I stood there smirking at the receiver. As it turned out, she was the only telemarketer I heard from all week.

Mary finished the dishes, left the casserole dish to soak in the sudsy water, and then she made tea. Again she arranged the pot, mugs, spoons, honey, and milk on my black lacquered tray. I carried it into the living room and set it down on the coffee table between two overstuffed armchairs upholstered in a geometric pattern of many shades of green. Scattered across the green are black shapes and figures, spirals and slashes that might be the letters of an undiscovered alphabet or a code of secret symbols just waiting to be deciphered. Behind the chairs are floor-to-ceiling bookshelves running the whole width of the room. Along the adjoining wall is a long couch in solid hunter green. On the opposite wall are more built-in bookshelves and the grandfather clock which was just then chiming seven o'clock.

I went back to the kitchen and returned with a plate of chocolate wafers, store-bought, probably a little stale. Mary waved aside my apologies and took two. She had settled herself in one of the armchairs.

Left to my own devices, I would probably have turned on the television and then, being chronically unable to watch television in an upright position, I would have sprawled on the couch with the remote control in one hand and my trusty *TV Guide* in the other. As comfortable as I was with Mary by that point, still I felt that some less insouciant behavior was in order. I put on my current favorite CD, Bach's *Goldberg Variations*, performed by Glenn Gould, and sat down in the other armchair.

While the tea steeped, we listened to the music and nibbled on our cookies. Just as I was about to pour, Mary stood up.

—There is something I could use your help with, she said, and left the room.

I suffered an immediate paroxysm of alarm. Having now lulled me into a false sense of complacency, was she indeed going to ask me to perform some superhuman feat of devotion after all?

She returned to the living room carrying the dress she had

been wearing when she arrived. I must have looked as puzzled as I felt.

—I need to wash this dress, she said. But first I have to remove these.

These, it appeared, were the tiny metal objects fastened to the skirt that I had at first mistaken for embroidery. Mary shook out the dress and it jingled. I moved the tea tray to the floor and she spread the dress on the coffee table.

—What are they? I asked.

—They're called *milagros*, Mary said. That's the Spanish word for miracles.

I leaned forward and looked more closely. Most of them were made of cast or stamped nickel or tin, a few of real silver, brass, or gold. Most were flat, a few were three-dimensional. There were hundreds of them, in the shapes of people, animals, and objects of all kinds. They were attached to the fabric with tiny gold safety pins, the kind I would use to fasten a broken bra strap, the kind my mother had hundreds of in a clear plastic box in her sewing cabinet and which I had once, on an interminable rainy Sunday afternoon, pinned all together in a chain that stretched the full length of the living room.

—What are they are for? I asked, quite astonished.

—As I said, Mary explained, I've just been in Mexico. It is the custom there for the faithful to bring these milagros to the shrines. There, the statues of Jesus, myself, and the other saints are often dressed in real clothes to which the milagros can be easily attached. They're a kind of votive offering, some from people praying for something, others given in thanks for prayers already answered. Once they were individually hand-made but now they're mass-produced, sold at religious and jewelry stores or at booths set up by street vendors near the shrines.

Many of them, I could see, were miniature human figures: men, women, children, and babies, kneeling, praying, standing, sitting, crawling, and lying down, sleeping perhaps or dead. Just as many more were individual body parts: heads, ears, eyes, arms, legs, hands, feet, breasts, stomachs, kidneys, lungs, lips, teeth, and tongues.

Mary carefully unpinned a pair of pointy silver breasts.

—This one was from a new mother who was having problems breast-feeding, she said, cradling it in the palm of her hand. She was praying for more milk.

Next to the breasts was the figure of a plump, smiling baby.

—The same woman offered this one in thanks after her prayers were answered.

Then she removed a man's head with a large bulge and a deep wound on the left side.

—This one was given in thanks by a man who had recently undergone surgery for a brain tumor. I get a lot of heads, for headaches, mental illness, memory loss, learning disabilities. I get a lot of hearts too. There are so very many maladies of the heart.

She pointed out several kinds: hearts sprouting flames, hearts pierced by swords, and hearts encircled by crowns of thorns. There were striated hearts, anatomically correct hearts, and perfect plump valentine hearts. Literal hearts, figurative hearts, diseased hearts, lonely hearts, broken hearts.

I went into my bedroom and took my old charm bracelet from the top dresser drawer. It was cold in my hand as I passed it to Mary. She admired the charms one by one: the Christmas and birthday ones, the typewriter, the bicycle, the horse, the diploma, and the rest. There was a winged Cupid with a quiver of arrows slung over his shoulder. And yes, there was a perfect silver valentine heart.

I remembered the extreme joy of receiving this one from a boy I dated when I was eighteen. I remembered the feel of his hand on my neck, his tongue in my mouth, but I could not make his face come clear.

What kind of heart would I choose now to pin on Mary's dress?

She continued unpinning and explaining: a set of teeth (prayer for relief from a toothache), an ear (thanks for a hearing aid), a stomach (thanks for relief from ulcers), a pair of lungs (prayer for help to quit smoking), a second pair of lungs (thanks for having been saved from drowning), a pair of closed eyes (thanks for a good night's sleep after six months of insomnia), a pair of open eyes (prayer not for a cure for blindness, as you might expect, but prayer for hope from a woman who said she had lost sight of the light at the end of the tunnel).

Soon Mary's hand was full of little body parts and safety pins.

—We'll need a box to put these in, she said.

Being something of a pack rat, I have an extensive collection of cardboard boxes of all sizes stashed in my basement. But an old shoebox did not seem appropriate in this instance. I had recently bought a beautifully carved wooden box with a hinged lid. I had not yet decided what I was going to keep in it. I got this box from my study and, from the kitchen, a plastic container for the pins.

Mary dropped the milagros into the box, the pins into the container.

—I was able to bring these ones away with me, she said, but over time they number in the thousands at any given shrine, and eventually the priests have no choice but to remove them to make room for more or to clean the statues. Sometimes they're kept in storage or buried, but other times they're melted down or simply thrown away. Myself, I just don't have the heart to dispose of people's prayers that way.

Neither did I.

I have since done some reading about milagros. I have learned that, between October 1988 and March 1993, the number of whole-body milagros left at the Church of Santa Maria Magdalena in the town of Magdalena de Kino, Sonora, Mexico, was 20,670. During the same period, 22,664 body-part milagros were also left at Magdalena. Among these were 1,312 hearts, 3,524 heads, 8,989 legs, 1,069 hands, 160 breasts, 193 navels, 140 stomachs, 93 kidneys, 26 lips, and 6 tongues.

We settled down to our task. The fabric of the dress was a thin, gauzy cotton that was soft and cool between my fingers. We unpinned the milagros one by one and dropped them into the box. Apparently sharing an inherent inclination toward orderliness, by unspoken agreement we removed them by categories: first, human figures and parts, then animals, then food, and finally miscellaneous inanimate objects.

There were horses, cows, donkeys, dogs, pigs, sheep, cats, turkeys, geese, peacocks, chickens, and snakes. There was a scorpion (prayer to ward off being bitten), a sow with six suckling piglets (thanks from a pig farmer for his animals' fertility), an elephant (thanks from a circus owner for the complete recovery of an ailing elephant).

There were apples, tomatoes, cucumbers, an ear of corn, a stalk of bananas, a sheaf of wheat, and a bunch of grapes.

—The fruits and vegetables are usually from farmers praying or giving thanks for a good crop, Mary said. But sometimes they're from hungry families too.

There were houses, cars, trucks, boats, airplanes, motorcycles, and buses.

—The houses, Mary said, are often from people praying for a mortgage from the bank. The boats are usually from fishermen. They pray for abundant fishing and calm waters. They give thanks for having survived bad storms. The cars are from people praying for money to buy a new one or to have the old one repaired. Sometimes they're from people who have survived car accidents.

One of the airplanes was three-dimensional, with the initials M.S. carved one on each wing.

—This was from a woman praying for a trip to Europe, Mary said, a trip she'd been dreaming of all her life but could never afford before, and now that her three children had grown up and moved away from home, surely she and her husband deserved a holiday before they got too old to enjoy it. I'm pleased to report that today for lunch they had the Terrine of Rabbit in Tarragon Aspic at a lovely little bistro on the Left Bank. Afterward they went to Notre Dame Cathedral and then they took a boat along the Seine to see the Eiffel Tower. Tomorrow they will be going to the Louvre. On Wednesday they will travel to Lourdes. On Friday they will fly to Rome.

I held the airplane in the palm of my hand. It was almost identical to the one on my charm bracelet, the one that I did not remember receiving, the one that made me think that when I was younger, anything had seemed possible, that I might indeed someday fly to Mexico, France, or Kathmandu.

There were two baseball bats and a football, given by people praying for success in sports. There was a martini glass, given in thanks by an alcoholic to mark the first anniversary of his sobriety. There was a pair of golden handcuffs and a jail, both of these, Mary explained, given on behalf of the same person, a young man who claimed he had been unjustly accused of murder. The handcuffs were given by his wife with a prayer that he be found innocent. When he was not, she returned with the tiny jail and a prayer that the appeal being launched would eventually be successful and that he would be returned to her and their six children who missed and needed him very much. So far this had not happened.

The box was filling up. There were radios, watches, padlocks, books, crosses, medals, crowns, keys, slippers, pillows, and liquor bottles. There was a purse, a guitar, a sewing machine, a pair of scissors, and a pair of eyeglasses.

—Some of these are from people praying for the return of lost or stolen objects, Mary said. Others are given in thanks for their recovery.

—Our Lady of the Lost and Found, I said.

—I like that, she said, and sang a few bars of "Amazing Grace."

I remembered the large wooden box that had sat in the main hallway of my elementary school. It was always overflowing with lost articles: scarves, hats, single winter boots, jackets, teeshirts, lunch boxes, and gym shorts. Several times a day the box was vigorously pawed through until it became an impenetrable tangle of sleeves and legs, zippers and buckles and twisted cloth. Once a pair of long johns, torn and yellowed at the crotch, worked its way to the top of the pile and everybody giggled every time they walked past. Once a year the box was emptied, its contents spread across the floor of the gymnasium for all to see. Parents were invited to the viewing. Each class would then file down to have a look, students often finding things they didn't even know they'd lost, parents discovering pieces of their children's clothing now two sizes too small because they'd been in the box so long. Whatever was not claimed was then bundled up and given to the poor people, as if they, by some heroic measure of resourcefulness spawned by desperation, would be able to make good use of all those single socks and mittens and shoes.

I thought about other things lost, other milagros that people might pin to Mary's dress. I pictured hundreds of single earrings and gloves. I imagined tiny scaled fish for all the ones that got away; locks of hair from balding men; brains or marbles from those in danger of losing their minds; and words, many little silver words from writers who were blocked or from others who had lost their voices, words like *love, sorry, please, promise, stop, go, come back to me.* I wondered what you would pin to her dress to represent those lost things bigger but harder to put your finger on, things like innocence, trust, hopes, dreams, courage, faith.

Each milagro contained a story. Going through them was like going through an old photo album and telling the story behind each picture—the way I might point out a black-and-white photograph of two little girls and a boy beside a lake and say:

—Here we are at the beach in 1963, my bathing suit was pink, my sister's was orange, my brother cut his foot, and we had to go home.

Or many pages later, I might put my finger on a colored picture of a tall, handsome, dark-haired man in a green shirt standing beside a red car with a bouquet of yellow flowers in his hands. And I might say:

—This is someone I used to love.

Finally the box was full and the dress was just a dress again, having given over into our hands all those miracles and moments of despair. Although this word is bandied about as a generic term for all manner of misery and unhappiness, now I could see that, in fact, despair is an utterly personal and private place.

Mary washed the dress by hand in the bathroom sink and hung it over the shower curtain rod to dry. I took the box into her room and left it on the bed, not sure what she wanted to do with it now.

We went back into the living room and sat down. Having told me all those strangers' stories, Mary started then to tell me the stories of her own life.

History (1)

Every child, and the child in every one of us, is ready to plead: Tell me a story. For the role of stories is to explain life, and the good stories, in their very substance and in the structure of their language, become revelation.

—Andrew M. Greeley

Since all of what I first learned about Mary came from the Bible stories I heard in the basement of Saint Matthew's United Church, I realize now that it was no wonder my early knowledge of her was so meager. In the New Testament, Mary is mentioned less than two dozen times, often not even by name. *But when the fulness of the time was come, God sent forth his Son, made of a woman, made under the law.*

In its skeletal outline of Mary's life, the Bible does not even say when she was born, who her parents were, what she looked like, or how and when she died. Mary herself speaks only seven times.

All the history and myth which now trail her, all the legend and lore which now ravel around her, came later: an apocryphal and eventually enormous body of details and interpretations that grew and changed through the centuries, fueled as much by faith and imagination as by documented factual information. Much of the official doctrine that now concerns her grew out of the unofficial stories of her birth, life, and death: articles of dogma forged from controversial narratives not contained in the Bible itself.

Even in what they do tell us about her, the authors of the four Gospels, Matthew, Mark, Luke, and John, do not always agree on the details. By the time their books were written, Mary had been dead for many years and was already making the earliest of her earthly visits.

Our Lady of the Pillar

In the year 40 A.D., some ten years after the death of Jesus, the apostle James has been dispatched to preach the gospel in Saragossa, a town on the banks of the Ebro River in northwestern Spain. It is a primitive and isolated region ringed with rugged mountains. Its natives are fierce and unholy, prone to excessive violence and immoderate bloodshed.

—This was just four years before James became the first of the apostles to be martyred for his faith, Mary told me. He was beheaded in Jerusalem by King Herod Agrippa I. This was seven and a half centuries before he became known as Saint James the Greater. This was back when he was still just plain James, son of Zebedee, and the word *Christianity* would not even be invented for another sixty years.

James is discouraged and depressed because he isn't having much luck converting the bloodthirsty pagans of Saragossa. They just won't listen to him, despite the fact that back in

Jerusalem he was already well known for performing miracles, including once having brought back to life a boy who had been dead for five weeks after having been unjustly hanged.

In Saragossa, nobody cares that he, along with Peter and John, was present at the Transfiguration when Jesus took the three of them up to a high mountaintop and the prophets, Moses and Elijah, appeared before them.

He was there in the Garden of Gethsemane, too, where Jesus took him after the Last Supper. James was one of the three apostles who slept while Jesus spoke to God. *Then cometh he to his disciples, and saith unto them, Sleep on now, and take your rest: behold, the hour is at hand, and the Son of man is betrayed into the hands of sinners.*

Stranded alone now in Saragossa, James feels like a failure. He wanders around listlessly, barefoot, with his robes muddied, his favorite hat all bent out of shape, and his staff dragging in the dirt behind him. Even the scallop shell which he wears like a badge has grown dull and chipped. He looks pathetic and he knows it. He looks like a lost soul, which, for the moment, he is.

—That shell was something of an affectation, Mary said, like a tattoo or an earring. But it was harmless enough and he loved it, his special symbol of the sea. Besides, even a future saint should be allowed a bit of vanity now and again, don't you think?

Bedraggled and beset by despair, one sunny morning James trudges down to his favorite spot along the Ebro and dangles his fishing line into the river.

—He was thinking, Mary said, that he might as well just give up on this mission and go home to Jerusalem. He was an excellent fisherman back in Galilee before Jesus called him and now, effortlessly, he caught one fish after another and tossed them carelessly onto the bank behind him. If only being a fisher of men were as easy as being a fisher of fish. He was losing his faith not in God but in himself, in his own power to spread the word, do good works, change history.

James stands on the riverbank in the sun, fishing and doubting, doubting and fishing, and then there are sounds in the bushes behind him. Rustling, sighing, a little genteel throat-clearing.

It is Mary. She has been transported from Jerusalem to Saragossa on a large gilded throne borne by a band of angels. They set her down softly and then stretch out on the riverbank to doze in the sun. Mary steps down from the throne and stands with her hands raised toward heaven.

—Some people have wondered if maybe I was still alive when this happened, Mary said. But I was not. I was dead, quite dead at the time. I never performed miracles in my earthly lifetime. Only later, only after I was dead.

Terrified and ecstatic, James flings himself to the ground at her feet and then clings briefly to her ankles. She is indeed a sight for sore eyes. As in: eyes sore and bloodshot from so many sleepless nights, so many wretched days. As in: eyes strained and gritty from so much fruitless soul searching. As in: *the glory of the Lord shone round about them: and they were sore afraid.*

Mary pulls him gently to his feet and brushes him off.

—We prayed together then, Mary said, for patience, perseverance, peace of mind. I woke the napping angels and we went back to his small dwelling for lunch. It was Friday. We cleaned the fish and fried them up. I reminded him that not only was the fish a mystical symbol of fertility and the life-giving force of all motherhood, but it was our secret sign, too, the sign by which the followers of Jesus could recognize each other even in the midst of the heathen hordes. We licked our plates and picked our teeth with the bones.

Then Mary gives James a six-foot pillar made of a green-colored quartz called jasper and a fifteen-inch wooden statue of herself cradling the baby Jesus in her left arm. A little bird sits in the baby's hand. Mary asks James to build a chapel in her name and there to place the statue on the pillar in her honor.

—We prayed some more, Mary said, James cried a little, and then the angels carried me back to Jerusalem. That very night, James cleaned up his act, washed his dirty robes, polished his precious scallop shell, and began to make plans for the chapel he would build, the chapel which was the first ever dedicated to me.

Many more miraculous and interesting things happen to James in the following years, both before and after his death. He is first buried in Jerusalem but his body is moved several times after that, finally ending up in Compostela, Spain, eight centuries later. The shrine of Santiago de Compostela soon becomes one of the most popular pilgrimage destinations in the world. The bones of Saint James are still there today, housed in a silver reliquary beneath an imposing statue of the saint seated on a throne, wearing garments of silver and gold. Embossed upon his voluminous cape are scallop shells, which the pilgrims fervently kiss and caress.

James becomes the patron saint of Spain, also of Nicaragua and Guatemala, and of soldiers, laborers, horsemen, furriers, and veterinarians.

Over the bloody centuries of Spanish history, Saragossa is invaded by various conquerors including the Romans, the Goths, the Moors, the Muslims, and the Vandals. The original chapel and several churches built to replace it are destroyed. But always the jasper pillar and the statue survive. They stand now before a green marble wall studded with 148 gold stars, eighty of which are set with precious jewels. Both Mary and Jesus now wear jeweled crowns and behind their heads is a large bejeweled halo and a golden aureole. The pillar is encased in intricately carved silver and bronze. The small patch of jasper left exposed and framed by a golden oval has been worn smooth by the kisses of millions of pilgrims including Saint John of the Cross, Saint Ignatius of Loyola, Saint Teresa of Ávila, all the kings of Spain, and Pope John Paul II.

That was the beginning. In the nearly two thousand years since then, Mary, according to several reliable sources, has made more than twenty thousand appearances. A well-traveled gypsy, she has been seen on every continent except Antarctica. (And no one, in all honesty, can blame her for this omission from her itinerary. The interior of Antarctica is, after all, permanently covered by 8,000 feet of snow, enjoys August temperatures as low as −130°F, and is populated only by penguins.) She has appeared to people of all ages, races, classes, and occupations, to the educated and the illiterate, to believers and nonbelievers alike.

The chronicle of Mary's miracles and apparitions tracks the entire timeline of human history, charts an annotated atlas of world geography, paints an illuminating picture of all mystery and magic, narrates an intimate story of all hope and despair.

What I now know (or think I know) about Mary, I learned in two ways: from the stories she told me while she was here and from the reading I have done since. For those of us with a bookish bent, reading is a reflexive response to everything. This is how we deal with the world and anything new that comes our way. We have always known that there is a book for every occasion and every obsession. When in doubt, we are always looking things up.

Not being especially fond of library books myself (mostly because you have to give them back when you're done but also because their spines are often broken, their pages sticky and dog-eared, marked up with other people's jottings and grease spots),

I would rather buy than borrow. Even a casual examination of my overcrowded shelves would quickly reveal the various areas of interest that have gripped me over the years. Add to these now a small shelf of books about Mary:

Mary Through the Centuries. Mary, Queen of Heaven. A Litany of Mary. A Dictionary of Mary. Miracles of Mary. Visions of Mary. Meetings with Mary. Portrait of Mary. In Search of Mary. The Secret of Mary. Encountering Mary. Mary's Message to the World. Mary's Journal. Mary's Way. Healing Words from Mary. Desperately Seeking Mary. . . .

My original intention was to write a fictionalized version of the story of Mary's visit to me, keeping my promise, of course, to publish it under a pseudonym and call it a novel. I knew this would work to the book's advantage because, ironically, calling it fiction would make it easier to believe. There are some truths that cannot be made credible in any other way. When I began to write this book, I thought it would be a simple story, one that would result in a slender pretty volume with gold lettering and a Renaissance painting of Mary and Jesus on the cover. But soon after I started reading about her, I realized that I could not write the story of Mary's visit to me, fictionalized or not, while ignoring her whole history, the history of the last two thousand years.

Each story of Mary that I have discovered could (and sometimes does) constitute a whole book in itself. For each one of the stories I've attempted to retell here, there are hundreds more that I haven't got room for. As the story of Mary that I was trying to tell grew ever more complex, I could not decide whether trying to get it all straight was more like untangling a gigantic ball of wool or like being caught in a labyrinth. Some stories are too small to be novels but others, I soon found, might just be too big. I could only hope Italo Calvino was right when he said that, while overly ambitious projects may be objectionable in many other fields, in literature they are not.

In my mind, the book began to resemble an octopus with its tentacles waving alarmingly off in all directions at once. Or sometimes it was like a giant squid squirting ink all over the place. When these deep-sea similes threatened to overwhelm me entirely, I kept reminding myself that many cephalopods, by way of a process called bioluminescence, are, like angels, saints, and fireflies, capable of producing light.

What kept me going was a vision not of Mary but of a stack of white pages covered with double-spaced typescript, clean and tidy with no arrows, scrawls, or angry red slashes; a stack of white pages perfectly squared, with no yellow, purple, turquoise, orange, and pink Post-it notes affixed to the edges bearing exclamatory notes to myself like NEEDS WORK, CHECK THIS, MORE HERE, CUT! I kept reminding myself that there is only one way to write a book: one word at a time.

As I tried to sift through and make some sense of all this material, it became more and more obvious to me that the whole story has not, cannot, will never be told. It also became clear to me that the whole story, the real story, and the true story are not always the same thing.

Our Lady of Einsiedeln

Born at the end of the eighth century to a noble Swiss family, the Hohenzollerns, young Meinrad is never especially interested in the advantages that nobility has to offer. Rather he is interested in holiness. At the age of twenty-five he becomes a priest and enters the Benedictine monastery at Reichenau. But even

the monastic life does not completely satisfy Meinrad's longing
for solitude.

Several years later, in 829, he moves to an isolated spot on
Mount Etzel, taking with him only a small collection of reli-
gious books and a wooden statue of Mary and Jesus that was
given to him by the Abbess Hildegarde of Zurich. It is a Black
Madonna, and in the crook of her left arm sits the naked baby
Jesus. His whole body is black too.

—For years, Mary said, people have been coming up with
theories to try and explain away this and the many other Black
Madonnas around the world. They say my skin in these images is
black by accident, because of the passage of time or fires in those
churches or from the soot of so many candles lit before them for
hundreds of years. But if that were the case, then wouldn't the
whole image be blackened, not just my face and hands, not just
Jesus' body? These artists made me black because sometimes I
am. Even way back then they knew that someday I would be all
things to all people. Remember the Song of Solomon: *I am black,
but comely, O ye daughters of Jerusalem, as the tents of Kedar, as the curtains of Solomon.* Have you never looked at your own face in the
mirror and thought that you both are and are not the same person from one day to the next?

Try as he might, Meinrad cannot hide the light of his holiness. Soon the pious and the curious alike find their way to his
hermit's cell in the forest. He puts up with them as best he can,
but seven years later, in 836, he moves again, to an even more
remote spot, now called Einsiedeln near Lake Lucerne. Here he
hopes to find perfect isolation at last and to spend the rest of his
life in private prayer and contemplation.

Rumors that Meinrad is being visited by angels at his new
location begin to circulate among the faithful. Soon they track
him down and begin traveling in large numbers to his hermitage

for spiritual instruction. Resigned now to only an imperfect peace, Meinrad agrees in 853 to the construction of a small chapel where mass may be celebrated, the sacraments administered, and the statue installed. Years pass. The pilgrims pray for miracles, marvels, and miscellaneous graces. Our Lady of Einsiedeln does not disappoint them.

News of the popularity of Einsiedeln reaches not only the penitents. It eventually comes to the attention of the unscrupulous as well. Two criminally minded hoodlums from Zurich, Richard and Peter, figure that all those pilgrims must be leaving jewels and other valuables at the shrine in thanks for favors received. They can just imagine the vast treasure that has been deposited there over the past twenty-five years. They decide to pay Meinrad a visit too.

—Richard and Peter arrived at Einsiedeln on January 21, 861, Mary said. I warned Meinrad that they were coming. I told him what was going to happen. Still he welcomed them just as he welcomed everyone. Still he remained true to his faith and his fate. It was a cold day. They had had a long journey. He stoked up the fire. He encouraged them to warm their hands and feet before it. He offered them freshly baked bread, chunks of fragrant cheese, big bowls of hearty stew, and steaming mugs of chocolate. He took them to the chapel and introduced them to his pets, two crows he had tamed. They were perched on either side of the holy statue. Meinrad prayed with the two visitors and then waited for them to make their move. I stood by and waited too. Meinrad could not see me but he knew I was there.

Despite his own love of solitude and his foreknowledge of the outcome of this particular visit, Meinrad is still a Benedictine and he lives every day by the Rule. Saint Benedict said that all guests at a monastery must be welcomed as Christ would be welcomed and so must be treated with generosity, courtesy, and love. A monk must pray with them, feed them, warm them, and bestow upon them the blessèd kiss of peace.

After Richard and Peter have warmed up, eaten their fill, and pretended to pray with Meinrad, they smash his head in with clubs they have kept hidden in their heavy winter clothes.

The murderers search for treasure and find nothing. Suddenly two candles standing near Meinrad's bloody body are mysteriously lit. Terrified, Richard and Peter flee. Meinrad's two pet crows, who witnessed the murder, now follow the criminals all the way back to Zurich. There they make a great racket and are soon recognized as Meinrad's pets. A group of citizens travels to Einsiedeln and discovers Meinrad's battered body. They carry it back to the abbey at Reichenau where it is preserved with great veneration. Richard and Peter are arrested and thrown in jail.

—On the day of their hanging, Mary said, the crows perched on the gallows until the two men were dead. Then they flew back to the empty hermitage where they and the holy statue remained the only inhabitants for many years. The pilgrims stopped coming. Without Meinrad, there was no point.

Forty-two years later, in 903, the chapel at Einsiedeln is visited by Blessèd Benno, a canon from Strasbourg. Benno decides to restore the building and live there. Eventually a community of Benedictine monks takes up residence, building a larger handsome church around Meinrad's little chapel and the statue of Mary and Jesus. Conrad, the Bishop of Constance, comes to consecrate the new church on September 14, 948.

—The night before the ceremony, Mary said, Conrad and some of the monks gathered in the chapel to worship. Just after midnight, as they prayed before the statue, the sanctuary was suddenly illuminated and two choirs of angels began to sing.

The angels are joined by Saints Stephen, Lawrence, Peter, Gregory, and Augustine. Then Jesus himself appears, standing at the high altar, preparing to consecrate the church himself. Seated near him on a throne of light, presiding over the ceremony, is Mary, surrounded by still more angels.

Bishop Conrad's vision is confirmed and approved by Pope Leo VIII in 964 and devotion to Our Lady of Einsiedeln becomes official. The pilgrims return in droves. In 1028, the large church is destroyed by fire. Only Meinrad's chapel and the miraculous statue are spared. When the church is rebuilt and consecrated, Meinrad is canonized by Pope Benedict IX and his body is moved from Reichenau and ensconced at Einsiedeln, his beloved hermitage.

Throughout history, the church is destroyed by fire four more times, in 1214, 1465, 1509, and 1577. Each time, Meinrad's chapel and the holy statue emerge from the blaze unharmed.

As far as my own Marian reading goes, I would not presume to claim that I have done anything more than scratch the surface of the subject. In Mary's case, there are tens of thousands of books. The Marian Library at the University of Dayton, Ohio, houses the world's largest collection of printed material about her. By recent count, it included over ninety thousand books in fifty languages, more than fifty-five thousand clippings from newspapers and magazines, and nearly twenty thousand holy cards bearing her image. I think it is safe to assume that Mary has been the subject of more literature, art, and music than any other woman in all of history.

I began my own excursion into the vast body of Marian literature shortly after she left. It would have been rude, I thought, to start reading about her right in front of her. It would have looked as if I wasn't about to take her word for anything, as if I were checking out her credentials, preparing to cross-examine her, hoping to trip her up and catch her out in a lie. When I sat down to read, I soon found that the writings are of many different types: theological, ecclesiastical, devotional, testimonial, inspirational, evangelical, historical, philosophical, sociological, psychological, and every possible hybrid of some or all of the above.

I quickly realized that I could spend the rest of my life reading about Mary and still never get to the end. Rather than finding this discouraging, I find it not only liberating but somehow comforting. This, I think, is a testament to what I have learned so far.

There are many volumes filled with detailed narratives of Marian miracles witnessed and received. There are thousands of pages of praise and prayers. There are imaginative reconstructions of Mary's life, some written from her own first-person point of view in the form of diaries in which she records the details of her daily life in the first century and reflects upon both the joys and the trials of being the mother of Jesus.

There are many accounts of direct communications the authors have had with Mary. Some have engaged in ongoing conversations with her about matters of both global and personal significance. Others have found themselves in a more one-sided situation: she talks, they listen. Some have heard from Mary only once or twice. They write about what she wore, what she said, how it changed their lives.

Others have been hearing from her on a regular basis for a number of years, receiving a series of messages which are frighteningly apocalyptic, filled with dire warnings about Armageddon and the end-time. There are lengthy predictions of volcanoes, earthquakes, tidal waves, hurricanes, tornadoes, floods, droughts, famines, colder winters, hotter summers, the extinction of many wild animals, increased UFO activity, the total disappearance of England, France, Greece, Japan, much of the Middle East, and parts of North America. Eventually all the planets will be realigned, including the earth, which will be flipped sideways on its axis. But Mary's real message, they say, is not to scare us but to show us how to seek and find God through prayer and meditation. Some slim comfort is then offered by the prophecy that once this is all over, we (or what is left of us) will enter the after-time in which there will be two suns, new lands, new plants and animals, and a whole new species of human beings. These new people will have complete psychic abilities enabling them to communicate mentally not only with each other but with animals and spirits as well.

In this new world, all the problems which now plague us will have been eliminated and all creatures will coexist in perfect peace and harmony. In this new world, there will be no suffering, no sadness, nary a whiff of doubt or despair.

Our Lady of Walsingham

In 1061, five years before the Norman Conquest, in the town of Walsingham on the eastern coast of England, Mary appears three times to the devout and wealthy widow of the manor Richeldis de Faverches.

—She was exceptionally devoted, Mary said, and had offered many times in her prayers to use her wealth to honor me in a special way.

Mary hears the widow's prayers and three times takes her in spirit to the House of the Annunciation, the little house in Nazareth where the angel Gabriel told Mary that she would be made pregnant by God.

—I asked her to measure the house and then build a replica of it in Walsingham, Mary said. Neither of us being very experienced in these matters, it took us three trips to get all the measurements and the details exactly right.

Once all the plans are in place, the widow hires the necessary contractors. When the men show up bright and early one morning to start work, they see that during the night a heavy frost has covered the proposed building site. But two rectangles remain clear and dry, each of them measuring 23 feet 6 inches by 12 feet 10 inches, the exact size of the house to be constructed.

—I thought I had made my wishes clear, Mary said, but there was a mix-up at the last minute and two spots were marked instead of one. These things happen. The best-laid plans of mice and women.

The widow decides that she prefers the spot closest to two wells on the property, so the workmen lay the foundation there. But then they find they cannot properly attach the house to the foundation.

Puzzled and dismayed, the widow sends the workmen home and then she stays up all night, pacing through her mansion, praying over this unforeseen problem. When the workmen return at first light, they find the widow on her knees on the cold stone floor of the kitchen. She is fast asleep with her eyes wide open.

They rouse her and together they go out to the building site. There they are amazed to discover that the foundation has been mysteriously moved during the night to the other spot two hundred feet away. Construction of the small wooden thatched-roof house then proceeds without a hitch.

During the next hundred years, many miracles and healings take place at the Holy House of Walsingham. It becomes a popular pilgrimage destination.

—Along the road to Walsingham, other chapels were built and crosses were erected to mark the way, Mary said. Rich and poor alike made the journey. They came on foot, on horses and donkeys, in wagons, carts, and carriages. A mile to the south of the holy house, in a small building they called the Slipper Chapel, the pilgrims took off their shoes and walked the rest of the way barefoot.

In the middle of the thirteenth century, a large church is built around the little house which now contains a small dark statue of Mary embellished with gold and silver and precious jewels, the offerings of the wealthy pilgrims. Also ensconced in the shrine is a piece of white-colored earth said to be from the grotto where Mary nursed the baby Jesus and her breast milk dripped on the ground. The shrine is so revered that many of the pilgrims believe the Milky Way leads directly to it.

Among the many English kings who make the pilgrimage is Edward I, who credits Our Lady of Walsingham with saving him from being crushed to death by a large stone that fell from the vaulted ceiling above a table where he was playing chess. Henry VIII and his first wife, Catherine of Aragon, visit the shrine several times.

—Henry brought me rubies, emeralds, a solid silver statue of himself, Mary said. He prayed on his knees for hours at a time. I offer no comment on what happened next. There are some things that even I do not understand. I am neither omniscient nor omnipotent. I am merely ubiquitous and immortal.

In 1534, Henry breaks with Rome and, under the new Act of Supremacy, declares himself Head of the Church of England. He orders the destruction of the shrine at Walsingham along with the rest of the Catholic churches in the country. In 1538, the church and the house are demolished, the statue of Mary is burned, and all the offerings that have been made to her are confiscated by the royal treasury. Among those who are executed for objecting to the Act of Supremacy is Sir Thomas More, scholar, lawyer, author of *Utopia*, former Lord Chancellor, and once Henry's trusted friend and adviser. He is imprisoned in the Tower of London and then beheaded on a charge of treason for his insubordination. Four hundred years later, Thomas More is canonized by Pope Pius XI.

During those four centuries, Our Lady of Walsingham is apparently forgotten.

—Out of sight, out of mind, Mary said. This happens all too often, but it was understandable enough. I was busy elsewhere and inadvertently overlooked Walsingham for a while. Besides, there was so much else going on in the world. Time was passing. History was happening, just like it always does. There was a lot of ground covered in those four hundred years.

Near the end of the nineteenth century, the Slipper Chapel is restored and reopened. Early in the twentieth century, the church, too, is restored and in 1934 twelve thousand people go to Walsingham in the first national Catholic pilgrimage in England since the Reformation.

—The historical significance of this pilgrimage was largely overlooked at the time, Mary said regretfully. It was overshadowed, no doubt, by the fact that 1934 was also the year when Stalin began his Great Purge and Adolf Hitler ordered the roundup and execution of four hundred prominent storm troopers and monarchists on the Night of the Long Knives.

The day after President Hindenburg's death, Hitler becomes the Führer of the Third Reich, in accordance with a law he had issued the previous day. Having thus eliminated his enemies and seized absolute control, Hitler began his reign of terror over Europe.

—The die was cast, Mary said. And so began the darkest chapter of history by which humanity's sense of itself was forever changed.

Knowledge

Like most people, my first exposure to a more or less consistent and organized study of history occurred back in high school. It was never one of my favorite subjects. I had no head for the past.

We studied mostly North American and European history, as if the other parts of the world did not exist or, at least, as if they possessed no past to speak of. Being a chronically good student, I dutifully memorized (and then regurgitated upon request) the names of kings and queens, presidents and prime ministers. All these dead people were presented to us like so many cardboard cutouts dressed up in their fancy period costumes but stripped of their humanity. It was as if having once become instruments of human history, they were hardly still human at all.

I memorized the dates of wars, revolutions, plagues, famines, and important inventions like the lightbulb, the cotton gin, and the telephone. Little of what I learned remained in my brain much past the day of the final exam. There are bits of that historical information still locked away in my mind, of course, patchwork pieces of the distant past that I don't even know I know—until they are released without warning by some passing reference in a book I'm reading or some obscure question on *Jeopardy!*

But for the most part, the history I learned all those years ago has been lost, either back then in the hormonal tumult of adolescence or lost since in the quotidian preoccupations of adulthood.

Where do they go, I wonder, all those facts we once knew, those memories we once treasured, those truths we once believed in, those people we once loved and now don't?

Back in high school History, I mostly couldn't see the point of having to study all those dead people, all that ancient stuff. Being an ordinary, self-absorbed adolescent, I could not (and did not much want to) entertain the possibility of the existence of a world that different from my own.

As a teenager, I had trouble even imagining my own parents as people before I was born, so how could I possibly take seriously a world without cars, airplanes, television, telephones, and rock-and-roll? As far as I was concerned, anything that had happened before my own lifetime was more like *pre*history than history, part of a past as distant and alien as the dinosaurs, those bloodthirsty, inarticulate giants with unpronounceable names, all of them lumbering blindly toward a mysterious demise.

But, much as I could not seem to stretch my imagination back that far, still I never doubted that it was all true. Not one of my teachers ever mentioned or even alluded to the idea of history as an inexact science. We were never encouraged, expected, or allowed to question history. Year after year, we were led to believe that the past was carved in stone and that the contents of the textbooks we studied were to be regarded as strictly gospel.

My favorite History teacher was Mr. Skinner, whose Grade Ten class I attended right after lunch on Tuesdays and Thursdays. A big muscular man with a red face, a receding hairline, hands and feet so large they looked swollen, he was also the football coach. Mr. Skinner struck me even then as a man absolutely untroubled by doubt. He was always in a good mood, even when the football team had just lost six games in a row.

After vigorously filling all four panels of the blackboard with names and dates, he would then pull out the colored chalk and draw stars and arrows all over the place, with blue circles and pink underlining for emphasis. These were probably similar to the diagrams he drew for the football team when laying out his strategy for the next game. Sometimes, with a magician's flourish, he would pull down the tattered world map from where it hung above the blackboard like a window blind and stab at it with a wooden pointer for a while.

Combining these methods with reading assignments of one or two chapters per week, he was able to cover vast stretches of time in no time. We galloped through the ages at breakneck speed. We gulped them down like long draughts of water. We piled them one on top of the other like bricks: a process that did not result in any recognizable or reliable structure, not a building, a house, not even a wall, but rather a tall and narrow tower of the past, teetering precariously in the fickle winds of the present, ever on the verge of collapse. We were not expected to draw conclusions, search for patterns, or wonder why one thing invariably led to another. We were expected simply to memorize and believe.

Every other Thursday we had a quiz, either multiple-choice or true-and-false. Not for Mr. Skinner the thought-provoking, anxiety-inducing ambiguity of essay questions. He was apparently not interested in interpretation, speculation, or protracted rumination. He wanted the facts. I was quite comfortable with this black-and-white version of the world and got 98 percent on the final exam. I was quite content to be operating under the assumption that history was a fixed commodity, something you could count on, put your faith in, bet your bottom dollar, if not your life, on. That facts were facts and that's all there was to it.

It was not until I got to university that I learned there is more than one way to tell the story of the past; that there is, historically speaking, more than one way to skin a cat, if the cat is the past and the skin is the shape into which it has been poured.

In my first year I was required, as a student in the General Arts Program, to take one history course. I chose Ancient History 101, mostly because it was offered on Friday mornings and so fit in well with the rest of my schedule. But partly also because the professor, Dr. Sloan, was rumoured to be an eccentric and entertaining character.

On the cool September morning of our first class, the lecture hall filled just before ten o'clock with at least a hundred freshmen. There was the usual noisy preamble of organization: shuffling, coughing, chatting, the scraping of chairs, the unzipping of jackets, the crinkling of chocolate bar and cigarette wrappers, the slapping open of notebooks, the clattering of coffee cups, ashtrays, and writing utensils. But as a group, we fell silent on the stroke of ten. We waited. We watched the clock and the door. We sighed, doodled, and grumbled. At 10:25 a handful of students mutinied: they packed up and left. The rest of us continued to sigh, doodle, and grumble. We told each other that we had better things to do than sit around all day and wait. But still we waited.

At 10:45 the door opened and Dr. Sloan strode in. He was a tall thin man with wild white hair like Albert Einstein. He wore a red tie, black trousers, and an extremely wrinkled white shirt with the sleeves rolled up to the elbows. He had a lit cigarette in his mouth and was pushing a metal cart stacked high with papers. He did not apologize for being late. In fact, he did not even acknowledge us but began placing on the desk in front of each student a stapled sheaf of pages covered with small black print. As he made his way up and down the rows, his cigarette continued to dangle precariously from his lips. He screwed his face up against the smoke curling into his eyes and did not look at any of us.

When the cart was empty, he flicked his cigarette butt into a nearby ashtray, went down to the front of the room, and hoisted himself wearily onto the desk.

Without introduction, he told us that Hammurabi was the king of Babylonia in the first dynasty, having reigned from 1795 to 1750 B.C. His great Code was carved in cuneiform in the Akkadian language on a black stone monument for all to read and obey.

I stared down blankly at the pile of papers in front of me.

Our assignment, he told us, was to write an essay on the Code of Hammurabi. It must be five pages, typed and double-spaced, and we were not allowed to consult any secondary sources in the process. He said he wanted *our* thoughts and only our thoughts. The essay was due in one week. He stood up and walked out of the room without a backward glance.

Eccentric? Indeed. Entertaining? Not so far.

Hammurabi in hand, I trudged back to my room. Heavy-hearted, I had to admit that I did not even know the meaning of the word *cuneiform* and had only a vague idea of where Babylonia had been. How could I be expected to have knowledge of, let alone an opinion on, something about which I knew nothing?

That evening I began with Hammurabi's bombastic introductory enumeration of his own many stellar accomplishments. Then I read his laws, all 282 of them, dealing with various high crimes and misdemeanors involving property, livestock, crops, slaves, mercenaries, merchants, sailors, wives, children, prostitutes, paramours, and virgins. Those convicted of the most serious crimes were to be exiled, impaled, burned, or tied up and thrown into the water. Other punishments included the knocking out of teeth, the breaking of bones, the putting out of eyes, and the sawing off of appropriate body parts such as tongues, breasts, ears, and hands, this last amputation to be performed upon sons who struck their fathers and surgeons whose patients died.

I had been a straight-A student all through high school, but nothing I'd learned there had prepared me for this. I knew that now I was in well over my smart little head.

I have absolutely no recollection now of what I found to say to Dr. Sloan about the Code of Hammurabi. But I did manage to come up with the requisite five pages, typed, double-spaced, on the blue Brother portable my parents had given me that summer for my birthday.

I handed in my essay the following week. The number of students present in the lecture hall that morning of our second class was, I noted, considerably smaller.

As Dr. Sloan collected our essays, he was muttering happily to himself, something about winnowing the wheat from the chaff, and then he started on the *Epic of Gilgamesh*. At the next class, our third, our numbers had shrunk still further, and Dr. Sloan was positively gleeful as he returned our Hammurabi essays, each marked with a big red A on the front page and nothing else.

By Christmas, we had studied, among other things, the creation myths of India and Iran, the development of Egyptian hieroglyphs and the Phoenician alphabet, the Carthaginian Law of Sacrifices, lists of kings (Hittite, Assyrian, and Sumerian, of which one, Alalgar, was said to have reigned for 36,000 years), and lists of gods and goddesses (Roman, Greek, and Hittite, of which one, Hannahannas, was also known as the Queen of Heaven). We worked strictly according to Dr. Sloan's two edicts that secondary sources were verboten, primary sources were all, and that in the beginning, history was an art form (awarded its own muse, Clio, by the ancient Greeks), a complex combination of myth, chronicle, and literature that was neither pure fiction nor pure fact but a sophisticated hybrid of the two.

Dr. Sloan took great pains to make it clear that the word *history* itself (from the Greek *historia,* meaning "knowledge discovered by inquiry") has since become loaded, a double-edged sword referring both to the flow of events unfolding and to the written record of them. We talked about *History* with a capital *H* as opposed to *history* with a small *h* and the more colloquial ways of using the word, the way you might use it when discussing your medical or personal history: I have a history of sinus trouble; there is a history of cancer in the family, or heart problems, or mental illness; I have a history of insomnia, of low self-esteem, of hating myself and/or the people who love me.

We learned how the meaning of the word *history* has changed over time, moving from "a story represented dramatically" through "a series of events (of which the story has been or might be told)" to "the aggregate of past events; the course of human affairs."

We stumbled along and Dr. Sloan occasionally despaired of our utter doltishness, at which point he either smoked furiously and paced vigorously or left the lecture hall in a huff. But mostly he was patient with our halting forays toward an understanding of what history really means. He was obviously a brilliant man and usually magnanimous enough to tolerate, perhaps even to take some measure of pride in, our small breakthroughs as we

each labored through what must have been to him our own rein-
ventions of the wheel.

The rest of Ancient History 101 was taken up with the
Greeks, of whom there were many. Although Dr. Sloan gra-
ciously left the more familiar names to the Philosophy Department, still there were plenty of others, most, like the dinosaurs,
with unwieldy difficult names: Hecataeus, Xenophanes, Anaxi-
mander, Pisistratos, and the rest. Dr. Sloan had a way of bringing
these men to life. And they were indeed all men and the events
and issues of which they wrote were all the province of men. It
was as if the ancient world consisted of one gender only. I could
not help but wonder what the women were doing while the men
were so busy philosophizing and trying to solve the mysteries of
the universe.

This question was at least partially answered the following
year in my Ancient Greek Theater course when we studied Aris-
tophanes' comedy, *Lysistrata*, in which the women of Athens get
fed up with their husbands being off fighting all the time and go
on a sex strike to force the men to vote for peace with Sparta.

Dr. Sloan clearly had his favorites among the old Greeks,
Pythagoras being one. I had already encountered Pythagoras by
way of his famous theorem: in a right-angled triangle, the square
of the hypotenuse is equal to the sum of the squares of the other
two sides. Or, to put it more succinctly: $a^2 + b^2 = c^2$. (This information was one of those pearls of wisdom I had garnered in high
school that I did not expect to ever find a use for. So far this has
proven to be true.)

To me and the rest of the class, Pythagoras was (merely) a
mathematician, but Dr. Sloan spoke not of his geometry but of
his creation of a secretive celibate utopian community at Croton

in the boot of Italy where people were said to live according to a set of philosophically determined laws. Pythagoras' beliefs in reincarnation and the transmigration of souls led to the establishment of some rather bizarre rules for the residents of Croton, not the least of which was the prohibition of eating beans, not because they caused flatulence but for fear that a migrating soul might inadvertently take up residence in a bean. Dr. Sloan found this extremely amusing.

Studying the Pythagorean theory that the entire universe was a closed system built solely upon numbers, we examined his idea that everything could be explained by a Table of Opposites which included ten pairs: Limit and the Unlimited, Odd and Even, Unity and Plurality, Right and Left, Male and Female, Straight and Crooked, Square and Oblong, Rest and Motion, Light and Darkness, Good and Evil.

This provided Dr. Sloan with a handy segue to the philosophy of Heraclitus, of whose writings only a hundred sentences survive. He believed that the constant conflict between opposites ultimately resulted in a harmonious whole. The struggle between opposites was everywhere and determined everything: winter and summer, night and day, war and peace, man and woman, love and hate, good and evil. Although we mere humans are prone to seeing only the opposites, God, according to Heraclitus, sees the harmony instead. With everything in flux, Heraclitus observed, one thing was always changing into another, often into its own opposite: ice into water, day into night, life into death. He concluded that nothing is stable or permanent, that change, with fire as its symbol, is the only thing you can ever know for sure. It was Heraclitus who said you can never step into the same river twice.

I began to see what Dr. Sloan was getting at: that history can only be lived once and any written record of it that follows must be read as a reconstruction, a simulation perhaps that must be deemed more or less accurate according to any number of variables.

I also began to appreciate how the study of history involves a constant slippage into other disciplines: mathematics, philosophy, linguistics, science, literature, and theology. I wondered why we call them disciplines anyway, *discipline* being a word so evocative of being made to stand in the corner because you colored on the wall, said a bad word, or tried to flush your teddy bear down the toilet. Why do we call them disciplines when they are so decidedly undisciplined?

After Heraclitus, we moved on to two writers who are customarily recognized as the first great historians: Herodotus writing on the Persian Wars and Thucydides on the Peloponnesian Wars. Both lived in Greece in the fifth century B.C. Their books were big, difficult, and daunting.

These two men are traditionally perceived as being on opposite sides of the historiographical fence. Their aims no doubt were similar: to chronicle past events in a truthful manner; to bring to bear upon them some kind of shape, order, plot, some analysis of the forces of cause and effect; to investigate a particular part of the past in hopes of illuminating lessons and caveats that would prove useful in both the present and the future. The means they used to accomplish these rather lofty ends were, however, quite different.

Herodotus of Halicarnassus is known as the father of history, but he has also been called the father of lies. Belonging to the romantic school of writing, he treated his subject in a grand manner, making full use of vivid description, lively characterization, colloquial speech, and lyrical language to dramatize and invigorate the raw materials of his research. He did not underestimate the importance of factual accuracy but felt free to engage in invention and conjecture when the facts were not available. He made no clear distinction between history and myth. His descriptions of Greece and Persia included elliptical, sometimes prolix, digressions into the details of their respective histories before the wars, as well as of climate, geography, commerce, religion, literature, and the other arts.

A generation later, Thucydides of Athens took a totally different tack. The ruling principle of his more scientific method was that facts, once unearthed by laborious research, must be rigorously scrutinized and then strictly adhered to. He apparently never questioned the ultimate importance and the intrinsic value of the facts. A champion of objectivity, he allowed himself no digressions, no anecdotes, no material that could possibly be construed as subjective or irrelevant. He was documenting an *event,* not a period, and so told nothing of the arts, commerce, religion, or manners and mores of the time. His was a cold-eyed chronological account, resolutely logical, intellectually focused, with no apparent interest in charm, drama, or entertainment.

Dr. Sloan, as usual, made no attempt to hide his bias. He had warned us early on that bias, in history no less than anything else, is inherent and unavoidable. It was best, he said, to declare yourself at the outset and make the most of it from there on in. He pointed out that, although carrying a concealed weapon is a crime according to American law, driving around with three or four rifles on a rack in the back window of your pickup truck is not.

Planted firmly in the camp of Herodotus, Dr. Sloan dismissed the critics who pilloried the man as a gossip, a liar, an altogether untrustworthy source, the original unreliable narrator. He admired Herodotus' jolly nonchalance and his unabashed assumption that his readers would be happy to indulge him, just as glad to be entertained while also being instructed.

I, too, found myself favoring Herodotus. I imagined him as a cheery, gregarious fellow who was most welcome at any dinner party. A jolly raconteur, he would amaze the other guests with his far-ranging knowledge and entertain them with anecdotes of the strange customs and creatures of foreign lands. I pictured him topping off the evening with his story of the Giant Gold-mining Ants of India, a tale that appears in his book. He said that when the Indians went out on their camels (which, he said, had four thighs and four knees in the hind legs) to gather the gold the ants had unearthed, they did it with stealth and speed in the hottest part of the day when the ants had gone under-ground and so would not give chase and eat them alive, camels and all. I imagined that, as a dinner guest, Herodotus would come early and stay late, help out with preparation and clean-up, and partake liberally of both food and drink all evening long.

On the other hand, I pictured Thucydides as a stuffy, stodgy man who was seldom invited to dinner parties. But when he was, he would spend the whole evening looking down his Grecian nose at the other simple-minded guests. He would place tiny tidy portions of food on his plate (nothing touching!) and then refuse seconds. He would not have another glass of ouzo. He would not, absolutely would not, gossip. I imagined the other guests' eyes glazing over while he droned on and on about the military strategies of the Peloponnesians. I could just imagine how relieved they were when he had to go home early and get a good night's sleep.

In retrospect, I can see that the most important thing I learned from Dr. Sloan and Ancient History 101 was that there is more to history than facts, more to truth than reality.

In retrospect, I can see that this is a piece of knowledge that will change your life if you let it. But once upon a time, I thought that history was carved in stone.

History (2)

We normally think of history as one catastrophe after another, war
followed by war, outrage by outrage—almost as if history were
nothing more than all the narratives of human pain, assembled
in sequence. . . . But history is also the narratives of grace, the
recountings of those blessed and inexplicable moments when
someone did something for someone else, saved a life, bestowed a
gift, gave something beyond what was required by circumstance.

—Thomas Cahill, *The Gifts of the Jews*

In the reading I've done since Mary left, I have discovered many interesting and unusual facts. For instance:

In the chapel of Our Lady of Altötting in Germany, the
hearts of twenty-four Bavarian dukes and kings are preserved in
silver urns. These men bequeathed their hearts to Mary as tokens
of their undying devotion.

On special occasions, the statue of Our Lady of Guadalupe
in Spain wears a headdress decorated with 30,000 precious
jewels.

In a pilgrimage that took place on July 14, 1950, the statue
of Our Lady of Miracles at St. Omer, France, was visited by forty

other statues of Mary carried on the backs of the faithful from shrines throughout the region.

In the Brides Corner of the church of Our Lady of Montevergine in Italy, there are hundreds of wedding gowns, complete with veils and bouquets, that have been dedicated to Mary in thanks for a husband found and in petition for a happy marriage.

In my reading, I have also discovered that some of Mary's appearances are much better documented than others. Typically, it is those apparitions that were eventually sanctioned by the Catholic Church that have generated the most literature. These frequently skeptical volumes come complete with lots of footnotes and references to many obscure sources in foreign languages. I looked at one especially robust book that, in its five-hundred-page examination of just one apparition narrative, included 2,020 footnotes and a twenty-three-page bibliography.

And further, by these, my son, be admonished: of making many books there is no end; and much study is a weariness of the flesh.

In their learned attempts to explain the apparitions of the Blessed Virgin Mary (who, for the sake of abbreviation, is sometimes referred to as the BVM, an unfortunate practice which invariably brings to mind others like BMW, IBM, and, of course, BVDs), these authors, I found, most often end up explaining them away. Even those writers in this group who seem to have begun their research wanting to believe, apparently find, in the end, that they cannot.

Paradoxically, I have also discovered that it is these more frequently chronicled apparitions that are hardest to get to the heart of. As the number of pages piles up, it becomes harder to ferret out the truth. It seems as though the more widely an apparition is known, the more versions of it there are likely to be: the more often a story is told, the more details will be added, altered, or taken away; the more extensively any given experience is written about, the more room there is for speculation, disagreement, error, and doubt.

As a writer, I found this somewhat dismaying but hardly surprising. In my own work I have sometimes belabored a scene, an image, or even a single sentence so long and hard that in the end it fell apart altogether. This is something like making pie-crust: if you handle or roll the dough too much, it will turn out too tough to eat.

(Speaking of piecrust . . . I recently read that, although in most countries, virginity was historically considered the most important requirement for a young bride, in Hungary, a girl was not deemed eligible for marriage unless she could make strudel dough so thin that her betrothed could read the newspaper through it. I have already mentioned that although I like to cook, I am not much of a baker. I do not know about making pie-crust from personal experience but only from what others have told me. Myself, I buy the frozen ones.)

Having found in my own writing that thinking or talking about an idea too much or too soon can cause it to evaporate altogether, it occurs to me now that the same paradox applies to faith. Searching too hard for God can get in the way of finding him. Sometimes you just have to stop looking and let yourself be taken by surprise. Sometimes God is as plain as the nose on your face. And sometimes you just can't see the forest for the trees.

In several of the books I've read recently, the authors make it clear that this business of finding faith is not an intellectual exercise: you cannot think your way to faith.

This strikes me as being in direct opposition to the philosophical school of Scholasticism that I studied at university. Prevalent throughout much of the Middle Ages, this theory of analysis held that the truth about *anything*, from the existence of God to the life cycle of the ladybug, could be discovered by thought alone. The Scholastics figured that if enough people thought about and discussed any given question long enough, eventually they were bound to come up with the right answer. Scholastic thinkers used impersonal formal reasoning, involving increasingly smaller logical components, based on repetitious formulas and divisions. They saw no need whatsoever for research based on experiment or experience. They were especially fond of what they called "speculative grammar," a belief that language was the faithful mirror of all metaphysical and theological truths. It was the practice of Scholasticism that led to protracted disputes about such arcane issues as the number of angels in heaven and the nature of a butterfly's soul.

The Scholastics sounded to me like the original ivory-tower thinkers, completely immersed in the life of the mind. I must admit that I found their approach rather appealing. The world of the Scholastics sounded rational and tidy. It seemed to offer an elegant and intellectual way of life unsullied by the nagging chaos of everyday reality, rife as it is with contradictions, randomness, irrationality, and a general existential messiness engendered by the sheer muddle of human nature. Not to mention the necessity of remembering that seeing is believing and that there is an exception to every rule. I imagined the exalted Scholastics descending (or condescending) to dabble in daily life every once in a while, just because they *wanted* to, not because they *had* to. All the Scholastics, of course, were men.

But Scholasticism was eventually debunked by the principle known as Ockham's razor. William of Ockham was a fourteenth-century Franciscan philosopher and theologian. The word *razor* here is a double-edged metaphor referring to the fact that this principle effectively sliced down Scholasticism while simultaneously cutting to the heart of things. Also known as the principle of economy or, more pejoratively, as the law of parsimony, it states that "entities should not be multiplied unnecessarily." That is to say, the simplest theory is the best.

Ockham held that all knowledge must start with the senses; that all reasoning must be inductive, moving from the particular to the general; and that all reality could be examined, measured, and experienced as a number of individual objective facts that were not part of any overall plan. In the world according to Ockham, there was no room for faith, theology, or revelation. Ockham's razor was the precursor to the development of modern-day empiricism.

As Ockham would have it, too much thinking leads to trouble. Having been often accused of thinking too much, I, in theory, am inclined to agree with him. But much as Ockham's razor may have become a rule in both science and philosophy, for those of us who live largely inside our heads, it is still sometimes hard to put into practice.

I can see now that, yes, in various circumstances, I have indeed tried to think my way to many things: self-confidence, peace of mind, patience, serenity, happiness, love. I have also tried to think myself out of all manner of things: misery, doubt, guilt, anger, despair, love. I can see now that, yes, they are right, those who say you cannot think your way to faith. And I suspect now that you cannot read or write your way to it either.

It was Saint Augustine of Hippo who said, sixteen centuries ago: *Seek not to understand that you may believe, but believe that you may understand.* Six centuries after Augustine, Saint Anselm of Canterbury offered his famous prayer: *I yearn to understand some measure of thy truth which my heart believes and loves. For I do not seek to understand in order to have faith, but I have faith in order to understand. For I believe even this: I shall not understand unless I have faith.*

Saint Anthony of Padua

In January 1220, the headless and otherwise mutilated bodies of five men are brought for burial to the priory at Coîmbra, then the capital of Portugal. These men are missionaries who have been brutally murdered in Morocco. They are the first members of the Order of Friars Minor, also known as the Franciscans, to be martyred for their faith.

Among the monks assembled to receive their remains is a young Portuguese man named Ferdinand Bulhom. Born into a noble and powerful Lisbon family in 1195, young Ferdinand joined the Augustinian Canons Regular at the age of fifteen, entering the monastery of Saint Vincent just outside the city. After two years, he asked to be transferred to Coîmbra where he would not be so distracted by the frequent visits of family and friends. By the time the bodies of the martyrs arrive, he has been praying and studying the scriptures there for eight years. Recently ordained to the priesthood, he is twenty-five years old, a short swarthy fellow who, much to his chagrin, tends to gain weight all too easily.

—He was still young enough to be impressionable, Mary said, but old enough to realize that he was not likely to ever achieve that fine figure of the lean ascetic to which he had once aspired. Having quietly practiced the monastic life for ten years already, now Ferdinand longed to give his life to Jesus, to God, to me, in a more active and dramatic way. As he meditated on and prayed over the remains of those five martyrs, an idea began to take shape in his mind. The gore and the glory that martyrdom offered became more and more attractive.

Ferdinand takes to fantasizing at length about fingernails

pulled out (his), entrails scooped out (his), gentle hearts yanked out (his), juicy tongues ripped out by the roots (his!) and flung into the desert by the bare bloody hands of the Moors. He dreams about bodies: short bodies, plump bodies, soft bodies (his, his, his!) dragged behind camels, torn apart by dogs, devoured by lions, stretched on the rack, boiled in oil, burned or buried alive.

—He prayed, Mary said, that when the fire was built to finish him off, he, like Saint Apollonia, would jump willingly into the flames, thus depriving his torturers of the pleasure of tossing him in. He had heard how the Roman Emperor Nero, in the first century, impaled live Christians on stakes and then set them on fire. They were carried through the streets like torches to light the city at night. The irony of this particular torture did not escape Ferdinand: those flaming Christians still shedding the light of God upon the pagan world. He could do it, too, given half a chance.

Eventually the Franciscans are convinced of Ferdinand's sincerity and in 1221 he is admitted to their order. He takes the name of Anthony, after Saint Anthony the Great of the fourth century, one of the original ascetic hermits, exemplar of the desert fathers, also called Anthony the Abbot or Anthony of Egypt.

—These Christian solitaries, Mary said, were both men and women, desert fathers and mothers, abbas and ammas, who chose to live in the deserts of Egypt and Palestine because they believed that there they would encounter God and garner divine wisdom. They practiced various levels of asceticism, perhaps the most extreme of which was that of the stylites. These were men who lived standing on small platforms atop tall pillars in the desert. One of the most famous stylites was Saint Alypius. After standing upright on his pillar for fifty-three years, Alypius found that his legs would no longer support him. Instead of coming down, which certainly no one would have blamed him for, he lay on his side and stayed up there for another fourteen years.

—This was not quite what Ferdinand, now Anthony, had in mind, Mary continued. Nor was he especially interested in becoming an anchorite, an increasingly popular ascetic practice during his time. These men and women, mostly women, were first laid out on a bier and given the rite of Extreme Unction to symbolize that they were dead to the world and risen with Christ. Then they entered the anchorhold, which was permanently bricked up behind them. Their only access to the outside world was through a small window that was opened to pass food in and refuse out. Anthony did not want to be shut away from the world. He was seeking a more active form of devotion.

As soon as possible, he sets out for North Africa, but after several months there, he falls gravely ill and is forced to return to Europe. Caught in a bad storm, his boat is blown off course and travels east across the Mediterranean, landing some months later at Messina in Sicily.

—Anthony had already put himself entirely at God's disposal, Mary said, in spirit anyway, if not in body in quite the way he had intended. So now he took this unexpected change of plans as a sign of God taking charge of his life and so he remained in Italy.

In May, Anthony travels north to Assisi to attend a great gathering of Franciscans. Saint Francis himself is present, seated humbly at the feet of the presiding vicar general, Brother Elias. Anthony is impressed and inspired. The gathering is remembered as the Pentecost Chapter of Mats, so called because there is not enough room for all the attendees and three thousand friars have to sleep on flimsy mats on the cold stone floor.

Afterward, Anthony is appointed to the isolated hermitage

of Montepaolo near the town of Forli southwest of Bologna. For nine months he is kept busy doing kitchen work and other menial jobs around the hermitage.

In 1222, he goes with the other friars to an ordination of Franciscans and Dominicans held at the Minorite convent in Forli. When it comes time for the ceremonial address, it turns out that, due to a misunderstanding, no one has actually been assigned to preach. The local superior asks several of the friars present if they will take over the pulpit but each declines, being unprepared. When Anthony is asked, he, too, excuses himself humbly, protesting that he is but a menial worker, accustomed only to washing dishes and scrubbing floors. The superior, growing impatient, insists that Anthony must stand up and speak whatever God puts into his mouth. Anthony, compelled by his vow of obedience, goes to the pulpit.

—He was very nervous at first, Mary said. His voice was shaky and he was mostly mumbling into his chest. The friars at the back kept calling out for him to speak louder. He was blushing and sweating and his voice was cracking. But soon he managed to master his stage fright, not by imagining the audience in their underwear as timid public speakers are now so often advised, but by turning to me and repeating my name over and over to himself. I was pleased to oblige. Soon he was speaking with eloquence and vigor. God was indeed putting words into his mouth and out they poured in a torrent. His explication of the scriptures was erudite, profound, and sublime. The assembly was collectively and completely astonished.

News of Anthony's stellar performance soon reaches Saint Francis himself who writes him a letter and bestows upon him the dual mission of preaching the gospel throughout the region and teaching theology to his fellow friars. Anthony thus becomes the first lector in theology of the Franciscan order.

In the next five years he makes nearly four hundred trips throughout northern Italy and southern France. He is not an overnight success. The sinners are not especially interested in hearing his long sermons denouncing luxury, avarice, tyranny, and heresy. On one occasion, Anthony is so frustrated by their lack of interest that he goes to the water's edge and preaches to the fishes who stand on their tails and listen.

—In a world without mass media, Mary said, a world, for that matter, largely undiscovered, unexplored, unimagined, uninvented, still news traveled fast. Stories of Anthony's charismatic preaching spread quickly, passing from mouth to mouth, town to town, like currents in the atmosphere. Soon enough, whenever he was scheduled to make an appearance, the shops of the town were closed and people lined up and waited all night to hear him.

Anthony especially likes to travel to those places where the heretics are most deeply entrenched. His remarkable success rate in converting them earns him the nickname *Malleus hereticorum,* Hammer of the Heretics.

—The key to his success, Mary said, was the relentless repetition of my holy names. I am not bragging, I am just telling you how he did it. To each and every heretic he met, he would chant the Litany of the Blessed Virgin as it had come to be ritualized near the time of his birth.

Anthony begins quietly enough:

—*Holy Mother of God, pray for us. Holy Virgin of virgins, pray for us. Mother of Christ, pray for us. Mother of divine grace, pray for us. Mother most pure, pray for us. Mother most chaste, pray for us. Mother inviolate, pray for us. Mother undefiled, pray for us. Mother most amiable, pray for us.*

By the time he reaches the middle of the list of forty-nine titles, a murmuring ripples through the crowd of heretics as a few of them begin to pick up the recurring line:

—Spiritual vessel, pray for us. Vessel of honor, pray for us. Singular vessel of devotion, pray for us. Mystical rose, pray for us. Tower of David, pray for us. Tower of ivory, pray for us. House of gold, pray for us. Ark of the covenant, pray for us.

As the end of the litany approaches, each and every one of the heretics has flung his arms up to heaven and Anthony's own seraphic voice is nearly drowned out by theirs:

—Queen of angels, pray for us. Queen of patriarchs, pray for us. Queen of prophets, pray for us. Queen of apostles, pray for us. Queen of martyrs, pray for us. Queen of confessors, pray for us. Queen of virgins, pray for us. Queen of all saints, pray for us. Queen conceived without original sin, pray for us. Queen assumed into heaven, pray for us. Queen of the most holy Rosary, pray for us. Queen of peace, pray for us. Lamb of God, you take away the sins of the world; spare us, O Lord.

The heretics, as if a single body, fall to the ground. Pressing their faces into the earth, they say the final prayer and their mouths fill with dirt:

—Grant, we beg you, O Lord God, that we your servants may enjoy lasting health of mind and body, and by the glorious intercession of the Blessed Mary, ever Virgin, be delivered from present sorrow and enter into the joy of eternal happiness. Through Christ our Lord. Amen.

The crowds grow exponentially, soon numbering thirty thousand or more. No building is sufficient to hold them, so Anthony preaches in public squares, marketplaces, meadows, and vineyards. He has to hire a bodyguard to protect him from the faithful who show up with scissors, eager to snip off pieces of his habit for souvenirs.

—Like the urban legends of modern times, Mary said, the stories of Anthony's many miracles became common currency throughout Europe.

In Toulouse, a heretic tells Anthony that he will not believe that the body and blood of Jesus reside in the Eucharist until his mule leaves its stable and kneels down before the sacramental bread and wine. A few days later when Anthony stands in front of the church with the Eucharist in his hands, the mule appears on the steps and goes down on its knees before him.

On another occasion, Anthony is served a sumptuous but poisoned meal by a group of Italian heretics hoping to do away with him. Anthony makes the sign of the cross over the food and it becomes wholesome and delicious again.

—At Padua, Mary said, a young man named Leonardo, remorseful and repentant, confessed to Anthony that he had kicked his mother in a fit of rage. Anthony told him that the foot of a man who kicks his own mother deserves to be cut off. So Leonardo ran home and chopped off his foot with an axe. Anthony came to the house, picked up the amputated foot, and miraculously rejoined it to Leonardo's leg. There is no record of what Leonardo's mother had to say about all this.

Shortly after the death of Saint Francis in October 1226, Anthony is recalled to Italy. Suffering general ill health due to his years of strenuous traveling and frequent fasting, Anthony is happy now to settle down at the Santa Maria monastery in Padua, where he is much honored and beloved. He devotes himself to teaching theology, studying the scriptures, and composing sermons on the lives of the saints.

In this time well before the invention of printing, two full centuries before the appearance of the Gutenberg Bible, the first substantial printed book, Anthony's most prized and essential possession is his psalter, a collection of scriptures, psalms, and canticles in manuscript form. It is invaluable not only for its own sake but also for the notes and comments Anthony has written in it to aid him in his teaching. He keeps it always close to him, even going so far as to sleep with it in his hands.

—But one morning, Mary said, Anthony awakened to find

his hands empty. He figured the psalter must have slid to the floor in the night. But it was nowhere to be found in his cell-like room. He alerted the other friars. Frantically they searched the entire monastery but instead of locating the psalter, they discovered that a number of other items were missing: a store of root vegetables they were recently given by a neighboring farmer and were saving for the next feast day, three loaves of bread just baked the day before, four bottles of sacramental wine, a healthy young mule, and a French novice who had recently been complaining at length about the deprivations of monastic life. Clearly it was he who had absconded with the psalter.

Anthony prays that it will soon be returned to him. The very next day, the remorseful novice comes slinking back. He tells a horrific story of being confronted by a hideous, axe-brandishing demon as he tried to make his getaway. The novice is forgiven, the psalter is restored to Anthony's hands, and there is much all-round rejoicing.

In 1231, after preaching through Lent, Anthony is stricken with dropsy and retires with two other friars to a woodland retreat at Camposanpiero. He lives there in a cell built under the branches of a walnut tree. When it becomes clear to him that death is near, he asks to be carried back to Padua. But the trip by wagon proves too much for him and, on June 13, he dies at the Poor Clare Convent at Arcella. He is just thirty-six years old.

On his deathbed, Anthony sings a hymn to Mary:

—*O Gloriosa Virgine: O Glorious Lady, exalted high in heaven above, the great Creator, mighty Lord, was nursed by thee with mother's love. What sinful Eve had lost of us, by thy dear Son thou didst restore.*

Immediately after his burial on June 17, 1231, miracles begin to occur at his tomb. In the fastest canonization ever, Anthony is officially declared a saint by Pope Gregory IX on Pentecost, May 30, 1232. Thirty-one years later, in 1263, his body is exhumed and moved (or "translated" as is said of moving such relics from one place to another) from the convent to the newly erected Basilica di Sant' Antonio at Padua. Although it is found that most of him has turned to dust, his tongue, which praised the Lord with such eloquence and wisdom, remains fresh and red. Present at the exhumation is Saint Bonaventure, another great successor of Saint Francis. Upon seeing the wondrous tongue, he takes it in his hands and kisses it fondly, declaring this the ultimate proof that Anthony had indeed found favor with God.

Neither his miracles nor his popularity subside over the following centuries. In 1350, his tomb is reopened and his jawbone is removed, it, too, having been part of what made him so eloquent. With its teeth still intact, the jawbone is placed on display in a head-shaped reliquary in the basilica near his tongue. In 1668, four hundred years after his death, Anthony, by royal decree, is made a soldier in the second infantry regiment of the Spanish army. Each time his regiment shares in a victory, Anthony is promoted. In 1889 he retires, having reached the rank of general.

In 1946, Anthony is declared a Doctor of the Church by Pope Pius XII. In 1981, his tomb is opened yet again. This time his vocal cords are extracted. After scientific testing determines that they too are undecayed, they are put on display in a crystal ball set upon an open book. Golden flames leap from its pages which are made of solid silver.

Anthony is such a popular saint that he has more places named after him than any other. Throughout the world, sixty-eight cities, mountains, bays, and reefs bear his name. He is the patron saint of many things, including harvests, the mail, sailors, fishermen, spinsters, barren women, American Indians, Portugal, Italy, Brazil, the poor, and the oppressed. He is called upon for help against infertility, fever, demonic powers, and plagues afflicting cattle. He is most often invoked as the finder of lost objects because of the story of his psalter, lost and found.

Busloads of pilgrims, more than a thousand a day, come from around the world to see his relics in Padua. In the basilica gift shop and at the stalls of vendors in the surrounding square, they stock up on souvenirs. They buy bookmarks, key chains, tape measures, school supplies, combs, and toothbrush holders, all with Anthony's image on them. They take home Anthony snow globes, dashboard magnets, lightswitch covers, ballpoint pens on which his figure moves up and down, and pink plaster Anthonys which predict rain when they turn blue.

In return, these pilgrims leave behind gold and silver ex-votos, colored snapshots of their loved ones, embossed thank-you cards, short notes dashed off on the backs of place mats and parking tickets, long letters handwritten on expensive monogrammed stationery. Ever obedient to the words of Jesus, Anthony, they believe, will not deny them: *Ask, and it shall be given you; seek, and ye shall find.* Anthony receives nearly four hundred letters a day.

Today to him the faithful pray: *The sea obeys, and fetters break, And lifeless limbs thou does restore; Whilst treasures lost are found again, When young or old thine aid implore.* Those who like to speak to him more casually say: *Tony, Tony, turn around. Something's lost and must be found.* He is the friendly finder of car keys, earrings, mittens, hats, money, wallets, homework, husbands, gloves.

—Anthony is, Mary said, the restorer of lost hopes, lost dreams, lost souls, the shining beacon for all those who have lost their way.

Walking

For the duration of Mary's visit, we fell into a comfortable routine that suited us both. She was the perfect houseguest. She was not noisy, demanding, messy, or intrusive. She was helpful without getting in the way, and she did not need to be constantly entertained. I sometimes asked her if she wanted to go out: for lunch or dinner, to a movie, an art show, or something. But she always said she was happy just staying close to home.

—Given a different set of circumstances, she said, I would have been a real homebody. But that's not the story that was written for me.

She insisted that I should just go on about my business and she meant it.

Each morning I got up at six o'clock as usual, brought in the newspaper, turned on the radio, and made the coffee. Mary would join me for a light breakfast and then go back to her room where, she said, she had some reading to do, some letters to write, some phone calls to make. I imagined that these calls might give the phrase "long distance" a whole new meaning. My anxiety about the resulting phone bill must have shown on my face.

—Fear not, Mary said. I've got my calling card.

I would then spend the rest of the morning doing exactly what I would have done if she were not there. I would read in the kitchen for an hour or so, then have a bath, get dressed, and go to my study. There I worked on whatever business needed tending to and continued making notes for my next book. Sometimes I could hear Mary moving around in her room or talking on the phone. I could hear her in the shower. But mostly she was silent.

Around noon or one o'clock, we would reconvene in the kitchen for lunch. After lunch, the rest of the afternoon was open.

Late on Tuesday, the second day of her visit, Mary suggested that we take a walk around the neighborhood. The prospect of some fresh air and a little exercise was appealing. We put on our shoes and went out. Mary wore her brown cardigan which, on her, did not look dowdy at all. It was close to five o'clock and many of my neighbors were just returning from work.

On any given weekday, myself and a handful of retirees are usually the only people home on the block, the others having gone off to fulfill their respective obligations in the real world. While I am at home here constructing my own fictional worlds, performing what I like to think of on a good day as my own minor miracles, they are out there making their various contributions to society. They are out there cutting hair, serving meals, nursing the sick, fixing cars, delivering mail, teaching the twelve times table, selling lawn mowers, dresses, refrigerators, life insurance, real estate, and shoes.

My neighbors do not seem to be unduly impressed or bothered by having a writer in their midst. I don't know for sure if any of them have ever read my books. If they have, they might or might not have recognized bits and pieces of themselves in the pages, stray details here and there: a description of a house, a garden, a trellis, a dog, a face in the window looking out at the rain. If they have noticed, they do not mention it.

They do usually notice when I get my picture in the local paper. One or another of them will cut out the article and bring it over in case I haven't seen it or might want an extra copy. The newspaper picture that generated the most excitement around the neighborhood was when, two years ago in the fall, I happened to arrive at the Health Unit Flu Shot Clinic at the same time as the newspaper photographer. So there I was the next day in black-and-white with my hair not combed, my sleeve rolled up, and my teeth gritted in an utterly unconvincing smile while the nurse stuck the needle in my arm.

As far as my neighbors are concerned, what matters the most about me is that I am a good neighbor because I do not have a dog that barks all night or a cat that digs up their gardens, I keep my lawn mowed in the summer and my snow shovelled in the winter, and, most important, I do not have wild parties to which the police must be called.

Now, as far as they were concerned, that day in April had been as ordinary a day as any other. When Mary and I set out on our walk, they were pulling into their respective driveways with relief, I imagined, at another day's work done, looking forward to dinner, a relaxing evening, early to bed, and a good night's sleep. At least that's how it looked from the outside. If any of them were coming home with reluctance or regret, dreading yet another boring evening, another scene, another argument, another phone call from the principal, the collection agency, or a spurned lover threatening to spill the beans, they did not let it show, and I did not have to know about it. Respect for each other's privacy is, I believe, an essential component in the loving of thy neighbors.

Just as Mary and I reached the end of my driveway, the woman who lives directly across the street pulled in in her new red minivan. She is a secretary at a real estate agency and her husband, who was bound to be home shortly, works for the city. Her three towheaded boys tumbled happily out of the van. The two older boys clutched their lunch boxes and several sheets each of colored construction paper, today's artwork, no doubt destined now for the fridge door. The youngest, who was still in day care, carried his teddy bear by one leg, its brown head dragging on the ground.

—Hello, hello, their mother called merrily across to us, juggling her purse, her keys, and a large bag of cat food, while gently herding the children toward the back door. Their big tabby cat sat in the front window, washing his face and waiting patiently.

We waved and called back.

—Who's that other lady with the long hair? I heard the oldest boy ask his mother, looking over his shoulder at us. I could not hear her answer but one of the questions I had not asked earlier had thus been answered.

—They can see you, I said with wonder.

—Children can always see me, Mary said. But yes, this time they can all see me, the mother too. Don't forget: seeing is not always believing. They can see me without seeing me, if you know what I mean.

Then she quoted Jesus from the Gospel of Saint Matthew:

—*Therefore speak I to them in parables: because they seeing see not; and hearing they hear not, neither do they understand.*

Mary was the only person I have ever met who could quote the Bible in ordinary conversation without sounding pompous, self-righteous, or overweeningly pious. When Mary spoke scripture, it sounded as natural and unaffected as anything else she had to say.

We turned right and headed down the street, falling smoothly into step, strolling at an easy pace.

Now considered part of the downtown area, my neighborhood, when it was originally developed fifty years ago, was one of the first suburbs of the city. Most of the houses are much like mine, three-bedroom bungalows in red brick or white stucco. There are a handful of larger homes with two stories and four or five bedrooms. Over the years, many of the houses have undergone changes. There have been renovations and additions, new porches, patios, windows, garages, and decks. There have been innumerable paint jobs. The neighborhood has thus long since lost that cookie-cutter look of newer suburbs and possesses now a comfortable character of settled respectability, kindness, decency, safety, and well-being.

The large deep lots contain mature trees of various kinds: maple, poplar, spruce, fir, cedar, weeping birch, black walnut, mountain ash. In the yards both front and back there are many kinds of bushes and shrubs: lilac, juniper, forsythia, weigela, mock orange, honeysuckle, hydrangea. Because it was only April, the deciduous trees and bushes were just beginning to glow green with leaves in bud, but Mary said she could imagine how lush it would all look in a couple of months and how glorious the leaves must be in the fall.

As we walked, Mary noted and sometimes paused to admire certain details of various houses. She liked the vine-covered wall of one, the cedar hedge of another. She liked a cobblestone walkway, a bay window, a split-level front deck, an old-fashioned screen door, and a bright blue pair of shutters. She liked a white wooden trellis that was bare now but would soon enough be completely hidden by a deep purple clematis so large and striking that cars passing in the street frequently slow down to admire it and, if the owners of the house happen to be outside, they wave and smile proudly from their chairs on the front deck.

We talked about gardening, which is something I have come to enjoy very much in recent years. Mary was quite knowledgeable and enthusiastic about the subject and lamented the fact that, because of her peripatetic lifestyle, she was not able to have a garden of her own.

—I have to let other people do my gardening for me, she said, and went on to tell me about Mary Gardens, a medieval tradition now enjoying something of a revival.

According to this tradition, each plant and flower cultivated in such a garden is either named for or symbolic of her possessions, her body parts, her virtues, and the events of her miraculous life. The rose and the lily, both symbolizing her purity, are the two flowers most commonly associated with Mary, but there are hundreds of others. Each flower has its own meaning and significance. Each plant is a prayer.

—Take that clematis, for instance, she said, pointing at the still-empty trellis. It's also called Virgin's Bower. The fuchsia is Our Lady's Eardrops, campanula is Our Lady's Thimble, Canterbury bells are Our Lady's Nightcap, thrift is Our Lady's Pin Cushion, and lily of the valley is Our Lady's Tears.

Mary Gardens, both public and private, have all these and more: Our Lady's Hair, Our Lady's Ribbon, Our Lady's Glove, Our Lady's Fingers, Our Lady's Comb, Our Lady's Looking Glass, Our Lady's Needle, Our Lady's Thumb, Our Lady's Meat, and Our Lady's Cheeses. There is Mary's Face, Mary's Gold, Mary's Nut, and Mary's Milk, a kind of thistle whose leaves are covered with white spots said to be drops of breast milk spilled while Mary nursed the baby Jesus on the road to Egypt.

—And don't forget navelwort, Mary said. Once it was called

Venus' Navel, but then it became known as Our Lady's Navel. Another one of the many interesting things I seem to have inherited from the early goddesses. I also share a lot with Artemis, the Greek goddess of both virginity and childbirth.

When we reached the stop sign at the corner, we turned right and then right again. Midway up that part of the block there lives an old but ferocious yellow bulldog. In fact, that is his name: Bulldog. His owners, much to the relief of the rest of the neighborhood, keep him in at night so his barking does not disturb anyone's sleep. But in the daytime he is mostly outside, tied up in the front yard on a sturdy rope just long enough to allow him to reach a spot on the outer edge of his lawn six inches short of the sidewalk. Bulldog cannot tolerate anyone walking past his house. No matter how sound asleep he might appear to be in his usual station beside a large forsythia bush at the foot of the steps, whenever a pedestrian approaches his yard, Bulldog comes flying out with his vicious little teeth bared and his watery brown eyes bulging. He tears hard and fast toward the street and, just as he reaches the edge of his lawn, Bulldog also reaches the end of his rope. He is then unceremoniously yanked off his feet and flipped over backward. Struggling upright again, he goes into a maniacal convulsion of barking and gagging while nearly strangling himself and spraying slobber everywhere. Once the pedestrian has passed, Bulldog plods back to his favorite spot at the foot of the steps and falls instantly asleep, exhausted, no doubt, by his valiant efforts.

As if on cue, the moment our feet touched Bulldog's stretch of sidewalk, he launched himself across the yard. Mary stopped walking. Bulldog kept running. That day, as always, he headed full bore toward us until the rope caught him up short and flipped him over. We both laughed as his stocky little legs pawed the air. He flailed about, righted himself, bared his teeth, and faced us down. His eyes bulged. His mouth opened. But nothing came out. He closed his mouth and sat down. Mary frowned at him. He cocked his head and eyed her suspiciously. Mary smiled. He stood up, turned around, and trudged back to his spot at the foot of the steps. He lay down and closed his eyes.

Mary laughed and we continued down the street. At the corner we again turned right. Several houses down we stopped to let a battered brown station wagon pull into the driveway of a red-brick house just like mine. There were children's toys scattered across the front lawn and a red and white stroller parked near the door. This, I realized, was the front of one of the houses whose backyards I can see from the window of my study. It was, in fact, the house whose laundry I had been contemplating the previous morning, the house with five identical shirts and a Jesus teeshirt on the clothesline.

The driver got out of the car, a short blond man wearing jeans and a teeshirt (a faded green teeshirt with nothing on it, no face of Jesus or anyone else). He came toward us smiling. He shook my hand and introduced himself.

—Hi, I'm Peter, he said. You live right there, don't you? he asked, pointing.

—Yes, I said and told him my name.

—Well, I'm pleased to meet you, Peter said. We've just moved here from the west coast. Myself and my wife, her name is Doreen, we're your new neighbors. We've got two kids. Jody is four and little Jenny is just eleven months. We've been married for five years now. This is sure a nice quiet neighborhood, isn't it? Have you lived here long?

He rattled on in a jovial, if somewhat disjointed, fashion for a few minutes, asking questions but leaving no room for answers, offering random bits and pieces of information about himself and his family but shedding no light on their laundry.

Suddenly he broke off and turned to Mary.

—Pardon my manners, he said, again putting out his hand.

—I'm Mary, she said simply.

—Pleased to meet you, he said. Do you live in the neighborhood too?

—No, Mary said. I'm visiting from out of town for the week.

—Well now, isn't that nice, Peter said.

They shook hands for a longer time than seemed necessary. Then Peter went into his house and we went on our way. Although the mystery of Peter's laundry had not been cleared up, still I was relieved to have another of my unasked questions answered. Not only could other people see and hear her, obviously they could feel her too. Her hand in Peter's had apparently been every bit as solid and unremarkable as mine, every bit as firm and warm as it was when she touched me.

In a few more minutes we were home. In the time it had taken to walk around the block, not more than half an hour by my watch, I had come to feel that spending time with the Virgin Mary was, if not quite something I had been doing all my life, then at least something I had been expecting or intending to do all along.

In the back porch we took off our shoes and hung up our sweaters. We went into the kitchen and began to make dinner as if this were the most ordinary thing in the world to be doing at this time of the day in this part of the world. Which, of course, it was.

History (3)

The world, the human world, is bound together not by protons and electrons, but by stories. Nothing has meaning in itself: all the objects in the world would be shards of bare mute blankness, spinning wildly out of orbit, if we didn't bind them together with stories.

—Brian Morton, *Starting Out in the Evening*

Over the years there have been many things I thought were facts that turned out to be untrue. Mostly these are relatively inconsequential things that everybody assumes are true, popular misconceptions that go largely unquestioned and unexamined unless or until they are eventually put to the test. The discovery that these things are false is interesting but, with any luck, has little or no bearing on life as we know it. Yes, lightning can strike the same place twice, and yes, bears can climb trees. No, porcupines do not throw their quills, bats are not blind, cats are not afraid of water, Chicago is not the windiest city in the United States, Frankenstein was not the name of the monster, Nero did not fiddle while Rome burned, and it is never too cold to snow. And in my first solo building project (a box to hold yard waste too large and woody for the composter), I learned the hard

way that a two-by-four piece of lumber does not actually measure two inches by four inches.

So too (but with far greater significance) has the notion of
history as an inviolable body of knowledge to which I was inured
back in high school since been completely dispelled, summarily
counteracted and corrected. First by Dr. Sloan and Ancient History 101 and, more recently, by Mary herself.

—Everything they have ever said about me has become true,
she said that Tuesday evening as we sat together in the living
room and she told me more about her life.

—Everything they have ever said about me has become true.
In one way or another.

And I was left to make whatever I could of that.

She obviously enjoyed watching my logical modern mind
trying to grapple with these mysteries, trying to set them in
order, put them in perspective, trying in vain to hammer each
piece of the puzzle into place and keep it there. She tossed out
such cryptic comments and contradictions as if hoping they
would be like grains of sand irritating the inside of an oyster
shell long and hard enough to eventually produce a pearl.

Think about pearls of wisdom falling from heaven. Consider
Botticelli's *Birth of Venus*, the goddess of all love and beauty born
out of the sea foam, a perfect pearl arising from an oyster shell
with one hand upon her breasts, the other trying to hide her
nakedness with her long golden hair. Consider also his earlier
Virgin and Child with Eight Angels. Notice that in these two
paintings Venus and the Virgin are the same woman. Do not
imagine this to be a coincidence. Consider Mary as the holy
embodiment of beauty and the beautiful embodiment of holiness. Consider Mary as the utterly pure oyster from which issued
Jesus Christ, most brilliant and precious pearl.

Think about Jesus saying: *Give not that which is holy unto the dogs, neither cast ye your pearls before swine, lest they trample them under their feet, and turn again and rend you.*

Think about the pearly gates: *And the twelve gates were twelve pearls; every several gate was of one pearl: and the street of the city was pure gold, as it were transparent glass.*

Think about glass. Created by superheating a mixture of sand, limestone, and other minerals at a temperature of about 2,400°F, it becomes a liquid. It is then supercooled back to a transparent solid. On a molecular level, glass is an amorphous substance because it is both and neither liquid nor solid. It is strong enough to emerge from the fire in a new and beautiful form, yet so fragile as to be shattered by a single careless brush of the hand.

Pour yourself a cold glass of water on a hot summer day and remember that the vessel was made by fire, Heraclitus' symbol of change. Think about transparent glass taking on the color of whatever is poured into it: green Kool-Aid, brown tea, red blood. Think about the glass being half empty and half full.

Sweet Mother of 's Hertogenbosch

Early in the year 1380, the Cathedral of Saint Jan in the Dutch city of 's Hertogenbosch is undergoing extensive renovation and expansion. This flourishing city with the unwieldy name began as a village beside the River Maas on the estate of Hendrik I, Duke of Brabant. It became a city in 1185 and was given this name meaning "in the Duke's woods." The locals, for simplicity's sake, call it Den Bosch. The cathedral, too, is nearly two hundred years old and needs to be enlarged to accommodate the ever-growing congregation.

Easter arrives and any hope of celebrating it in the newly

renovated cathedral must be abandoned as the work is far from done. On Maundy Thursday, an apprentice stonemason eating his lunch in the builders' shed discovers a mutilated statue of Mary buried beneath a pile of stones and rubble. Being a practical sort, the young man finds an axe and is about to chop up the statue for firewood. But the architect for the project, uneasy at the thought of such sacrilege, stops him and tells him that since it is the custom to arrange all movable statues around the Easter Sepulcher, he had better carry this one inside and find a place for it among the rest.

—When the parishioners of Den Bosch saw that dirty old statue, Mary said, they were shocked and disgusted. They began murmuring to each other in growing consternation. Some of the more outraged covered their eyes and refused to look at it. Admittedly, the statue as it was then did not show me to my best advantage. But still there was no need to overreact, no excuse for such a commotion.

The parishioners' voices grow louder and louder until soon they are mocking and sneering at the statue's disfigured face, pointing their fingers and shrieking insults at the young mason who brought the hideous thing inside. Finally losing his temper, the mason jumps to his feet and yells at them all, saying they are just as old and ugly themselves so they have no right to criticize. Whether chastened by his rebuke or rendered speechless by his audacity, the congregation falls silent. The statue stays in the sepulcher all through the Easter celebrations.

Afterward, when the other statues are returned to their usual places, a lay brother named Wouter, who has taken quite a liking to the miserable old statue, moves her to a side chapel. Still the parishioners are annoyed. Tired of all the complaints, the sacristan tells Brother Wouter he can do whatever he wants with the statue as long as he keeps her out of sight. But now

Brother Wouter discovers she has become too heavy to move. She stays in the chapel.

The cathedral is still swarming with workmen involved in the renovation. One of the painters, the kind of clownish man who will do anything for a laugh, smears the statue with yellow paint. The other workmen think this is hilarious. They gather round laughing and pointing and slapping their knees. Later, someone drapes a length of embroidered linen around the statue's shoulders in an anonymous attempt to recover her dignity.

Meanwhile, Brother Wouter has come to the conclusion that the statue is incomplete. Both of Mary's hands are extended. In the right she holds an apple but the left is empty.

—A year later, in 1381, Mary said, Brother Wouter found the missing piece. He came upon a group of children playing with a wooden doll on Orthen Street. Bribing them with candy and guilders, he persuaded them to give up the doll. It was the baby Jesus and it fit perfectly into that empty left hand.

The statue is restored and moved to a more prominent position in another chapel. Still, the parishioners are not about to accept this abomination. Even after the statue has been repainted and repaired, the insults and abuses continue.

—It was time to take action, Mary said, time to fall back on that old standard of reward and punishment. The next visitor who laughed and asked if the statue had jaundice fainted on the spot. She was confined to her bed for two weeks until she apologized and promised to make amends. Punishment. But there was another visitor, a housewife named Hadewych van Vichten, who had been lame for three years with a mysterious malady that the doctors could not cure. She prayed to the statue for healing. She brought a miniature tin leg to the chapel and laid it at my feet. She was instantly cured. Reward, Mary said. Now I was speaking their language. Now they understood.

The miracles in Den Bosch continue. Those who believe are rewarded with graces, favors, and cures. Those who disparage the statue are punished, not violently, not excessively, but gently, with fainting spells, aches and pains, headaches, nightmares, disappointments, indigestion, and acne. Soon there is no more talk among the parishioners of ugliness or jaundice.

Eventually the Sweet Mother of 's Hertogenbosch is restored to her rightful splendor. Her gown is painted scarlet and the baby Jesus' garment is green. Her hair is frosted with gold and luminous roses adorn her tunic. In this small country known for tulips, dikes, canals, and windmills, devotion to Mary continues through the centuries, even when the statue herself is removed from the chapel and hidden during nearly three hundred years of conflict and iconoclasm. Over the years, the shrine is visited not only by thousands of regular citizens but by many members of royalty as well, including the Emperor Maximilian, Ferdinand of Castile, Ferdinand of Naples, Edward IV of England, and Philip I of Spain. The statue is finally returned to the chapel in 1828 and in 1878 Pope Leo XIII orders her coronation.

Today the shrine is crowded with miniature wax and metal body parts, including the little leg given in thanks by the housewife, Hadewych van Vichten, more than six hundred years ago.

Mary told me stories from her past in the same way most people do. They resurrect details and dramas from years ago, offering amusing anecdotes and wry confessions delivered with fluctuating measures of pride and regret. Exorcising and exercising their various demons and gods, excavating all possible parallels and patterns, they are, in effect, inventing themselves as they go along. Every life is open to interpretation. Every history is subject to exegesis.

Consciously or unconsciously, we reconstruct our recollections as we construct our stories, succumbing not infrequently to the temptations of embellishment and exaggeration. Being a writer, I already knew that all stories change with the telling. Immortal though she might be, Mary was no exception to this. Apparently, immortality does not guarantee infallibility or objectivity any more than it guarantees omnipotence, omniscience, or absolute truth. It all depends on memory, which has its own irrepressible tendencies to make meaning, magic, or mischief.

I learned about Mary from her stories in the same way you learn about any new person who comes into your life: a little bit at a time. As she doled out more and more pieces of the puzzle that comprised her life, I listened carefully and stockpiled contradictions, enigmas, and ambiguities. In the beginning, I assumed that it would all make sense in the end, that all my questions would be answered, and all the mysteries would be solved.

In the beginning was the Word, and the Word was with God, and the Word was God. In the beginning I assumed that in the end I would know everything there was to know about Mary.

Our Lady of Czestochowa

Back when Mary is still alive, she sometimes has her portrait painted by the apostle Luke. Although Luke is a physician by trade, he also becomes an accomplished artist over the years. He is eventually revered as the patron saint of artists, doctors, and butchers, this last not because of his proficiency with the knife but because his emblem is a winged ox.

—I spent many long hours sitting for Luke, Mary said. This was after Jesus was killed, after I had gone to live in Ephesus with John, who loved me like his own mother, just as Jesus had told him to. That was John the Evangelist, not to be confused with all the other Johns. There have been so many. John the Baptist, of course, and John of the Cross, John the Divine, John the Good, John the Silent, and John the Dwarf, just to name a few. The confusion is compounded even more by the fact that John the Evangelist is also called John Before the Latin Gate, a name that arose after Emperor Domitian sentenced him to be boiled in oil near the Roman gate that led to the town of Latinum.

—Anyway, Mary continued, it was Luke who painted me, and while he worked, I sat very still and tried not to sweat or twitch, tried not to think of how my neck was aching, my shoulders were cramping, and my nose was starting to itch. While he painted, I talked. He did not know Jesus himself, so I told him about my son's life and later he wrote it all down in his gospel.

Mary is one of Luke's favorite subjects and he paints her in many different poses and attitudes. If the large scrolls on which he prefers to paint are in short supply, Luke will use almost anything that comes to hand, including the furniture. He paints Mary on the cypress top of a table made by Jesus himself. After Luke completes Mary's face, he paints Jesus as a baby nestled in the crook of her left arm. He dresses them both in blue and red robes laden with gold and gems. Then he crowns them with more gems, more gold. Mother and child, they are both black.

—This painting was apparently lost or just plain forgotten, Mary said, until nearly four hundred years later when Helen, mother of Constantine the Great, discovered it in Jerusalem, along with the nails used to crucify Jesus and the True Cross itself. Helen gave the painting to her son, who was by then the Emperor of Constantinople, absolute master of the Roman Empire. Constantine built a church to house the painting and soon the miracles began, not the least of which was the saving of Constantinople from the attacking Saracens.

A thousand years later, in the fourteenth century, after a treacherous and complicated journey through Eastern Europe, the painting becomes the property of Prince Ladislaus of Poland. He keeps it in a special chamber in his castle at Belz, which is attacked by the Tartars in 1382. An arrow shot by one of the Tartars flies through the window and hits the Black Madonna right in the throat.

In his precipitous flight from Belz, Prince Ladislaus takes the precious portrait with him, fearing that if he leaves it behind, it will be destroyed by the Tartars. Ladislaus spends a night in the town of Czestochowa where he puts the painting in a small church. On the morning of August 26, 1382, when he picks up the painting and tries to leave town, the horse pulling his carriage will not move. Ladislaus takes this as a sign that God wants the painting to stay in Czestochowa. A Pauline monastery is built to house it on the Jasna Góra, Mountain of Light.

Fifty years later, in 1430, the monastery is invaded by the Hussites, who try to steal the painting. One of the thieves slashes the Black Madonna twice with his sword. He then falls to the ground screaming in pain and dies. The rest of the Hussites flee in terror and the monastery is saved.

Despite repeated attempts to repair them, these two cuts on Mary's cheek and the earlier wound to her throat are still visible on the portrait today, more than five hundred years later.

—Some wounds never heal, Mary said. People should know that by now.

The history of Our Lady of Czestochowa is as long and complicated as the history of Poland itself. Her power and her miracles continue unabated through all those wars, invasions,

partitions, and political upheavals. In 1717, she is crowned
Queen of Poland by Pope Clement XI and more than two hundred thousand pilgrims gather for her coronation.

No matter how hard the Russians and the Nazis have tried to
control her, still Our Lady of Czestochowa has remained at the
spiritual heart of the country. After the Nazis claim Warsaw and
Hitler forbids all pilgrimages, more than five hundred thousand
Poles travel secretly to the sanctuary. When Poland is liberated
in 1945, a million and a half people make the trip to the shrine
to give thanks. When the Russian army captures the city three
years later, again hundreds of thousands of pilgrims journey to
the site, moving as if invisible right past the Communist soldiers
who are patrolling the streets.

In 1979, more than two and a half million pilgrims visit the
shrine. One of them is Pope John Paul II, who was born in
Krakow in 1920. He is the first non-Italian pope to be elected in
456 years and he is the first pope in history to visit a Communist
country. To the multitudes gathered in the Assembly at Jasna
Góra, he speaks of how the history of Poland has been written in
many ways, but the Polish heart writes it, reads it, and lives it
through the history of Mary, their Mother and Queen.

Listening to Mary's stories, I soon realized that it was no more
possible to know everything about her than it is to know everything about anybody. Just when you think you have another person all figured out, they are just as likely to throw you a curve
that leaves you bewildered and scratching your head.

The man who dumps you because he isn't ready for a serious
commitment marries a cocktail waitress named Candi six scant
months after breaking your heart. The woman who hates big
cities and small children meets a new man named Lance and

follows him to Manhattan, where they proceed to have four children and live blissfully ever after. The man who is afraid of heights takes up skydiving. The woman who hates traveling goes on a Mediterranean cruise.

The man who apparently has everything going for him lowers and locks his garage door one Sunday morning, tucks a note under the windshield wiper like a parking ticket, gets into the car and starts it. His lovely wife and their two children are away visiting relatives. His body is discovered the next day by the mailman. The note, addressed to no one in particular, says: *I'm sorry. It's not your fault.* The car is a brand-new black BMW. The man, safely strapped into the driver's seat, is wearing neatly pressed khakis and a yellow teeshirt. On the passenger seat beside him is a half-eaten bag of salt and vinegar potato chips, an empty can of Coke, and a book called *Planning Your Retirement* with a bookmark carefully inserted at the last chapter. On the bookmark is a painting of a field of sunflowers before a black mountain below a blue sky. At the bottom is a quote from Anatole France: *To accomplish great things we must not only act but also dream, not only plan but also believe.*

When all is said and done, you have to admit that learning about another person invariably involves putting two and two together and getting five.

You have to admit that another person, any other person, is, in the end, an enigma: inscrutable, unpredictable, ultimately unknowable. But no less compelling for that.

There were whole days when the more Mary told me, the less I knew for sure.

Our Lady of Good Counsel

In 1467, in the tiny village of Genazzano, Italy, situated on a hilltop thirty miles southeast of Rome, Mary delivers a miraculous gift to the faithful.

—I quietly advised a widow named Petruccia de Geneo to begin rebuilding an old church in Genazzano, Mary said. Originally built more than ten centuries before, this church was now in a sorry state, not much more than a pile of crumbling stone.

According to legend, the spot on which the abandoned church stood was, in pagan times, the site of a temple dedicated to Venus, the Roman goddess of love. When early Christians denounced her as a harlot, the temple was razed and the church dedicated to Mary was built on the site. Ironically enough, Venus eventually became a Christian saint called Venerina or Venere, to whom young girls are still known to appeal for help in finding a good husband. It was Venus who was first known as Stella Maris, Star of the Sea. But now, as far as the Genazzano faithful are concerned, this title belongs to Mary: Stella Maris, Our Lady of the Mariners, the guiding star by which all sailors steer their ships.

It is to Mary that they sing "Ave Maris Stella": *Hail, thou star of ocean, God's own mother blest, Ever sinless Virgin, Gate of heavenly rest. . . . Virgin all excelling, Mildest of the mild; Freed from guilt preserve us, Meek and undefiled.*

—Petruccia tried to have the church fixed up, Mary said, but she was not wealthy and she soon ran out of money. Instead of helping her out, as you might think they would, her neighbors ridiculed her mercilessly, and work on the church was stopped. I told her to never mind them. I promised her that someday soon I would come and take possession of the church and then wouldn't they be surprised? Of course, when Petruccia told her neighbors what I had said, they just scoffed and laughed all the harder.

On April 25, 1467, the citizens of Genazzano gather to celebrate the feast day of Saint Mark.

—How many of them, Mary said, could be expected to know that this date was also once a pagan feast commemorated to Venus? It is no coincidence that so many early Christian celebrations and ceremonies fall on the same days as pagan rituals and festivals. The first Christians had to be clever. Knowing that they would be killed if their faith was exposed, they carefully timed their celebrations to take place on the days when the pagans were celebrating something too. That way the Christians just blended in with all the other revelers and so countless lives were saved.

With or without a thought to Venus, the citizens of Genazzano are honoring Saint Mark, who is said to have been the favorite disciple and the ever-faithful companion of Saint Peter.

—I was always quite fond of Mark myself, Mary said, although, like so many young men, he was impulsive and prone to extremes on occasion. I remember a time when he found himself sexually aroused by a beautiful young woman who had innocently kissed his hand. He was so disgusted with himself that he chopped off his own hand with an axe. I thought this was quite unnecessary and immediately restored the hand myself. I reminded him that he was, after all, only human and should not be so hard on himself. I reminded him that much as self-control was necessary, self-mutilation was not. Many things have been done in my name that I would rather not be held responsible for.

It is a perfect spring day. All the village shops and businesses are closed for the occasion. The trees seem to have sprung into bud overnight and the sky is that high clear blue dome only possible at this time of year. The villagers are in high spirits and, following a rather boisterous procession through the streets led by the village priest, they congregate in the town square to continue their revelry. There is much praising and praying, singing and eating, liberal partaking of wine.

Of course Petruccia is there, too, lingering self-consciously on the sidelines, hurt at still being snubbed by her former friends but not willing to miss the celebration either. She ignores the rest of them and offers her prayers separately, silently. She cannot help but pray that Mary will make good on her promise soon. She is trying to be patient. Over and over again she reminds herself that God's time is not our time: *But, beloved, be not ignorant of this one thing, that one day is with the Lord as a thousand years, and a thousand years as one day.*

But still Petruccia's patience is wearing thin and she is more than a little tired of being treated like the village idiot.

Suddenly, in the midst of the festivities, at about four o'clock in the afternoon, the sky above Genazzano grows dark. The crowd falls silent. A giant white cloud descends from the sky in slow motion. It settles upon one of the unfinished walls of the church, which some of the more malicious villagers have taken to calling Petruccia's Folly. Although the church is quite empty, its bells begin to ring vigorously. The air fills with their music, the cloud parts, and the darkness lifts. There, standing without support on a narrow stone ledge in front of the ruined church, is a beautiful painting of Mary and the baby Jesus, mother and child cheek to cheek. Jesus, wearing red, has one little hand wrapped around his mother's neck while, with the other, he tugs at the gold-brocade neck of her black dress.

The townspeople stare first at the painting and then at Petruccia with their mouths hanging open like foolish dogs. Their heads bounce back and forth like balls. Petruccia smiles and then falls to the ground weeping.

In the following four months, 171 miracles occur in the village of Genazzano, more than one a day, all credited to the painting.

When the painting is examined, first by the village priest, then by the bishop, and finally by a papal commission hastily dispatched from Rome, it is found to have been rendered on a thin layer of porcelain no thicker than an eggshell. When the painting is viewed straight on, Mary appears to be smiling, but when looked at from an angle, she is very sad. Her cheeks sometimes change color from red to pink and at different times of the year, the whole tone of the painting changes.

—They called it *Madonna de Paradiso*, Mary said, because they thought the angels had brought it down from heaven. But there was more to the story than that.

Genazzano is soon visited by two men from the Albanian city of Shkodër on the shores of Lake Scutari. These men say they were suddenly overcome by an inexplicable urge to visit this town of which they know little or nothing. They say they want to see the painting. When these men are taken by the townspeople to the church, they are shocked and amazed. These men say they were praying on their knees before this very painting back in Shkodër when suddenly it disappeared and they were left dumbstruck before a blank stone wall. Now they realize why they were compelled to travel to Genazzano. Now they realize that the painting flew off the wall in Shkodër at the exact moment when the Turks invaded Albania. The townspeople shiver. There can be no doubt that it is a miracle wrought by Mary herself.

—The villagers were suitably humbled by the whole experience, Mary said. They finished rebuilding Petruccia's church, and when she died, they buried her in the chapel there. The whole town came to the funeral and everybody cried. They were sorry for being so mean to her. They understood that by doubting her, they had been doubting me too. Human nature being what it is, they could not see the error of their ways until it was too late. They were remorseful, repentant, begging me for forgiveness and a second chance. I did not have the heart to punish them. I let them have their church, I let them have their miracles, I let them give their hearts and souls over to Our Lady of Good Counsel. I was not disappointed. Those men and women and each of their succeeding generations have been devoted to me ever since.

Four hundred years later, during World War II, the village of Genazzano is caught in the middle of the war zone. A bomb is dropped directly onto the church, destroying its roof, its walls, and most of its interior. But the portrait on porcelain, the portrait so fragile that even the reverberations of the explosions could have shattered it to smithereens, the portrait remains untouched. Today it still hangs suspended in the air without support, defying gravity, logic, and disbelief.

Time

—Another beautiful morning, Mary said.

It was Wednesday. She had come into the kitchen for more coffee. I was reading at the table. I had almost finished Allende's *The House of the Spirits*. Mary commented that she, too, had recently reread it and loved it. She stretched and yawned and filled her mug. We were not dressed yet. She was wearing her pale green nightgown with smocking across the bodice. I had on my old pink chenille housecoat over a sleeveless white cotton nightgown. Although I like to get up early, I have never been one to rush into getting dressed. Neither, apparently, was Mary.

It was, indeed, another perfect spring morning. The sun was shining softly in a high blue sky dotted here and there with ragged wisps of cloud. I had opened the kitchen window, and the curtains rose and fell lazily on the breeze coming in through the screen. The air was clean and fresh, the birds were singing, and the hours spooled out before us. The whole day lay ahead, inviting us into its boundless realm of possibility. We were poised at the beginning of another stretch of time in which anything might happen, for which a to-do list was not necessary, and for which we did not need to be anything but ready.

Mary added a generous measure of milk to her coffee and

then took her watch from the windowsill above the sink where she'd left it the night before after we did the dishes.

—This is what is called Ordinary Time, she said, strapping on the watch.

It did not feel ordinary to me. Although it seemed as if two centuries had passed since she arrived, in fact it had only been two days.

She tapped her watch face on which there was a tiny intricate painting of a curly haired medieval angel playing the lute.

—According to the Catholic liturgical calendar, she explained, all the days of the year that are not Lent, Easter, Advent, or Christmas are called Ordinary Time. So here we are: Easter is over and Christmas is still a long way off. I guess you could say this is the time in which we're meant to feel that we have all the time in the world.

I could see then what she meant. Ordinary Time is all those days that blend one into the next without exceptional incident, good or bad; all those days unmarked by either tragedy or celebration. Ordinary Time is the spaces between events, the parts of a life that do not show up in photo albums or get told in stories. In real life, this is the bulk of most people's lives. But in literature, this is the part that doesn't make it into the book. This is the line space between scenes, the blank half-page at the end of a chapter, and the next one begins with a sentence like: *Three years later he was dead.*

Ordinary Time is all those days you do not remember when you look back on your life. Unless, of course, the Virgin Mary came to visit in the middle of it and everything was changed: before and after; then and now; past, present, and future.

* * *

Looking back on it now, my time with Mary seems to have passed all too quickly. But at the time, each day unfolded at a leisurely and luxurious pace. The hours opened before me one after another like an infinite series of doors, each admitting me into yet another room where I could stay as long as I liked. For the time that Mary was with me, I wore time as effortlessly as I wear my housecoat, my slippers, my skin.

This was nothing like my usual relationship with time, which has always been somewhat adversarial. When I was younger, there most often seemed to be too much of it. I was consistently guilty of, as my mother often pointed out, wishing my life away. Now that I am older, there never seems to be enough of it. I do not recall exactly when I crossed that invisible line between slouching and scrambling through time. But cross it I did. Just as everyone does.

My friends and I have often puzzled over this apparent acceleration of time as we age. We usually conclude that this must be a matter of perception, a phenomenon provoked by our growing awareness of our own mortality, our burgeoning consciousness of the fact that we have crossed the halfway point and it is getting harder and harder to think of the glass as being half full rather than half empty. But current medical research suggests that this change in how people experience time may have a physiological basis after all, that it may be the result of the lowering of dopamine levels in the brain as the body ages. If my sense of time speeding up is all in my head, it's good to know that maybe it's the product of a neurological process and not just my imagination.

Perception or physiology, too much or too little, either way I have always harbored a certain resentment toward time. I have often looked back with regret for all the time I've wasted over the years. Growing older, I began striving to make the most of

every day, but still I was never satisfied. Still I went to bed at
night and nagged at myself about all the things I didn't get done
that day.

In my heart, I knew there must be something more to a day
than how many things you had checked off your list at the end of
it, how much you had accomplished in it. But, also in my heart,
I did not know what that something was.

In recent years, as time has speeded up, I have become
increasingly fond of calendars. Each New Year's morning I make
a small ceremony of taking down the old ones and putting up
the new. I begin buying them in the fall so that when the time
comes, I am ready. I comb bookstores and gift shops searching
for just the right calendar to hang in each room.

This year in the kitchen I have one called *Kitchen Garden*.
Each month features a full-color photograph of carefully arranged
and labeled examples of a certain food group. January is bread,
March is pasta, June is salad greens, August is peppers, September is mushrooms, October is cheese. If I had had this calendar
the year that Mary was here, we would have been looking at
April's mixed herbs: savory, sage, marjoram, mint, parsley, basil,
rosemary, chives. But time has passed. It is not April and Mary is
not here. It is July and I am looking alone at summer fruits:
peaches, pears, cherries, plums, blueberries, raspberries, figs.
They are so beautiful that my mouth waters and I think of William Carlos Williams's poem "This Is Just To Say":

> I have eaten
> the plums
> that were in
> the icebox
>
> and which
> you were probably

saving
for breakfast

Forgive me
they were delicious
so sweet
and so cold

Also, I imagine, so purple and plump in a plain white bowl
on a hot July afternoon and his teeth pulled the flesh from the pit
and the succulent juice was divine on his tongue.

Later this month it will be my birthday and another year of
my life will have passed.

This past New Year's morning, the pleasure I took in my
calendar-hanging ritual was deepened by now knowing that,
according to the sanctoral cycle of the liturgical year, the first
day of January is one of the Solemnities of Mary, the day on
which she is celebrated as the Mother of God. I am certain it
is not by accident that on the kitchen calendar, the January
food is bread, no less than twenty-eight varieties of it: poppy
seed, whole grain, rye, bagel, brioche, baguette, crusty, braided,
unleavened.

Remember that Jesus said: *I am the bread of life: he that
cometh to me shall never hunger; and he that believeth on me shall never
thirst.* Remember the repeated miracle of the loaves and the
fishes. Remember the Last Supper: *And he took bread, and gave
thanks, and broke it, and gave unto them, saying, This is my body
which is given for you: this do in remembrance of me.*

I know that if I bought my calendars after New Year's, I
could get them at half-price and save myself some money. But
that is not the point.

The point is that no matter what has or has not happened in
the previous twelve months, still I enter each new year with

optimism, imbued with the promise held out to me by those twelve blank pages, those 365 (or 366) empty numbered squares. To me, each new calendar is the unwritten book of the coming year, the as-yet-unread liturgy, not of the hours but of the months to come.

And yet sometimes I suspect that my fondness for calendars has a darker side too. Sometimes I suspect it comes from believing that if only I can keep close enough track of time, then I will be able to control it. Ironically, I have to admit that more often than not, the opposite is true. As I keep turning those pages one after another, indeed my calendars haunt me.

Each morning as I sit at the kitchen table reading and drinking my coffee, I invariably find myself looking at the calendar on the wall. Directly above it hangs the clock with its round white moon face, plain black numbers, slim elegant hands that are never still. It is framed in dark blue like my new plates. These are two of the things that I would pin to Mary's dress: two more votive offerings, two more shiny milagros: a tiny silver calendar and a miniature golden clock.

Many of the once-empty squares on each month's page are already the past, filled up now with the unrelenting details of my daily life: appointments with the doctor, the dentist, the accountant, the optometrist; deadlines, interviews, meetings; lunch, dinner, and movie dates with friends. On the following months' pages, I note the days on which I will have the furnace cleaned, the trees trimmed, and a new ceiling light installed in the living room. I note the days on which I will travel to give readings, attend a formal dinner party in honor of a visiting famous writer, celebrate a friend's birthday.

I know this marking of the future is more than a matter of good organizational skills. It is a hedge against despair, an act by which I imagine that not only will I still be here but I will be appreciating the applause of an audience, engaging in a lively literary conversation over coffee and a sinfully rich dessert, toasting a friend's birthday with Perrier and lime while wearing a new red dress. My marking of the future is a way of reassuring myself that yes, indeed, time will continue to pass and I will continue to be part of it.

—Where does the time go? I wonder as I sit at the table and look at my calendar: *Kitchen Garden*, summer fruits, strawberries, blackberries, melons, and plums.

Although William Carlos Williams ate his plums more than sixty years ago, they are as real to me now as they were to him then. He died when I was only nine years old, and yet still those plums remain, the perishable made permanent with words. A physician as well as a poet, he went to his grave at the age of eighty, still full of plums, I imagine, still full of words, time having been outwitted (if not outstripped) not by medicine but by the power of words. Ten years after the plums and nineteen years before dying, he wrote "A Sort of Song":

> Let the snake wait under
> his weed
> and the writing
> be of words, slow and quick, sharp
> to strike, quiet to wait,
> sleepless.

Everybody knows that time, like words, is quick and slow, sharp and quiet, long and short, true and false, all of these at once. Everybody knows that time, like history, is not a fixed commodity. We hardly need science to tell us that Sir Isaac Newton was wrong: time is not mechanical, uniform, steadfast, or absolute. Time, like beauty, is in the eye of the beholder. There is no universal clock ticking off the seconds by which we all grow older, no giant calendar hung on a star past Pluto with its pages flapping into the vacuum of space. Everybody knows that time is relative, slippery, illogical, and moot.

The week I spent with Mary had little to do with those numbered squares on my kitchen calendar. The word *week* no longer meant what it used to, was no longer seven equal blocks of time with Sunday at one end and Saturday at the other. A *day* was no longer the predictably proportioned sequence of morning, noon, and night. An *hour* was no longer the numbers from one to twelve tidily arranged at equal intervals in a circle on my wrist or the wall. *Minutes* and *seconds* were no longer the decreasing increments ticked off relentlessly by the hands of the clock.

I finally understand that these instruments (calendar and clock), these words (week, day, hour, minute, second), are all human inventions, historical means of measurement that have themselves been often altered over the centuries, evidence of our desperate attempts to nail down time and make it behave. I am not eager to admit that these words, like all words, are not sacrosanct; that they, too, as Dr. Sloan had shown us back in Ancient History 101, are subject to change over time.

But persistent (if not consistent) as we are in trying to take the measure of time, still it eludes us, from nanosecond to light-year and back again. Still, time itself is something else again, not a *thing* at all but an inexorable force like the wind: undeniable but invisible, and yet evidence of it is apparent everywhere, for better or worse, its effects incarnate all around us.

I have written about time before and found in the process, then and now, that most of what I think I know about time comes out as metaphor or simile. The clock and the calendar, too, are metaphors that stand in for the elusive truth about time. In the vernacular, most of what we say about time is also figurative. Time passes, we say: like a football, a parade, a ship in the night. Time flies: like a bird, a plane, like Superman. Time flows: like a river, like sand, like blood. Time, we have been told, is a reef, a hand, a wheel, a gift. Time is avenger, devourer, destroyer, a disordered string. Time is the great physician, the wingèd chariot, the subtle thief of youth. Time, we hope, heals all wounds.

We talk about spending time (like money), serving time (like dinner), doing time (like lunch). We talk about buying time (like a car, a refrigerator, a new pair of shoes), borrowing time (like a library book, a cup of sugar, an egg), stealing time (like hubcaps, third base, a kiss). At one time or another, we have all had time on our hands, time to squander, time to kill. More often we say that we are pressed for time: like a shirt, like grapes for wine, like a flower in a book, like a hand against a heart. Time, we say, has run out on us: like milk, luck, or an unfaithful spouse. So much time, we complain, is lost: like mittens, sheep, or souls.

Time, I once wrote, *has always been the monkey on our backs. . . . Time, like gravity, is irrefutable, a clear glass ball rolling down a silver slope.*

Time, I once read on a bathroom wall, *is just God's way of keeping everything from happening at once.* This sentence was written with a fine red marker in a stylized calligraphic hand.

God's way, I wonder now, or our way?

We teach our children to tell time: like a fortune, a lie, or a story. The truth is you cannot tell a story without it. Time is the medium of history and change. Without time, history does not exist. Nor does story of any kind. Narrative depends on it. In a story, one thing happens after another . . . and then and then and then. Time is the natural propellant of narrative, and one of the luxuries of story is being able to move around in time in ways you never can in real life.

The truth is you cannot write even a single sentence without it. Language itself is predicated on the passage of time. Remember all those verb forms and tenses you were forced to learn back in high school: each one of them has something different to say about time. Each step in a verb's conjugation is a step forward, backward, or sideways in time. Try to remember the meaning of grammatical words like: *transitive, intransitive, indicative, subjunctive, anterior, conditional, perfect, imperfect, pluperfect.* Think about split infinitives and dangling participles: *split* as in logs, personalities, the ends of your hair; *dangling* as in earrings, legs, a dead man from the gallows.

Consider the fact that the most irregular verb in the English language is the verb *to be.* It is so irregular, in fact, that it cannot be classified and so must be treated as a special case.

Consider the possibility that a sentence is akin to Heraclitus' famous river: you can never step into the same one twice.

Be thankful that it is not necessary to know any of these things in order to put together a coherent sentence about time or anything else. Be thankful that it is enough to be able to say: I was, I am, I will be.

Past, present, future. Yesterday, today, tomorrow. Beginning, middle, end. Sooner or later. Then and now. In Tennessee Williams's play *The Glass Menagerie*, Tom Wingfield says, ". . . time is the longest distance between two places." One of those places is always *then* and the other is always *now.* Perhaps it is no accident that we use the word *then* to refer to both the past and the future, while the word *now* is just a metaphorical attempt to isolate the present moment. Do we have a choice as to which segment of time we may inhabit?

Much as I may be preoccupied with the passage of time, paradoxically, I find it impossible to imagine the end of time itself. I can imagine the end of my time on earth, the end of my loved ones' time on earth. I can even imagine, in certain moments of fear and trembling, the end of the earth itself. I, too, have averted my eyes and hurried past those dishevelled men on street corners proclaiming that the end is near. But much as I have tried to ignore them and dismissed them as cranks, still their doomsday message has worked its way into my consciousness. I realize that I have spent my whole life assuming that the end is near, believing that we are near the end of the story and that Armageddon is just around the corner, if not *this* corner, then the next one or the next.

And yet, much as it is not impossible for me to imagine the end of the world, still I also believe that time itself will continue even if all else ends. I am predisposed to eternity. I find infinity easier to believe in than some future moment when time itself will stop.

Paradoxically, the more I think about time, the less I can grasp it, the less sense I can make of it. The same can be said about dreams, words, love, and God.

All I know for certain is that for the time Mary was with me, I was living both inside and outside of time (ordinary, extraordinary, or otherwise). I was both *in* time and beyond it. Just as she has always been. Just as she is, was, and ever will be.

History (4)

The truths of fiction and the truths of biblical religion are not unrelated. Certain aspects of reality can be captured only in narrative. Paradox and parable must in this sense be enacted or witnessed to, not analyzed away. Like liturgy, literature uses language and drama to immerse us in a re-created and revivified world.

—Paul Baumann, "A Family Man," in *A Tremor of Bliss*

As I listened to some of Mary's longer stories, the more meandering ones, those more liberally punctuated by tangents, digressions, and tantalizing asides about other saints, other shrines, other times, I trusted her in the way a reader trusts a good writer. I trusted that no matter how disparate or disjointed the stories might seem in the telling, still they would indeed amount to something in the end. And I, like Herodotus, appreciated the impossibility of telling one story without also telling all the others, without also telling what came before and what came after, what came first and what came later.

This realization came to me not so much as an epiphany or a revelation but rather as a recognition of something I had known all along but had not recently contemplated, articulated, or put to any good use. As a writer, I have always known there is no such thing as a simple story.

Much as I know better, still sometimes I find myself longing and trying to do just that: to write a simple story composed entirely of simple sentences about simple things.

I write: *A dog barked in his sleep.*

This start seems as promising as any other so I continue: *A woman stood by the window.*

I have no idea where this is going but I like it. I write some more: *A car passed. The rain fell.*

I think I'm really getting somewhere now. I stop and read over what I have written so far. This is my first mistake.

Now I cannot resist my own inclination to elaborate, embroider, and explain. I cannot let that sleeping dog lie. I decide to make him an arthritic old black Lab named Jet. His bark is plaintive and directed, in this instance, at a dream cat he is chasing down a dream blind alley. He is sleeping on a braided rug under the kitchen table. On the table there are four empty containers of Chinese food.

Before all this came up, that amorphous dog was any color, all colors. But having gone ahead and made the dog black, he is no longer yellow, brown, or white. Having made him a Labrador retriever, he is no longer a German shepherd, a Saint Bernard, or a Lhasa apso.

My simple story quickly gets out of hand. The next thing you know, the woman is a thirty-two-year-old hairdresser named Annette, the window is in the kitchen of her third-floor bachelor apartment, the car passing in the street below is red and going too fast, the rain is falling heavily, it is April, it is Friday, it is eight o'clock. The next thing you know, Annette will be pulling her fortune out of a cookie and reading it aloud to Jet. The next thing you know, there will be a knock at the door and the lives of Annette and Jet will be changed forever.

I already know how stories are made.

Saint Ignatius of Loyola

Early in the summer of 1521, a gallant Spanish nobleman named Iñigo López de Loyola is grievously wounded while trying unsuccessfully, with a mere handful of citizens, to defend the fortress at Pamplona against over three hundred French soldiers. This is the man who will eventually become Saint Ignatius of Loyola.

In the battle at Pamplona, Ignatius's right leg is shattered by a cannonball. His left leg is also wounded, but less severely. His injuries are so grave that on June 29, 1521, the feast day of Saints Peter and Paul, a priest is called in to administer the last rites. That night Saint Peter himself appears to Ignatius and, in the morning, his attendants find him not dead as they had expected but well on his way to recovery instead.

Ignatius is transferred to the family castle at Loyola in northern Spain, where his extended recuperation will take place. Without benefit of anesthetic, he undergoes several brutal operations. The last of these is requested by Ignatius himself. Horrified to discover that his nearly healed right leg is now deformed and considerably shorter than the left, he insists that the bones be rebroken and chiselled down so the leg will heal properly.

—Pure vanity, Mary said, shaking her head. He was thinking of those glorious days he intended to spend again in the royal court, showing off for the ladies, strutting around in his fancy tights and his knee-high boots. Sometimes I think he should have been made the patron saint of plastic surgeons instead of soldiers.

Indeed, prior to his injury at Pamplona, Ignatius was something of a swashbuckling dandy. A swaggering *caballero,* he was known for his hot temper, his quick wit, his proficiency on the dance floor, and his elegant wardrobe. Born in 1491, the last son of thirteen children of a wealthy Basque family, Ignatius showed no early signs of sanctity. As a young man, his favorite occupations were gambling, dueling, and sex.

While recuperating at the castle, Ignatius asks for books to help pass the time. He is hoping for some good old-fashioned romances, heroic chivalric tales of knights in shining armor, ladies-in-waiting, and damsels in distress. Instead, he is brought a four-volume biography of Jesus and a collection of the lives of the saints. Overcoming his initial lack of enthusiasm, Ignatius reads and rereads these books many times. He is increasingly impressed and inspired. A change begins to come over him.

At the age of thirty, Ignatius vows to renounce his formerly frivolous and immoral ways and dedicate his life to God. One night, so inflamed with his newfound religious passion that he cannot sleep, he gets out of bed and kneels before a picture of Mary that hangs in his sickroom. As he prays, the castle is convulsed with a tremor that opens a large hole in the sickroom wall. Then Mary herself emerges from the gaping hole with the baby Jesus in her arms.

—I did not stay long, Mary said. But it was long enough for Ignatius to dedicate himself forever to me. In those few minutes, he enjoyed what he later called "an excess of consolation." Such a lovely phrase, don't you think?

In February 1522, although still not fully recovered from

his injuries, Ignatius travels two hundred miles east on a mule to visit the shrine of Our Lady of Montserrat near the city of Barcelona.

—Forgive me if I digress, Mary said, but here is a story within a story. They say that once upon a time the whole area of Montserrat was a smooth, unbroken plain. But at the moment of the Crucifixion, the earth rose up in anguish and formed those jagged rocky peaks like the teeth of a saw. And so it was called Montserrat, the serrated mountain.

It is Saint Peter who first brings to Barcelona a life-sized wooden statue of Mary and Jesus carved by Saint Luke himself. It is another Black Madonna, Mary seated on a heavy chair, wearing a golden gown and a crown of twelve stars. In her right hand she holds a globe from which bursts a bouquet of lilies. The baby Jesus sits on her lap, holding a pinecone in one hand, while making a gesture of blessing with the other. They are both smiling.

For seven centuries the statue is worshipped and revered by Spanish Christians. They call her *La Moreneta*, the Little Dark One. Then the city of Barcelona is invaded by the Saracens. The citizens manage to hold them at bay for three years, but then the tide begins to turn. On April 22, 718, fearing that the beloved statue will be destroyed, the bishop and governor of the city hides it in one of Montserrat's deepest and most secret caves.

—As so often happens when you put something away in a safe place, Mary said, no one could find the statue again after the danger had passed.

In 890 a group of shepherd boys tending their flocks near the base of the mountain see a brilliant light emanating from one of the caves. The air fills with music and the boys are afraid. In the following days, both the light and the music are observed by others, first the boys' parents, then the parish priest, the rector, and finally the bishop, who orders that the cave be entered and examined. Inside, they discover the statue that has been lost for a hundred and seventy-two years.

After much amazed rejoicing, those present form a procession to carry the statue down the mountainside to the bishop's church in the town of Manresa. Midway down the steep slope, those bearing the statue suddenly find themselves unable to continue. Their feet simply will not move another step. After some grunting and groaning and much furrowing of brows, they decide it is a miracle. Mary is making her wishes known. The bishop orders a magnificent church to be built on that very spot. It is the shrine on the mountainside that will be known forever as Our Lady of Montserrat.

It is to the Benedictine monastery erected on the same site in the eleventh century that Ignatius of Loyola travels in 1522. On the road to Montserrat he meets a Moorish gentleman.

—As is so often the way with people traveling alone, Mary said, the two strangers struck up a conversation. After the usual pleasantries and many complaints about the winter weather, the conversation worked itself around to God who, as usual, was being blamed for the bone-chilling wind and the relentless cold. My name came up too. The Moor said I could not possibly have been a virgin after I had Jesus. Ignatius did his best to explain it, but by the time the two parted company, the Moor was still not convinced. Ignatius rode on, stewing and brooding. He thought he should turn around and track down the Moor and punish him for his blasphemy. But his mule balked and refused to go back. The animal, with a gentle nudge from me, carried Ignatius down a different road. And so at least one crime that might have been committed in my name was averted.

Upon reaching the monastery at Montserrat, Ignatius offers a full confession that takes three whole days. He then gives his fine clothes to a poor man and dons a penitent's sackcloth robe. On March 24, 1522, the eve of the Annunciation, Ignatius prays all night to Mary and in the morning hangs up his rapier and his dagger forever.

Then, having given his mule to the monks, Ignatius descends the mountain on foot and goes to the poorhouse of Saint Lucy at Manresa.

—As a wealthy Sicilian maiden, Lucy was betrothed to a pagan nobleman at the age of fourteen, Mary said. But she was having none of that. She had other ambitions. She aspired to be a virgin martyr. So she gave all her worldly goods to the poor and spurned her fiancé. Outraged, he denounced her as a Christian to the authorities and she suffered much persecution at their hands. In response, Lucy gouged out her own eyes and presented them to her fiancé, who had always admired them. She became the much-loved saint serenaded in the song "Santa Lucia," and is always portrayed bearing two bulging eyeballs on a plate.

Ignatius stays at Manresa for one year. Like Lucy, he renounces all vanity, all pleasure, and all pride to be taken in the physical body. He flagellates himself for his former sins, lets his hair, beard, and fingernails grow unchecked, and lives on bread and water, with some herbs thrown in for Sunday dinner. He weeps so copiously at mass that the monastery doctor warns him that he will go blind if he does not stop. He prays for seven hours a day and spends the rest of the time in a cave. Tormented by guilt for his own sins, he prays that after death his corpse will be laid upon a dung heap so it can be eaten by vultures and wild dogs.

—An excess of penance, I'd say, Mary commented. He grew so thin and weak that he suffered hallucinations and psychotic mood swings. He made himself so miserable that he began to contemplate suicide. Clearly he had gone too far. I had to step in and set him back on track. Fortunately, it worked. And the rest, as they say, is history.

While at Manresa, Ignatius writes much of his famous *Spiritual Exercises*, a work which is, in effect, a step-by-step course in mysticism. In the following years, he travels to the Holy Land, is imprisoned for forty-two days by the Inquisition, studies at Barcelona, Alcala, Salamanca, and Paris. He and several of his friends are ordained priests in Venice in 1537 on June 24, the feast day of Saint John the Baptist.

—More body parts on a plate, Mary said ruefully. As quick as you can say, Bring me the head of John the Baptist, King Herod had him hunted down and Salome had the plate in her hands. In those days in that part of the world, it was called a charger, not a plate. Do not let this confuse you. Do not let this bring to mind an image of a dashing white knight, armor glinting in the sun, on a fine white stallion, mane blowing in the wind. Hold in your mind the picture of a severed head, a yellow plate, and blood, red blood, lots of wet red blood.

In 1534, Ignatius is given the title Master of Arts. With his friends, he forms a group called the Society of Jesus, which is confirmed by Pope Paul III in a papal bull on September 27, 1540. The members of the Society are known as the Jesuits.

Ignatius continues to pray, preach, study, and write, always a mystic, always seeking the greater glory of God. He teaches that, although only God can save us, still it isn't all up to him: we must cooperate in our own salvation. We must pray as if everything depends on God (it does) while at the same time living and working as if everything depends on us (it does). He continues to be too hard on himself, not eating properly, burning the candle at both ends, exercising his spirit but not his body. His health fails steadily. He is plagued by stomach ailments, high fevers, exhaustion, and hardening of the liver. On July 31, 1556, he dies at the age of sixty-five.

In 1622, when he is up for sainthood, the judges of the Rota have sixteen hundred witness statements to consider on his behalf. These testify as to his purity, his piety, his relentless devotion to God. More than two hundred miracles are attributed to him.

—There was the surgeon who had headaches and eye problems, Mary said, and when he held Ignatius's signature to his forehead, he was instantly cured. There was the nun whose broken leg was healed when a piece of his robe was applied to her thigh. There was the woman who pressed his picture to her swollen stomach and her dropsy disappeared.

On May 22, 1622, Ignatius of Loyola is canonized by Pope Gregory XV. Patron saint of the military and of religious retreats, he is frequently invoked against being overly conscientious.

I already know how stories are made.

I already know how a story is subject to centrifugal force, radiating outward from the center in all directions, like a web catching flies or a net catching fish. But remember, when marveling at how much light a story can shed, that it can also be mysterious, ambiguous, both a wonder and a weapon.

Remember that light can be both wave and particle.

In 1678, Dutch astronomer Christiaan Huygens said that light was made of waves. In 1704, Isaac Newton said that light was made of particles. As it turned out, twentieth-century scientists proved that they were both right. Experiments showed that, much as light, in its essence, must be understood as being both wave and particle, at any given nanosecond, it is one or the other, not both simultaneously. Discovery of the wave-particle duality of light marked the end of classical either/or thinking. It constituted a paradigm shift, the beginning of a radical new way of understanding reality as the province of both/and possibility.

Remember that God said: *Let there be light: and there was light.* Remember that Jesus said: *I am the light of the world.*

I already know how a story can become a vortex, spiraling ever inward, turning and turning upon and into itself, like the Ouroboros, the serpent forever swallowing its own tail, ancient symbol of eternal return; the cycle of birth, death, and rebirth; the union of opposites, light and dark, male and female, yin and yang, agony and ecstasy, heaven and earth. Remember the Garden of Eden: *And the serpent said unto the woman, Ye shall not surely die: For God doth know that in the day ye eat thereof, then your eyes shall be opened, and ye shall be as gods, knowing good and evil.*

Remember also that Jesus said: *Behold, I send you forth as sheep in the midst of wolves: be ye therefore wise as serpents, and harmless as doves.*

Now I understand how one thing does invariably lead to another, although the path between the two is seldom well lit or predictable, and has little enough to do, in the end, with the logical exercise of action and reaction, cause and effect.

History, after all, as Dr. Sloan made clear back in university, is not prophecy.

I think about *History* as global: the story of big things, of important public events, both tragic and triumphant, that have changed the world for better or worse. I think about *history* as local: the story of so-called ordinary people who have lived (or died) during the unfolding of those same cataclysmic events, never having had any intention or hope of changing the world.

I begin to see how people, ordinary people, are, at any given moment, both wave and particle, both a part of and apart from history. How history, like time and light, goes on in spite of, not because of, us. How history is ever moving forward, both with and without us. I am not the first person to wonder when they took the *story* out of *history.*

Much as Mary herself exists beyond the usual time/space continuum which all history must inhabit, the thousands of recorded apparitions do not. They did not happen in a vacuum: they happened in the world, the *real* world, so to speak.

Everything has a history and you cannot follow the thread of Mary's history in isolation from all the rest any more than you can write the history of pain, for instance, without also writing the stories of the people who suffered it, or the history of gardens without the people who planted, weeded, and harvested them, or the history of astronomy without all the people who reached for the stars.

I have always known that writing is an act of faith, the one which has always been my own salvation.

Saint Teresa of Ávila

In the summer of 1561 Mary appears to Teresa de Cepeda y Ahumada while she is kneeling in prayer in the chapel of the Church of Saint Thomas in the walled city of Ávila in the rugged and arid mountains of central Spain. Teresa of Jesus is forty-six years old and has been a nun for twenty-five years. She is already known for her divine ecstasies and rapturous visions.

—Only two years had passed, Mary said, since Teresa experienced what became known as her most famous vision: the Transverberation. That time she was visited by a short, handsome angel who was obviously a member of the highest group of angels, one of the seraphim who surround the throne of God in heaven. According to the Bible, the seraphim have six wings, two to cover their faces, two to cover their feet, and two with which they fly.

Describing this vision later in her *Autobiography*, Teresa writes of the angel's golden flame-tipped spear piercing her heart and penetrating down to her entrails. And when the angel drew out his spear, she was overcome by a love for God which was a pain so sharp she was moaning, a pain so sweet she wanted it to last forever.

—It was this vision that was immortalized in the gigantic marble sculpture, *The Ecstasy of Saint Teresa*, Mary said. Nearly twelve feet tall, it was created by the Italian Baroque artist, Bernini, in the second half of the seventeenth century. He portrayed Teresa as a helpless swooning woman, with her eyes closed, her head flung back, and her mouth hanging open in the presence of the angel. She looks to be on the verge of either fainting or having an orgasm. The angel has only two wings. I have never been especially fond of this piece. I like to think we have a lot in common, Teresa and I, and she was anything but helpless or hysterical, not by any stretch of the imagination.

By the time Mary appears to her in 1561, Teresa has grown more or less resigned to being the recipient of such divine apparitions. She has already been visited by a multitude of saints and several times by Jesus himself, who once took her on a guided tour of her own specially reserved spot in hell.

—Teresa did not much appreciate these visitations, Mary said. She found them disruptive, frightening, and very embarrassing if they occurred when she was out in public. She had even gone so far as to ask the other nuns to please hold her down if she began to levitate outside the convent walls. She had begged God to find another way to make his presence known to her and talked sharply back to him when he refused. Known for her wit, her charm, and her passionate energy, Teresa was a large, capable woman, a stubborn, sensible, shrewd, persuasive, ironic, edgy extrovert. She was always a precocious creature of contradictions, Mary said. But then aren't we all?

Born in Ávila in 1515, Teresa is one of ten children of an aristocratic family. Her inclination toward the spiritual life shows itself early. At the age of seven, she and her brother Rodrigo decide to run away to Africa where they hope to be beheaded by the savage Moors, thus ensuring early martyrdom and a quick trip to heaven. They don't get very far before they are caught by their uncle and returned to their parents. Disappointed, the two children vow to become hermits instead and live lives of purity, humility, and devotion right there at home. This proves to be even more difficult than they expected.

When Teresa is thirteen, her mother dies. Teresa grows into a beautiful, rather vain young woman, who is much distracted from the spiritual life. She spends a lot of time trying on dresses, choosing perfumes, fixing her hair, and reading racy romantic novels. Alarmed by his daughter's increasing frivolity, her father sends sixteen-year-old Teresa to board with the Augustinian nuns at Santa Maria de Garcia in 1531. On November 2, 1535, she becomes a nun at the wealthy Carmelite Convent of the Incarnation at Ávila.

During her early years at the convent, Teresa suffers many bouts of debilitating illness. In 1539, she falls into such a deep coma that her attendants believe she is dead. This happens on August 15, the feast day of Mary's Assumption when, after her earthly death, she, like her son, was taken up to heaven in her body as well as in her spirit. A grave is ordered to be dug for Teresa while the nuns keep vigil over her apparently lifeless body. Four days later she revives, a miracle she attributes to the intervention of Saint Joseph. But her legs remain paralyzed for the next three years.

—Teresa was not happy with the way things were done at the convent, Mary said. She thought life there was too worldly, too easy, too trivial, filled as it was with tea parties, juicy gossip, and clever discussions of culture, philosophy, and that most treacherous of notions, platonic love. Teresa resolved to reform both herself and her order, to bring it back to its more proper practices of piety, poverty, hardship, and humility.

This is not an easy task, and for many years Teresa runs into strong opposition from both civil and ecclesiastical authorities. Teresa does not give up. Her resolve is much strengthened by Mary's visit in 1561, again on the feast day of the Assumption.

That morning Teresa is meditating on the Bible passage that is always read on that day: *And there appeared a great wonder in heaven; a woman clothed with the sun, and the moon under her feet, and upon her head a crown of twelve stars: And she being with child cried, travailing in birth, and pained to be delivered.*

As Teresa prays for forgiveness, mercy, and strength, Mary appears before her with Saint Joseph at her side. Mary and Joseph wrap Teresa's body in a brilliant white robe.

—We came in quietly, Mary said. We dressed her gently in a pure white robe and explained that this meant she was now cleansed of any residual sinfulness she might have been still harboring in her soul.

Mary takes Teresa's hands in her own and assures her that her dream of founding a new convent dedicated to Joseph will indeed come true. Mary promises that she and Joseph will watch over it when the time comes. She places a shimmering gold collar around Teresa's neck. Hanging from the collar is an expensive gold cross decorated with dozens of precious gems unlike any found on earth.

Mary and Joseph stay with Teresa for a while and then they rise into the sky escorted by an army of angels. Teresa feels no fear but rather an indescribable sense of peace, comfort, and exaltation.

Teresa continues her reformation campaign with renewed vigor. Now that she knows Mary and Joseph are behind her, nothing can stop her. A year later, she opens the first convent of Saint Joseph at Ávila. Thirteen novices don the coarse wool habit of the new order known as the Discalced Carmelites.

—The word *discalced,* Mary explained, has nothing to do with calcium, milk, or bones, nothing to do with calcination either, that being a burning down to ashes, a complete combustion, a consumption or purification by fire. Discalced means to go without shoes, a custom adopted by certain severe religious orders to further demonstrate their rejection of all earthly comforts and luxuries. Of course Teresa liked this idea, believing as she did that all physical suffering was but another step on the road to heaven.

Over the next twenty years, despite continuing ill health, Teresa travels constantly and founds sixteen more convents. She chooses her nuns for their intelligence, common sense, and good judgment. Her motto is: God preserve us from stupid nuns.

—Amen, Mary said.

Although Teresa frequently claims to hate writing, she is, in fact, a fast and prolific writer, author in her lifetime of many other books besides her *Autobiography.* She writes all the time, whether she is well or seriously ill. Often she writes in a small, cold cell without even a table or chair. She has the soul of a writer: a soul overflowing with contradictions, irony, self-doubt, stubbornness, wonder, and faith.

On October 4, 1582, Teresa dies at the age of sixty-seven. Mary, Joseph, Jesus, and several saints gather at her deathbed and ferry her soul back to heaven. She is canonized by Pope Gregory XV in 1622. Three hundred and forty-eight years later in 1970 she is declared the first female Doctor of the Church by Pope Paul VI. Also honored with this title in the same year is Saint Catherine of Siena.

—Catherine was born in 1347, more than two hundred years before Teresa, Mary said. She was the twenty-fourth of twenty-five children. She had her first vision of Jesus when she was only six years old. In her extreme devotion to God, she was even more obsessive and rigorous than Teresa. She practiced every kind of self-mortification she could think of. She lived on herbs and water, and for eight years took no solid food other than Communion wafers. She wore a hair shirt by day and wrapped herself in iron chains at night. Her bed was a board, her pillow a brick. She drank the pus from the sores of lepers and cancer victims. Her brief and bizarre life was marked by many miraculous events.

One day when Catherine is singing the Song of Solomon, Jesus comes to her and kisses her right on the mouth. Another time when he appears, she drinks the blood flowing from the wound in his side. Later she becomes his bride in a ceremony presided over by Mary herself and attended by Saints Paul and Dominic. On Catherine's right hand Jesus places a ring set with four pearls and a large diamond. After Jesus and Mary and the others disappear, the ring remains, although only Catherine can see it. In 1375, on the fourth Sunday of Lent, Catherine receives the stigmata while staring at a crucifix. As the blood from her wounds flows hot and red, she is transported to ever higher ecstasies.

In 1380, Catherine dies an agonizing death, which she believes to be the torment of demons. She is only thirty-three years old, the same age as Jesus, her Holy Bridegroom, when he died on the cross.

—Shortly after Catherine's death, Mary said, her tomb was opened and they discovered that her body had not decomposed.

The same thing has happened with many other saints, including Teresa. Their long-dead bodies were found to be completely incorrupt, still fresh and fragrant as newly picked flowers. Carnations, some said when trying to describe the smell. Clover maybe, or lily of the valley, Our Lady's Tears. Personally, I thought it was more like datura, Angel's Trumpet, whose smell is so intoxicating they say you shouldn't plant it below your bedroom window for fear of not waking up in the morning.

—Their flesh was found to be still juicy and sweet, Mary continued. So they were neatly dismembered and their body parts were distributed as sacred relics. Pieces of Catherine were spread all over Europe: shoulder blades, ribs, arms, hands, teeth, feet, the finger on which she wore Jesus' wedding ring. Pope Urban VI ordered and oversaw the ceremonial removal of Catherine's head, which was then taken to Siena in a gilded copper reliquary. As for Teresa, one arm was sent to Lisbon, one cheek to Madrid, one breast and one foot to Rome. A slice of her heart, like a slice of liver, was removed and taken to Milan. The rest of her heart was given a small jeweled crown and is still displayed in a glass case at the convent in Ávila. If you look closely enough, you can see the wide gash where the angel plunged his spear in all the way to her entrails. If you look closely enough, you can see her face or mine or your own reflected in the glass.

Shopping

On Wednesday afternoon we went to the mall. It was my idea, one that I suggested over lunch with some trepidation, well aware of the possibility that inviting the Virgin Mary to the temple of Mammon might be, if not exactly a mortal sin, then at least outrageously inappropriate. But I had some errands to run and I felt it would have been rude to rush off without asking her if she wanted to come along.

Much to my relief, she said she thought it was an excellent idea, that she had, in fact, been about to suggest a shopping trip herself. She was still using my shampoo and thought it was high time she bought some of her own. Plus she needed to pay a visit to the bank machine and there were a few other odds and ends she wanted to pick up. The word *Mammon* was not mentioned and she did not quote to me those familiar lines: *And Jesus went into the temple, and began to cast out them that sold and bought in the temple, and overthrew the tables of the moneychangers, and the seats of them that sold doves.* I was fairly confident that we would find no doves for sale at the mall—budgies, parakeets, cockatiels, and parrots perhaps, but not doves.

Right after lunch we got ready to go. As we gathered up our

purses, I noticed that Mary's was almost identical to one I had bought a few years ago but have since given away.

Sometimes I think I've spent the better part of my adult life in search of the perfect purse. Frequently I think I've found it, feeling sure that each new purse is the perfect purse at last, and that I will quite happily carry this one with me forever and ever. But then, sometimes quickly, sometimes more gradually, it becomes evident that this purse is *not* the perfect purse after all. With regular usage, it proves to be too big or too small, the strap is too short or too long, there are too many compartments or not enough. Or it proves to have been shoddily made: the lining rips, the zipper breaks, the fastener won't stay closed or else it closes so tightly that I have to wrestle it open with both hands every time.

Once, the strap of an apparently perfect purse let loose just as I was sprinting across a busy street in the pouring rain. I ended up down on my knees in the middle of traffic, trying to gather up my wallet, my hairbrush, a pack of gum, and three tampons that were rolling around on the wet asphalt. Brakes squealed, horns blared, drivers shook their fists and cursed at me.

Soon enough I found myself back on the trail, searching once again for the perfect purse. Upon reflection, I cannot help but conclude that in this aspect, men are a lot like purses.

Mary and I got into the car, buckled up, and headed to the large mall in the heart of the suburbs on the western side of town. We did not talk much on the way. Mary seemed content to look out the window while I concentrated on getting us there safely. Although I have been driving for more than twenty years and have never been involved in a serious accident, still I am nervous behind the wheel. I have little faith in my own driving ability, even less in that of the strangers piloting the cars all around me.

My car, having miraculously healed itself the week before, continued to behave well and carried us smoothly through a long stretch of urban landscape now so commonplace that this part of the city is completely indistinguishable from any other on the continent.

Both sides of the road were lined with a relentless cacophony of signs, each vying for our attention in hopes of convincing us to come on in and open our wallets. We passed between them as if running a gauntlet of colorful, shouting, oversized words. We passed gas stations, car lots, fast-food restaurants serving burgers, tacos, chicken, pizza, and submarine sandwiches. We passed sprawling superstores selling electronics, sports equipment, home and garden supplies, toys, furniture, and books. We passed strip malls where clusters of smaller stores offered carpets, computers, bathroom accessories, kitchen cabinets, party supplies, lighting fixtures, hot tubs, menswear, beer-making equipment, air conditioners, and pets.

We passed a funeral home that resembled an oversized ranch-style house. There was a large green sign in front that proclaimed the name of the home while also giving the exact time and temperature in a flashing red digital display across the top. Judging by the number of cars in the parking lot and the discreet presence of a black hearse at the side door, there was a funeral in progress. Mary crossed herself and closed her eyes for a minute.

We waited at a red light beside a new video store announcing its grand opening with a banner and red and silver flags strung across the parking lot. Beneath this stood a person in a gorilla suit thumping his chest with one hand and waving at the traffic with the other. I could not see the connection, but Mary seemed to be amused. She waved back and the gorilla jumped up and down until we drove away.

A few minutes later we turned left into the mall parking lot and found a spot near the large department store on the eastern side. This is where I always park. Even on a Saturday afternoon a

week before Christmas, I can always find a space in this part of
the lot. I come to this mall often enough to know that there is
never any room at the other end near the supermarket.

I come to this mall more often than I would care to admit in
certain circles. Not long ago, at a literary gathering, I inadvertently made passing reference to something I had seen at the
mall. One of the younger writers present immediately seized
upon this offhand remark, obviously aghast at my confession.

—Oh my God! he shrieked. I just can't picture *you* at the
mall!

I suppose he meant this as a compliment, as if my being a
writer meant that I must be like those early Scholastics, living the
life of the mind in their ivory towers, above all such uninspired,
unenlightened, quotidian activities. I suppose he also could not
picture me cleaning the toilet, washing the kitchen floor, or
watching silly sitcoms all evening in my pink chenille housecoat
while eating popcorn or doing my nails. The truth was I could
not picture him at the mall either, slinking around in his black
beret and his distressed leather jacket, wolfing down a burger and
fries at the food court while scribbling out his angst on a grease-
spotted paper napkin. Had I had a chance to say as much, I would
not have meant it as a compliment. But fortunately, the conversation had swirled on ahead before I could muster a reply.

When I was in my twenties, I, too, viewed shopping malls
with great disdain. I considered the mall to be the epitome of
crass commercialism and conspicuous consumption, the boorish
domain of the bourgeois, the soulless castle of the status quo, the
ultimate monument to materialism, meaninglessness, vulgarity,
vacuity, and all that is wrong with the world. Shopping malls, I
felt, were an affront to my dignity, my intelligence, my indi-
viduality, and my aesthetic sensitivity. I could not even drive
past one without feeling offended.

When I was in my thirties, I still disliked shopping malls, although for different reasons. Whenever I went to the mall, especially on weekends or near Christmas, I ended up feeling demoralized and depressed. As if all that fluorescent light and recycled air weren't enough to contend with, I also had to deal with the fact that everywhere I looked, all I could see were loving couples and happy families. There were young lovers holding hands across the tables in the food court, making eyes at each other in the lingerie department, kissing in the shoe store. I could see their tongues burrowing into each other's mouths. There were handsome fathers and beautiful mothers milling about with their rosy-cheeked children toddling along between them, bouncing wide-eyed through the toy department, waiting in line to sit on Santa's knee. There were babies sleeping like angels in strollers. I could see their eyelashes quivering on their cheeks. And there I was: alone. In those days, a trip to the mall only served to confirm my suspicion that I was a freak.

But now that I am in my forties, I find a kind of comfort at the mall that I cannot quite put my finger on. It has something to do with the fact that, because one is so much like another, when I am at the mall, I could be anywhere. There I know exactly what is expected of me: I am supposed to look and admire and then, if I can afford it, I am supposed to buy something. Usually I do. Maybe it sounds ridiculous, but I also find comfort in the orderliness of shelf upon shelf, rack upon rack, row upon row of all those brand-new products arrayed for my perusal.

Maybe I like being at the mall because there I can believe that the most weighty and pressing questions I will ever have to face are:

1. Will I sleep better between these 200-thread-count, 100% cotton sheets?

2. Will this sixty-piece collection of pop-top stackable plastic containers keep my leftovers fresher longer?
3. Which is more flattering: the red shirt or the blue?
4. What color nail polish should I buy: Antique Lace, Iced Mocha, Luscious, Flesh, or Buff?
5. Do these shoes pinch my toes?
6. Do these pants make me look fat?

When I am at the mall, I feel as normal as the next person and I like it.

We went into the department store. Nobody paid the least bit of attention to us. As far as anybody else was concerned, we were exactly what we appeared to be: two middle-class, middle-aged women out for an afternoon at the mall. We were close to invisible. As I have said, anonymity has its own rewards. Mary seemed as comfortable here as she would have been in one of the great cathedrals of Europe.

Just inside the door was the housewares department on our left and, on our right, ladies' lingerie. The aisle display in housewares consisted of a set of outrageously expensive, generously proportioned stainless steel pots and pans arranged on an antique stove the size of a small car. Directly across the aisle was the lingerie display: two mannequins (torsos only, no arms, no legs, no heads) sporting see-through underwire bras and minuscule matching bikini briefs, one in lime green, the other in hot pink. They, too, were generously proportioned and outrageously expensive.

—Not my style, Mary said. More suited, I'd say, to that *other* Madonna, the really famous one.

I snorted in agreement. I could not picture myself wearing

this underwear either, especially not while standing at the stove stirring a big pot of spaghetti sauce, with or without all my appendages intact.

We strolled through linens, televisions, and greeting cards. In the cosmetics department, we were accosted by a perky young woman in a tight red skirt who wanted to spray our faces with a pink purse-sized atomizer of Evian Water.

—Used regularly, she said, it will moisturize, tone, nourish, and refresh your skin. It is especially recommended for expectant mothers and babies.

I could not help but think that it might be even more useful for women of a certain age, those of us in the menopausal years who find ourselves suffering hot flashes at unpredictable (and always inconvenient) moments.

—It will change your lives forever, the young woman said earnestly.

—Holy water, Mary whispered.

I was shocked by her irreverence and laughed with my hand over my mouth. The young woman did not get the joke and walked away looking hurt. Clearly, Mary's sense of humor was not without a certain edge. In fact, she was becoming positively giddy, a result perhaps of inhaling the fumes of a hundred different fragrances all at once. Or maybe it was the dazzle of all those little bright lights reflecting off the mirrored countertops and a million glass jars of magic potions.

In the next aisle, an elegant, long-necked woman in an ivory-colored linen suit tried to convince us to buy the latest brand of anti-aging face cream.

—It's a miracle, she enthused breathlessly. I've been using it for only six months and just look at me. I'm fifty-four years old and I don't look a day over thirty.

We slipped away while the woman admired her own face and

neck in a small mirror she had produced with a flourish from her jacket pocket.

—Heaven forbid that a woman should look her age, Mary said, slipping her arm through mine. Imagine what that stuff could do for me. I'm two thousand years old and don't look a day over two hundred.

This time I laughed out loud.

We went into the mall proper. In the middle of the afternoon, in the middle of the week, it was not overly crowded. In all the times I've been to this mall, I have almost never run into anybody I know. This day was proving to be no exception. Our camouflage was holding up well and still, nobody gave us so much as a second glance.

We stopped at the bank machine. If I had expected Mary to marvel slack-jawed at the technological conveniences of modern life, I was wrong. Clearly she was as up-to-date on these advances as the next person. I should not have been surprised. After all, she was not some primitive *naif* who had been popped into a time machine and then dropped down unceremoniously into this day and age. She did not exist in a vacuum and she had not spent the last two thousand years in a cave. She had been here all along. Televisions, telephones, bank machines, microwave ovens, computers, and the Internet: all these things were no more startling to her than they were to me. She was as much at home in this world as in the past or the next.

At the bank machine, she went first. I found myself inching up behind her until I was peeking over her shoulder, trying to see the name on her card. I was practically on top of her and still could not read it. She, of course, caught me.

Laughing, she held the card up so I could have a good look: MARY THEOTOKOS, it said. This was obviously a Greek name but I had no idea what it meant.

—God-Bearer, Mary said, smiling. It means God-Bearer or Mother of God. It's a name first given to me at the Council of Ephesus in 431 A.D.

I used the machine and took out a hundred dollars.

Next to the bank was the pet store. We joined a small group of people that had gathered at the window where three black kittens were tumbling, boxing, and chasing their own and each other's tails. A fourth kitten, marmalade-colored and very dainty-looking, sat in the corner and ignored the others, washing her face and yawning. The audience was charmed and so were we. All at once, the three rambunctious kittens were tired. They collapsed in a furry heap and fell instantly asleep. The orange kitten walked over and flopped down on top of them. The crowd laughed and dispersed, except for an elderly woman in a powder blue cardigan who seemed about to go inside and make a purchase.

At Mary's suggestion, we wandered into the store just to look around. As I had suspected, there were no doves. There was, however, a fierce-looking, multicolored parrot perched not in its cage but on top of it, a peach-colored canary happily singing its heart out, and a fat blue budgie admiring himself in a little mirror with a bell attached. The left side of the store was lined with fish tanks: goldfish, guppies, kissing gourami, mollies, rainbows, harlequins, angelfish, algae eaters, and three small piranhas. I remembered what Mary had said about the fish being a symbol of Christianity and wondered if any of these exotic tropical varieties would qualify.

On the right side of the store were the rodents and the reptiles. There were hamsters frantically spinning their wheels, guinea pigs nibbling with their fur sticking out all over, mice curled up into little gray balls, and large white rats blinking their red eyes and twitching their long pink tails. Four small green iguanas stood like statues in their tank. Although the sign said not to, I tapped my finger gently on the glass, and one came forward, eyeing me in a friendly way with his head cocked to one side.

—He likes you, Mary said. Then she made a strange face and pointed at the tank directly below.

At first glance it appeared to be empty. I leaned in for a closer look and then drew back sharply, elbowing Mary in the process. There in the far corner was a cluster of large brown insects. There were six or eight of them, each about three inches long and half as wide. The sign said: MADAGASCAR HISSING COCKROACHES, $9.99 EACH.

Mary shivered and we fled.

—All God's creatures, she muttered and then hummed a few bars of "La Cucaracha."

—Yes, indeed, I said. Sometimes you have to wonder: What was he thinking?

As we left the store, the elderly woman in the blue sweater was standing at the cash register with her wallet in one hand and the marmalade kitten in the other. They both seemed to be purring.

Next we went into the drugstore, where Mary bought shampoo, vitamins, and a bar of oatmeal soap. I bought deodorant, mouthwash, mascara, a pair of yellow rubber gloves, and a Scratch-and-Win lottery ticket. Mary raised her eyebrows at that.

—I hope you don't think I can help you with that, she said.

—No, of course not, I said quickly, although the thought had crossed my mind.

—Many people pray to me about this sort of thing, she said, but, the truth is, lotteries are not my department. There are angels who take care of that.

I have since done some reading about angels. I have read that, according to fourteenth-century Kabbalists, the number of angels abroad in the world was 301,655,722. That was over six hundred years ago. It seems safe to assume that the number has increased substantially since then.

Having been crowned Queen of Heaven seven days after her Assumption, Mary has held dominion over all of them for the past two thousand years. I have looked at a dictionary of angels and I'm sure that some of them are delightful, if somewhat eccentric: Angel of Aspirations, Angel of April, Angel of Friday, Angel of Fruit, Angel of Fascination, Angel of Food, Angel of the Footstool, Angel of Small Birds, Angel of Summer, Angel of Sunday, Angel of Sweet-Smelling Herbs, Angel of Vegetables, and Angel of the Odd.

I have also looked at a children's alphabet book with charming, whimsical illustrations of twenty-six angels: Angel of Oranges, Angel of Books, Angel of Chimneys, Angel of Ink, Angel of Planets, Angel of Rooftops, Angel of Windows, Angel of Yonder, and Angel of Eggs.

Some of the fallen angels, I imagine, are less than cooperative: Angel of Annihilation, Angel of Confusion, Angel of Corruption, Angel of the Abyss, Angel of Earthquakes, Angel of Dread, Angel of Fornication, Angel of the Fiery Furnace, Angel of Horror, Angel of Hurricanes, Angel of Lust, Angel of Perversion, Angel of the Plagues, Angel of Quaking, Angel of Scandal, Angel of Rage, Angel of Vengeance, Angel of Winter, Angel of Wrath.

Nowhere have I found mention of the Angel of Lotteries. He or she must be a recent addition to the roster.

—The funny thing about lottery tickets, Mary mused as we waited in line at the cash register, is that people keep buying them even if they never win. Week after week, month after month, year after year, still they never give up hope. But if they pray for something two or three times, they expect immediate results, and if it doesn't happen, then they say that God is unfair, disinterested, or dead. Why is it easier to keep believing in the lottery than in God?

I assumed this was a rhetorical question and made no attempt to answer. If Mary herself had not figured it out, then I was not prepared to even hazard a guess.

—I only buy them once in a while, I said in my own defense. Once in a while, just for fun. I don't expect to win.

In fact, it is only when I have a lottery ticket in my hand that I truly understand the difference between hope and expectation. When I was younger, looking for love and all too often having my heart broken again, my friends were always advising me to be more careful. They said it was okay to hope (although not too much) but that I should not have so many expectations. I did not know the difference between hope and expectation or how much was too much of either. But when I buy a lottery ticket, it all makes sense.

I carry the ticket hopefully home, happily dreaming of what I will do with my winnings: new wardrobe, new car, new house, maybe a yacht or a sailboat, maybe a cruise to Alaska, the Caribbean, the Mediterranean, or maybe all three. (In my lottery fantasies, I know how to swim and I like traveling.)

Then I scratch my ticket and win nothing. I am hardly even disappointed. I drop it into the kitchen garbage can on top of coffee grounds, used Kleenexes, and the remnants of last night's dinner. Then I walk away and do not give it a second thought.

When I buy a lottery ticket, I *hope* to win but I don't *expect* to. Translating this lesson from the lottery to life, however, is more difficult than you might imagine.

Back home after our shopping trip, I scratched my ticket and won three dollars. It was better than nothing, of course, but not enough to do much else with besides buy another ticket.

* * *

Our last stop at the mall was the jewelry store. Mary needed a new battery for her watch which, she said, had stopped that morning at precisely ten o'clock. I wondered briefly if there might be some significance to this.

Mary removed the watch and asked the woman behind the counter if she would please put in a new battery for her as she always had trouble removing the back herself. While we waited, I looked at dozens of other watches displayed in a revolving rack on the counter. They were all stopped at different times. Again I wondered if this was significant.

Does time pass if the clock is not ticking? Does time pass if there is no one there to measure it? I have no doubt that it does. I have also never doubted that a tree falling in the forest does indeed make a sound even if there is no one there to hear it. I cannot explain why I believe these things. I do not know if they are significant.

I reminded myself that not everything is a sign, that some things simply are what they appear to be and should not be analyzed, deconstructed, or forced to bear the burden of metaphor, symbol, omen, or portent.

Beside the watches was a rack of silver charms, just like the ones on my bracelet, just like some of the milagros we had unpinned from Mary's dress. I wondered if it was still young women who bought charms or if it was now mostly middle-aged women, women like me trying to buy back their own innocent and aspiring selves, trying to find those parts of themselves they had lost on the journey from then to now.

From behind the counter, the salesclerk said she couldn't get the back off Mary's watch either. She took it into the back room where, apparently, there was someone who was better at these things.

Still waiting, Mary and I looked down into a large locked

glass case which held the more expensive jewelry: diamond necklaces, bracelets, and rings, pure gold earrings and tiepins, a selection of heart-shaped lockets in both silver and gold with spaces on the front where you could have your initials engraved.

The salesclerk returned triumphant and, while Mary retrieved her resurrected watch, I leaned in to take a closer look at the lockets. I caught a glimpse of my own face reflected in the glass, superimposed upon all those little hearts, and I remembered what Mary had said about Saint Teresa's heart displayed in a glass case at the convent in Ávila and on it, you could see the gash where the angel had plunged in his spear.

I have since read about other hearts under glass, most notably that of Saint Chiara, an Italian abbess who experienced the stigmata and visitations from both heaven and hell, and who, shortly before her death in 1308, proclaimed that the crucified Christ was present in her heart. When her body was later exhumed, her heart was found to be much larger than a regular heart and, when it was sliced open, images were revealed on the still juicy tissue. There was a thumb-sized crucifix with a red spot marking the wound in Jesus' side. There were images of a lance, nails, a crown of thorns, and the marble column against which Jesus was scourged. Chiara was canonized in 1881 and her miraculous heart is still on display in a glass case at the Augustinian monastery in the tiny walled village of Montefalco.

I have often been accused of wearing my heart on my sleeve. And if it, too, were sliced open and spread apart for all to see, I wonder what images might be found there, what pictures might have been inscribed by a fine steady hand into its succulent, glistening meat?

History (5)

I am the dreamer and the dream. I am the everything that is nothing, the spark of the soul, fire of the heart, ember of love. I am up and down, top and bottom, strange and charmed. I am the woman clothed with the sun and the child swaddled in darkness. I am the tissue of contradiction, the eye in the needle, the needle in the eye. I am the insubstantial and absolute idea and the hammer that shatters your skull. I am the color you have not named, the light which makes all visible except itself. I am the wave of reason, the particle of faith. I am the star in the cosmos and the atom with the universe inside. I don't seek, I find. I am the writing on the wall, the unutterable speech of the stone.

—John Dufresne, *Louisiana Power & Light*

To the enormous accumulation of written literature about Mary must now be added her ubiquitous presence in cyberspace. Soon after her visit, I discovered that Marian Web sites, like the books, number in the tens of thousands and they, too, come in an assortment of styles and approaches. They are, by turns, documentary, devotional, academic, personal. Some aspire to be comprehensive while others are of a more specialized nature.

One of my favorites is *Hail Mary! Six Thousand Titles and Praises of Our Lady*, the Web site of a doctor in Missouri named Florent E. Franke, who began collecting names of Mary while recuperating from a gallbladder operation in 1945. Many of the names included on Dr. Franke's exhaustive list are just what you would expect: Our Lady of Grace, Our Lady of Peace, Our Lady of Mercy, Our Lady of Consolation, Our Lady of Providence, Our Lady of Pity, Our Lady of Charity, Our Lady of the Rosary, Our Lady of the Cross, Our Lady of the Crown, Our Lady of the Little Ones.

But some names of Mary that appear on Dr. Franke's list and in other sources are more surprising, more intriguing, even whimsical: Our Lady of the Girdle, Our Lady of the Milk, Our Lady of the Precious Blood, Our Lady of the Bowed Head, Our Lady of the Swoon, Our Lady of the Smile, Our Lady of Pottery, Our Lady of Power, Our Lady of Hal, Our Lady of the Eraser, Our Lady of the Cradle, Our Lady of the Crib, Our Lady of the Thorns, Our Lady of Dull Students, Our Lady of Fertile Rocks, Our Lady of Anguish, Our Lady of Infibulation, Our Lady of Ransom, Our Lady of the Underground, Our Lady of the Willow Tree, Our Lady of the Window Pane, Our Lady of a Happy Death.

I would add to these now Our Lady of the Internet, Our Lady of Cyberspace, Our Lady of the World Wide Web.

There are hundreds of Web sites listing the major Marian apparitions. Some offer descriptive details and full-color images, while others simply state location, date, and names of the visionaries. On some lists, each apparition is classified according its standing with the Roman Catholic Church. The approval code consists of five little colored balls reminiscent of rosary beads. A yellow bead indicates that an apparition has received full church approval while a blue bead signifies a bishop's approval only. Green means the apparition is still under investigation, pink means belief in an apparition is discouraged by the bishop, and red means total disapproval by the church.

For those modern-day apparitions which are ongoing, these lists provide direct links to the Web sites of the visionaries themselves. They post in several languages the regular messages they receive from Mary. Some of these are every bit as apocalyptic and terrifying as those in the books. Others are more therapeutic and remedial in nature, relaying Mary's suggestions on how to live an exemplary life. Here she offers kindly advice on the importance of patience, prayer, forgiveness, and solitude. She gives gentle warnings about the dangers of gossip, materialism, seeking revenge, being too hard on yourself, and frittering away your time on pursuits that do not glorify God.

There are also thousands of Web sites devoted to individual Marian shrines around the world. Some of these are quite plain and simple, showing a photograph of the shrine and briefly describing its history. Others are more complex and sophisticated, using the latest computer technology to show off their particular Mary to her best advantage.

At the Web site called *Our Lady of Guadalupe: Patroness of the Americas*, for example, you can listen to a stirring rendition of "Ave Maria" while reading, in English, Spanish, French, or Portuguese, a lengthy timeline of events related to the miracle, from Juan Diego's birth in Cuautitlan in 1474 to his beatification by Pope John Paul II in 1990. You can also read in translation the complete text of *The Nican Mopohua*, the first written record of the Guadalupe apparitions ascribed to the sixteenth-century Aztec scholar Antonio Valeriano.

Our Lady of Guadalupe

On the morning of Saturday, December 9, 1531, a Mexican peasant named Juan Diego is on his way to mass. It is still dark when Juan leaves his humble home in Tolpetlac to make the nine-mile trek through the rocky barren hills to the nearest church in Tlatilolco. Orphaned as a young boy, Juan is now fifty-seven years old, a lonely childless widower, his beloved wife, María Lucía, having died suddenly two years before. He and his wife, along with the uncle who raised him, Juan Bernardino, were among the earliest converts to Christianity, which was brought to Mexico with the 1521 conquest by Cortés.

—Before that, Mary said, the Aztecs worshipped a pantheon of pagan gods and goddesses, chief among them being the feathered serpent god, Quetzalcoatl. The main feature of the Aztec religion was the practice of human sacrifice, which they performed daily. Black-robed chanting priests ripped the hearts out of their living victims, offering some twenty thousand men, women, and children a year to nourish, appease, and flatter their bloodthirsty and demanding deities. It is said that, in 1487, eighty thousand Aztecs were sacrificed in a single four-day ceremony. But Juan Diego, always a devout and mystical man, had renounced all that and dedicated his life to Christ. He walked to the church in Tlatilolco several times a week to partake of the sacraments and receive further Christian instruction.

This morning, as he reaches the base of Tepeyac Hill, Juan is startled to hear music like a delicate chorus of songbirds. He peers up at the mist-shrouded summit a hundred and thirty feet above him, once the site of a stone temple dedicated to the great mother-goddess, Tontanzin. There he sees a glowing white cloud shot through with streaming rays of light and a dazzling rainbow. Then he hears a woman's sweet voice calling him. He clambers up the rocky hillside and there she is: a beautiful Mexican girl, so radiant that even the surrounding rocks and cacti are splashed with her multicolored light. She looks nothing like Tontanzin, whose head was made of snakes' heads and her skirt of their writhing tangled bodies.

The young woman speaks to him in his native Nahuatl dialect. She is kind and concerned. She calls him the smallest and dearest of her children. She wants to know where he is going. She tells him who she is: *I am the perfect and perpetual Virgin Mary, Mother of the True God, through whom everything lives.* She says she wants a *teocali*, a church, built in her honor on this spot. She says he must go to the bishop and make her request.

—Juan, without question, fear, or doubt, agreed immediately, Mary said. He headed for Tenochtitlán, the large settlement that would one day become Mexico City. When he reached the house of Bishop Zumarraga, he was greeted by servants who, suspicious of this coarse, scruffy native, reluctantly ushered him into a small room where he waited alone for hours. Finally the bishop appeared and, with the help of the official church interpreter, Juan Diego told his story.

The bishop listens patiently enough but, in the end, he is condescending and skeptical. He says he will have to think about it and sends Juan away. Disappointed, Juan leaves the city and heads for home. Mary is waiting for him at Tepeyac Hill. Juan tells her what happened. Discouraged, he says maybe she should find a better messenger since he, obviously, sadly, has failed. Mary assures him that he is her chosen one. He will have to go back to the bishop tomorrow and repeat her request.

The next day, Sunday, the bishop is not so patient with this foolish old peasant who keeps pestering him with his outlandish story. Again he sends Juan away, this time saying he must have a sign from this mysterious woman claiming to be the Mother of God. When Juan again finds Mary waiting at Tepeyac, she tells him to come back the next morning and she will indeed provide the requested sign. If Juan is feeling frustrated, not to mention exhausted by all this trekking back and forth, he does not let on.

—When he got back to Tolpetlac, Mary said, he found that his uncle, Juan Bernardino, had fallen ill with the dreaded fatal fever, *cocolixtle*. Juan Diego remained by his uncle's bedside all that night, all the next day and the next night. He tried not to think about me waiting for him at Tepeyac. By Tuesday, December 12, it seemed that the end of his uncle was near. Juan set out for Tlatilolco to fetch a priest to perform the last rites. When he reached Tepeyac Hill, afraid that I was annoyed with him, Juan sneaked around the other side, hoping to avoid me.

But there she is again. Juan apologizes profusely and explains about his dying uncle. Much to his relief, Mary is not mad at him. In fact, she assures him that his uncle is already fully recovered and now he can quit worrying and get on with the task at hand. But first there is the matter of that sign.

Following her instructions, Juan climbs once more to the top of the hill. There, in the midst of thistles, cacti, mesquite, and prickly pear, he finds a profusion of Castilian roses in full fragrant bloom, bathed with a delicate summery dew. Having no container, Juan makes an apron with his *tilma*, a cape made of ayate fiber, a coarse fabric woven from the threads of the maguey cactus. He fills it with the moist blossoms and goes back down to Mary. She rearranges them carefully, ties up the tilma, and sends him again to the bishop. Bearing this miraculous treasure before him, Juan makes the journey with joy, certain that this time the bishop will believe him and honor Mary's request.

—Not surprisingly, Mary said, Juan was again abused by the servants, who cursed him and made him wait for hours outside the gates. Finally, he was allowed inside and this time he found the bishop accompanied by an entourage of important-looking men. Juan told his story and then loosened his knotted tilma. The roses, still fragrant and dewy, fell to the floor. So did the bishop and the other men.

What they see on the tilma where the roses have been is a life-sized image of the woman Juan Diego has been describing.

She is indeed a beautiful young woman, apparently of mestizo descent, with olive skin, rosy cheeks, dark brown hair, and dark liquid eyes cast down in prayer. She is framed by the sun which radiates behind her in more than a hundred pointed rays. She wears a floor-length, rose-colored gown patterned with finely drawn gold blossoms and leaves. A dark turquoise mantle dotted with stars and edged with gold flows in graceful folds from her head to her feet. At her waist is the black sash traditionally worn by pregnant Mexican women. It is fastened in a large bow just below her praying hands. Under her feet are a black crescent moon and a winged cherub happily holding up the hem of her robes.

The tilma is secured safely in the cathedral and Juan stays overnight at the house of the bishop who is now, of course, completely convinced and very sorry that he was not more receptive to Juan in the first place. By the next day, crowds are already coming to marvel at and worship before the miraculous image. Juan leads the bishop to the exact spot on Tepeyac Hill where Mary appeared and asked that the church be built.

—Then, accompanied by an escort of honor, Mary said, Juan went back to his uncle's house in Tolpetlac. There he was overjoyed to find that Juan Bernardino was indeed fully recovered and he too had been paid a visit by the Mother of God. I healed him and then I told him the whole story of the image on the tilma so he wouldn't be worried about his nephew's delay. I told him to rest and drink plenty of fluids. We had all had more than enough excitement for one day.

Juan Bernardino tells his nephew that just before Mary left him, she said they should call her Santa María de Guadalupe. The Spanish clergy are overjoyed to hear this as it pays homage to their most revered Marian shrine established two centuries earlier in the province of Estremadura, birthplace of Cortés, the mighty conqueror of Mexico. Cortés himself is devoted to Mary. He is said to have given a gold scorpion set with rubies, emeralds, and pearls to the Spanish Guadalupe in thanks for saving him from a scorpion bite.

—Later, Mary said, there were many questions and theories about the name. I did, after all, speak to Juan Bernardino in his native Nahuatl dialect and it does not contain the consonants *d* or *g*. I don't suppose he had heard of the Spanish Guadalupe anyway. Maybe what I said and what he heard were two different things. It would not be the first time. Maybe I said *Tlecuauhtlacupeuh,* She Who Comes Flying from the Light Like an Eagle of Fire. Or maybe it was *Tequantloaxopeuh,* She Who Banishes Those That Ate Us. Or maybe *Coalaxopeuh,* She Who Crushed the Serpent's Head. Nahuatl was a difficult language and, mangled no doubt by my awful pronunciation, any one of those words could have come out sounding like Guadalupe. Or maybe I said all these things. There is no reason to have it only one way or the other. The truth is, the name made everybody happy, Spaniards and Mexicans alike. And to this day, many Mexicans still call me Tontanzin, the name of their own ancient mother-goddess. A rose by any other name is still a rose.

In accordance with Mary's wishes, Bishop Zumarraga immediately orders the construction of a chapel on Tepeyac Hill. It is completed by volunteer Mexican and Spanish laborers in just thirteen days.

On December 26, 1531, Juan Diego's tilma is carried from Tenochtitlán to the new chapel. The huge procession is led by the bishop and Hernán Cortés and his wife. They are followed by clergymen, noblemen, judges, trumpeters, drummers, dancers, and thousands upon thousands of common folk. At one point, a throng of Mexicans, carried away by the excitement, begins to shoot volleys of arrows into the air. A spectator is accidentally struck in the neck and killed instantly. The crowd parts to allow his inert body to be placed before the sacred image. As the people pray, the dead man opens his eyes and gets to his feet. Mary has wasted no time: this is the first miracle. In the next few years, between eight and nine million Mexicans are converted to Christianity by the sheer power of the Virgin of Guadalupe.

—Juan Diego took up residence in a hut adjoining the Tepeyac chapel, Mary said. There he spent the rest of his life tending to the sacred tilma and telling its story to an unceasing stream of pilgrims. His uncle died in 1544 at the age of eighty-four and his home in Tolpetlac became a chapel. Juan Diego died four years later on May 30, 1548. I consoled him on his deathbed and he was not afraid when God called him home. Bishop Zumarraga, recently appointed the first archbishop of the New World, died just three days later.

As the centuries unfold, Our Lady of Guadalupe is given credit for everything good that happens to the Mexican people. She saves them from all manner of natural disasters including pestilence, flooding, and fire. She provides guidance and strength throughout the many revolutions and uprisings that characterize the country's tumultuous history.

—The sacred image, Mary said, was displayed unprotected for over a hundred years. Yet it was never damaged or worn, not even by the kisses, caresses, candles, and tears of millions and millions of pilgrims. Nor has the fabric, which would normally

have disintegrated in about twenty years, shown any signs of
decay after more than four hundred and fifty years.

The tilma is repeatedly and intensively examined by an assortment of scientific experts, all of whom must conclude that it
could not have been created by human hands. Among these
experts are a group of astronomers who discover that the stars on
Mary's mantle are not merely random decoration. Rather they
are an accurate duplication of the constellations as they were
positioned at precisely 10:40 A.M. on December 12, 1531. Physi-
cians, opthamologists, anatomists, and oculists study Mary's eyes
on the tilma and spot up to seventeen different people reflected
in her pupils.

The tilma has been housed in many different churches over
the years and has also traveled extensively to visit the many other
Mexican Madonnas: Our Lady of the Remedies, Our Lady of the
Light, Our Lady of the Miracles, Our Lady of the Round, Our
Lady of the Angels, Our Lady of Compassion, Our Lady of the
Thunderbolt, Our Lady of Santa Anita, Our Lady of Zapopan,
Our Lady of Ocotlán, Our Lady of San Juan de los Lagos, Our
Lady Health of the Sick. These Madonnas travel, too, carried in
processions from one city to another, from one church to the
next. Dressed in all their queenly finery, they are accompanied by
mariachi bands, choirs, dancers, jugglers, and military honor
guards. The citizens set off fireworks and airplanes drop flowers
down upon them as they proceed. In a country so full of Marys,
there is always a procession going on somewhere, always one
Mary on her way to visit another, with a thousand or more Mexicans following along joyfully behind, their hands full of tiny
milagros to be pinned to her dress.

Since 1976, the tilma has resided behind bulletproof glass in
the New Basilica of Guadalupe in Mexico City, a seventy-
million-dollar circular temple with room for ten thousand wor-

shippers. The basilica is visited by more than twelve million people every year.

Our Lady of Guadalupe is an inextricable part of daily life in Mexico. Her image appears in every church in the country, as well as on lottery tickets, medicine and soft drink bottles, baseball caps, taxi dashboards, calendars, lampshades, playing cards, key chains, coffee mugs, ashtrays, pillows, belts, purses, towels, tattoos, and computer mousepads.

At the Guadalupe Web site, it is possible to pray the rosary from your computer terminal at home, school, or office. Here, little boxes stand in for rosary beads. Each mystery is illustrated by a painting of the event and each instruction is preceded by a small red rose and followed by an empty box. Mark each box with an X as you complete each step. If you do them all at once, by the time you are finished, you will have meditated on the Five Joyful Mysteries, the Five Sorrowful Mysteries, the Five Glorious Mysteries, made the Sign of the Cross three times, said the Apostles' Creed and the Hail, Holy Queen three times each, said the Our Father and the Glory Be to the Father eighteen times each, said 159 Hail Marys, and put an X in 304 little boxes.

As I continued my exploration of the site, I came to a page called "My Prayer to Our Lady of Guadalupe." Here I was invited to light a candle and send my own prayer of petition or thanksgiving. There was a blank rectangle into which I was to type my prayer. Then I could click on the "Send the Prayer" bar and off it would go: to heaven, I presume, via Mexico and cyberspace.

I have to admit that I was laughing—but not out loud, not exactly. I was making the face and sound that pass for laughter when I am alone: a wry smile with my mouth tightly closed, half of it pulling up, the other half pulling down, while repeatedly making short, heavy exhalations through my nose. Full-blown laughter, I have found, is seldom a solitary activity. I couldn't help but wish that Mary was still with me: I could not quite imagine what her reaction would be.

In the middle of this page, in large letters, was the sentence: SEE THE LIGHTED CANDLES AND PRAYERS. I couldn't resist. I clicked on it.

It took a long time for the page to load. First came the black background dotted with twinkling white stars. Then came the full-color image of Our Lady of Guadalupe flanked by two glowing red candles. Below this was the title: *ORA PRO NOBIS*. PRAY FOR US. Then came the prayers in a tiny yellow font, each with a lit candle flickering beside it on the left.

I scrolled through them quickly. There were hundreds, maybe thousands. Each was dated, the most recent having been posted that very morning. The majority were in either English or Spanish, with a few in other languages: French, Italian, German, Swedish, Dutch. They addressed Mary in many ways: *Dear Mother, Dear Lady, Dear Virgin, Madre Mia, Madre Amorosa, Madre Bendita, Madre Santísima, Madre Purísima, Madre Llena, Querida Virgencita, Reina del Cielo y de la Tierra, Hi there Mary*. Some were anonymous but most were signed: with a name, both first and last, or just the first, or initials only, or with phrases like *Your devoted daughter, Your loving son, Your most miserable child, Your humble servant, Your faithful servant, Your faithless servant, Your desperate friend, A believer, A sinner, A mendicant, A small soul lost in the sea of sorrow, You know who I am*.

I went back to the top of the page and began to read the prayers more carefully. I was still feeling amused in a superior and cynical sort of way, wondering about the gullibility of all these people who were obviously smart enough to use a computer and yet foolish enough to believe that this could possibly be a meaningful or reasonable way to pray.

Most Holy Mother, please help my friend Donna who has just been diagnosed with breast cancer.

Blessed Virgin, please comfort the family next door. Their son died yesterday. He was twenty-three. Please give them strength.

Heavenly Queen, I thank you for the safe delivery of my baby boy last Sunday. He weighed 7 pounds, 6½ ounces. I named him Alexander. Please help me to raise him up right.

Mother of Jesus, I have lost my job again. It was not my fault. Please help me find another one so I can pay the rent and feed my children.

Merciful Virgin, please ask Jesus to cure my high blood pressure, my sinus infection, my sore back, my swollen feet, and my insomnia.

Oh Mary, please don't be mad at me. Please forgive me. I promise I'll never do it again. I know I've said that before, but this time I really mean it.

Mother Most Divine, please help my daughter to get away from that boyfriend who is hitting her and spending all her money on drugs and beer.

Hail Mary, full of grace, I sent you a prayer last week but have heard nothing yet. Please Mary, I need my prayer answered by the end of the month.

Dear Holy Lady, please forgive me for yelling at God and for thinking that you had all abandoned me. I will try to be more patient.

Blessed Mother, please show yourself to me. I promise I will not be afraid.

Holy Mary, thanks a million!

There were prayers that were lists of the names of loved ones needing to be blessed, protected, healed, returned to the fold, saved from Satan or themselves. The longest of these prayers contained 243 names. Some of these were names of the dead who

needed ferrying from purgatory up to heaven. Another list
included each person's problem or affliction in parentheses after
the name: Leonard (prostate cancer), Ida (gall stones), Martha
(migraines), Jennifer (pregnant), Billy (broken leg), Tony (liar),
Jimmy (thief), Bobby (drug addict), Angelina (single mother),
Doris (depression), Janet (loneliness), Stuart (suicidal tendencies). There were less personal pleas, too, prayers for the hungry,
the homeless, the victims of war, terrorist bombings, domestic
abuse, and abortion. There were prayers for the pope and the
American president.

I couldn't read the Spanish prayers in their entirety, but I
could pick out a word here and there, mostly those similar to the
English: *salvación, compasión, protección, desesperación, prisión, cáncer.*
With the help of my Spanish-English dictionary, I translated
others. There were, I discovered, several different words for prayer:
oración, rezo, ruego, súplica, plegaria, petición. In English, the word
prayer is most often used generically, encompassing all those
moments when a person talks to God. In doing so we are also
talking to ourselves, describing and addressing our own deepest
fears and needs. But theologically speaking, I now know that
there are five different categories of prayer: Adoration, Confession, Petition, Praise, and Thanksgiving. It seems quite likely
that the first prayer ever uttered was a desperate cry for help, a
petition. Human nature being what it is, I'm quite sure that
Petition is still the most frequently practiced form of prayer.
Many people, in fact, think that's all there is to it.

I continued studying the Spanish prayers with my dictionary
in hand. Some words showed up over and over again. *Ayuda,*
help. *Peligro,* danger. *Tristeza,* sadness. *Lágrimas,* tears. *Malo,* evil.
Miedo, fear. *Perdido,* lost. *Fe,* faith.

Even as I was reading them, I was reflecting on what a total
invasion of privacy this was. Thanks to the wonders of modern

technology, I was actually peeking into other people's prayers. I was sickened and thrilled by my own voyeurism. It was like chasing an ambulance or gawking at a car accident while a policeman waves you past, and you are both hoping and afraid that you will catch a glimpse of blood, a dismembered arm, a mutilated teddy bear facedown on the asphalt.

What an invasion of privacy and what a privilege. I was no longer feeling amused, superior, or cynical. I was no longer making my solitary-laughter smile and sound. I knew too much. I did not know nearly enough. I could not stop reading. I wanted to know more. I wanted to forget what I already knew. I wanted to know whose prayers were answered and whose were not. But there was no way of knowing how these stories would end.

I went back to the page for sending prayers. Into the blank rectangle, I typed: *My dearest Mary, I miss you.* I sent it unsigned. Then I sat at my computer and I wept.

Sightings

On Thursday afternoon Mary suggested that we go for a drive. It was another warm clear day and she said she would like to see the rest of the city. I thought this was a good idea. What we had seen the day before on our way to the mall had certainly not given her a true picture of the place.

In fact, this is a very old city, but traveling to the west had taken us to the very newest area. If we had gone beyond the mall, we would have found the suburbs, acres and acres of shiny, identical houses huddled together in an impenetrable maze of crescents and cul-de-sacs. Some streets there are still under construction. The houses are still just empty shells and the streets are filled with large yellow machines and lengths of colored pipe waiting to be set into the ground.

I did not suppose that was what she wanted to see. So this time we set off in the opposite direction. I was happy to play tour guide, narrating as I drove, pointing out interesting buildings and explaining the history of the city as best I could.

To the east is the downtown, a quaint conglomeration of boutiques, bookstores, banks, drugstores, coffee shops, and restaurants. Most of these businesses are housed in heritage buildings, which have been carefully restored and are now lovingly maintained. The streets are clean and attractive, decorated in the summer with flowers in concrete planters and hanging baskets, and in the winter with Christmas wreaths and colored lights. At the end of downtown is the waterfront where there is a marina and a large park complete with fountain, benches, a hulking black steam engine, hot dog stands, an information booth, and live music in the summer. Tourism is an important part of the economy here, and we take pride in the beauty of our city.

We circled around to the south, which is the upper-class residential district, the sizes and prices of the homes increasing steadily as the tree-lined streets slope down to the waterfront. Mary marveled at the stately old limestone mansions and I hoped she did not regret having come to stay at my house instead. Also in this district is the university, a prestigious old school with vine-covered buildings and tree-lined walkways. We drove then toward the north end, the homes becoming smaller and smaller and then being superseded by lopsided duplexes, triplexes, and fourplexes with old appliances and broken-down cars in the driveways. These in turn give way to a ramshackle housing project, a trailer park, and finally a desolate industrial area on the northernmost edge of town. Beyond that is the highway.

We turned around in the parking lot of an auto-body shop and headed back the way we had come. At a red light between the trailer park and the housing project, we found ourselves idling beside a place that sold concrete and plaster lawn ornaments. Arranged in tidy rows were hundreds of brightly painted gnomes, elves, lambs, cows, raccoons, foxes, rabbits, swans, turtles, bears, and flamingos. There were frogs in funny costumes, burros pulling little carts, red-jacketed jockeys with and without lanterns, groups of seven dwarves with and without Snow White, and whole families of ducks, skunks, and pigs.

Tucked away in a corner past the fountains and the birdbaths was a selection of religious statues. There were lots of angels, some sitting, some standing, some with their wings extended as if they had either just landed or were about to take flight. Some were only heads, with flowers or clouds where their shoulders should have been. There were statues of Jesus, of course, and of several saints whom I could not identify from that distance. And there was Mary.

In fact, there were many Marys. Painted in various combinations of white and blue and gold, she was short, tall, sad, smiling, praying, and pressing her hands to her chest. In each of these incarnations, she was pretty, pale, and patient. In some of them, she bore a distinct resemblance to Snow White.

—I hope their prices are reasonable, Mary in the car beside me said as the light turned green and we drove on.

Although these religious statues had undoubtedly been there all along, and I had probably driven past them a hundred times or more, I had never noticed them before. I knew that the fact of my finally seeing them now was a matter of neither miracle nor coincidence. Rather it was another instance of what Mary had talked about before: of seeing and not seeing at the same time.

I have had occasion to reflect upon this many times since Mary was here. I have found that since I began to think about Mary, she has begun to show up everywhere. These sightings have been numerous and frequently surprising. Sometimes it has seemed as if Mary's name were right on the tip of everyone's tongue.

There was the newspaper story, for instance, of Notre Dame de Bonsecours Chapel in the city of Montreal, where water damage to the roof had caused the paintings on the ceiling to come unglued, revealing the original oil frescoes beneath. These turned out to be a series of scenes depicting Mary's life that had been painted more than a hundred years before. In front of the church, built on the banks of the Saint Lawrence River, there was a statue of Mary overlooking the harbor. Originally, the article said, the statue had faced the city, but one day it had miraculously turned to look out over the water where the sailors on a ship stranded in a storm were praying to Mary for rescue. The article did not say whether the sailors were saved or not, but it seems safe to assume they were, and the statue continues to be much revered.

A week later, in another newspaper, there was a report of a new trend in designer clothing. Hand-painted and jeweled images of Mary were appearing on high-fashion runways in Paris, New York, and Milan. There, on the breastless bodies of *haute couture* models with long necks, large mouths, high cheekbones, and jutting hips, was Mary's face imprinted on see-through sleeveless tops costing thousands of dollars and accessorized with Miraculous Medal earrings in silver and blue. Some of the people interviewed in the article could not decide whether they were more offended by the prices or the pictures. The general consensus was that these designs would not catch on in this country because we are too conservative.

She made the front cover of *Life* magazine with a feature article called "The Mystery of Mary." The cover photo was of a pure white marble statue of Mary and inside, each page of the article was illustrated with a mosaic of nearly a hundred different icons of her. There were photographs too:

A crowd of worshippers is gathered in front of a large lighted dome in the dark. They are mostly young women waving their hands above their heads. One girl is wearing blue polish on her bitten-down fingernails. On the stage there is a white statue of Mary holding Jesus flanked by colored spotlights and gigantic black speakers like those you see at rock concerts.

A dark-haired woman tilts her head back and drinks holy water from the spring at Lourdes out of a clear plastic bottle shaped like Mary.

A blond woman in a white sweater and blue jeans helps her small blond daughter light a candle inside a replica of the Lourdes grotto in Belleville, Illinois. Behind them a statue of Mary glows in a niche carved into the simulated rock. All around them hundreds of candles in glass jars flicker. Beside them a sign says: VOTIVES $2.00.

She keeps showing up on television too. As I click through the channels in the evening searching for something worth watching, I am often startled to see her face smiling out at me from the screen. Usually the program is a documentary on one of the educational channels, another biography of her perhaps, or an investigative look into people's increasing preoccupation with miracles, angels, and all things divine. Sometimes there she is in prime-time on a major network in a program about visions and apparitions both past and present.

I have recently watched video footage of the sun spinning, dancing, pulsating, and changing color in the sky while Mary speaks to young visionaries; of statues, paintings, and other icons of Mary weeping blood, tears, and oil; of two different women, one in Bolivia, the other in Syria, receiving the stigmata, writhing in their beds before the cameras as blood oozes from their hands, their feet, and their foreheads, and within hours their wounds are healed over and they are in the kitchen drinking tea and talking to reporters.

I have seen the American actress Lola Falana declare that her multiple sclerosis went into complete remission and stayed there after she went to Medjugorje, a town in the former Yugoslavia where Mary has been appearing regularly since 1981. Ten million other pilgrims have also made the trip. A handsome man in a

business suit, who has been there five times, says that, in Medjugorje, the miraculous is commonplace.

I have seen thousands of colored crystals appear on a large
print of Our Lady of Guadalupe in the hallway of the home of
Katya Rivas in Cochabamba, Bolivia. These crystals look like tiny
jewels or those sugary sparkles used on birthday cakes. As they
continue to grow in the dark during the night, one area begins
to glow softly. When a bright light is shone on the image, this
area flares phosphorescent green. The reporters are mystified but
Katya Rivas is not. This, she says, is the womb of Mary in which
Jesus became a man. Although Katya never finished high school
and speaks no English, she records messages from Mary and Jesus
in Polish, Latin, and Greek. These writings, which now fill nine
spiral-bound notebooks, are eloquent, intelligent, and theologically sound.

I have seen a woman named Hermilla Carrazco mopping the
floor of her humble two-bedroom house in Monterrey, Mexico,
and there, in the living room in front of an old plaid couch, an
image of Our Lady of Guadalupe has appeared. Thousands of
people come to pray at the little altar she has set up in the room.
They leave candles, rosaries, milagros, pictures, letters, and rose
petals. I have seen the intricate etched images of Mary and Jesus
that appear on these petals when they are placed between the
pages of Bibles and prayer books. Each tiny image is different, so
clear and detailed that you can see the stray hairs on Jesus' forehead and the six-pointed stars on Mary's gown.

I have seen a crowd of thousands descending upon a farm
in Conyers, Georgia, where Mary gives frightening apocalyptic
messages to a woman named Nancy Fowler on the thirteenth of
every month. Traffic is backed up for a hundred miles, and there
are dozens of Greyhound buses lined up in the parking lot, some
with pictures of Mary tucked under the windshield wipers. These

pilgrims look like ordinary tourists in their shorts and teeshirts. They are carrying coolers, umbrellas, lawn chairs, and camcorders. In one scene shot in the dead of winter, millions of rose petals fall from the sky. In another scene, a cluster of people huddles around a large white statue of Mary bedecked with flowers. They press up against her. They say they can hear her heart beating. While thousands of people remain staunch and unwavering in their belief in Nancy Fowler, some local skeptics sport bumper stickers that read: EAT, DRINK, AND SEE MARY.

I have seen a children's program which is a retelling of the story of Mary appearing as Our Lady of Guadalupe in 1531. In this episode, Juan Diego is played by a Jack Russell terrier named Wishbone and Mary gently teaches him a lesson about the importance of loving his mother.

I have had several sightings of Mary in other places, too, places much closer to home.

Shortly after she left, new people moved in two doors down from a friend of mine. They immediately erected a backyard shrine. The plaster Mary which serves as the centerpiece for this changing diorama is about four feet tall, painted blue and white like all the others, but often draped with a red velvet cape. She has been joined, at various times, by several smaller versions of herself, by an assortment of Jesus statues, by a battalion of saints gathered in a semicircle at her feet, and once, by three Barbie dolls and a bust of Beethoven. This Mary, like all the others, gazes placidly over the tidy lawn and garden stretching before her. She is apparently neither pleased when she has company nor troubled when she does not. Rain or shine, she just stands there, smiling. In the winter, as the snow piles up to her waist, still she keeps on smiling.

The last time I went to get my hair cut, my hairdresser was wearing a Miraculous Medal and an abalone cross together on a silver chain around her neck. Tucked into the frame of the mirror at her station was a photograph of her baby daughter in a voluminous white christening gown and, above that, a laminated holy card of Mary as Our Lady of Fatima. Dressed all in white with a circle of white stars at her head, she was standing barefoot on a cloud, gazing fondly down at three blond children kneeling in prayer before her.

One day at the grocery store the man checking out in front of me opened his wallet and there, in the plastic sleeve that might have held a picture of his wife, his children, or his dog, was a picture of Our Lady of Czestochowa. He took out some money, crossed himself, and slipped his wallet into the back pocket of his jeans.

One rainy afternoon when I stopped at my favorite restaurant for coffee, the woman at the table near the window was praying the rosary while she waited for her food to come. The rain ran down the windowpane and soft jazz music floated through the room. The woman's head was bowed, her eyes were closed, her lips were moving, and the white rosary beads slipped through her fingers like pearls.

Just last week I received a catalog from a mail-order stamp company from which I used to regularly buy sets and special issues to add to my collection. In recent years I have not tended to my stamps as often as I once did. After I had failed to place an order for more than a year, this company dropped me from their mailing list. But suddenly, here they were again. The first item in this new catalog was a set of stamps called "Raphael's Madonnas."

The set included fifty stamps featuring Raphael's paintings and drawings of Mary. There were enlarged colored pictures of and detailed information about several. I recognized some of the paintings I had studied back in university.

Madonna of the Pomegranate from Austria. *Coronation of the Virgin* from Lesotho. *Madonna of Saint Anthony* from Liberia. *Madonna Esterhazy* from Hungary. *Madonna of the Diadem* from the Ivory Coast. *Madonna Connestabile* from the U.S.S.R. *Madonna in the Meadow*, *Madonna in the Garden*, and *Madonna with the Goldfinch* from Paraguay. *Madonna del Gran'Duca* from San Marino, Italy. This painting, according to the catalog, was the first Raphael did in Florence in 1504 or 1505. Nearly three centuries later, it became the property of Grand Duke Ferdinand III of Hapsburg. He carried it with him everywhere, and so it also became known as *Madonna of the Journey*. This painting alone has appeared on stamps at least twenty-three times.

The catalog informed me that in the past two decades nearly three hundred such stamps have been issued by seventy-five countries, a veritable world geography of Mary.

I had no memory of any such stamps in my own collection. Having been a more or less avid collector for so many years, how could I possibly have missed these? Considering the thousands of stamps I had accumulated, how could I not have at least some of them?

I hauled out the three large binders that comprise my collection and began flipping through them. I quickly discovered that I had not missed the Mary stamps at all. In fact, I had dozens of those with Raphael's Madonnas on them, as well as hundreds of others featuring pictures of Mary by all the famous painters.

I did not remember putting them into the albums along with all the others. But I suppose I must have because there they were. There was Mary's face looking out at me alongside poisonous snakes from Guinea, musical instruments from Germany, equestrians from Hungary, elephants from Laos, cosmonauts from Russia, dogs and cats from Poland, cows and chickens from

Romania, and a whole page of flamboyantly colored beetles from Burundi.

This new proliferation of Marys in my life would seem to give lie to the popular notion that you are most likely to find something when you're not looking for it. This idea is most often offered in the spirit of consolation and encouragement to a single woman looking for a man and repeatedly coming up empty-handed and/or broken-hearted.

—Don't worry, people say. You'll find him when you least expect it. Once you stop looking, you'll find him for sure.

These well-meaning advisers may or may not go on to mention how a watched pot never boils.

In light of my recent experience of running into Mary everywhere I turn, it now seems to me that, much as the old notion of finding something when you're not looking for it has often been proved true, the opposite is also and equally true: you find what you are looking for. Sometimes, once your blinders have been removed, you find it over and over and over again.

So there was Mary: on television, in newspapers and magazines, in a friend's neighborhood, in my stamp collection, at the beauty salon, the grocery store, and my favorite downtown restaurant.

And, on a Thursday afternoon in April, there she was among the lawn ornaments just where she had always been. If only I had thought to look.

History (6)

Just as the divine might manifest to us in a variety of ways, so on a subatomic level, an electron can be in many places at once, as a particle *and* as a wave. It seems strange, but on the subatomic level, only potentialities exist for the electron's location—that is, *until one actually observes what is there.* In the act of observation, the potentialities collapse into an actuality, and the electron appears in one place only.

—G. Scott Sparrow, *Blessed Among Women*

While contemplating the long and complex history of Mary, I find that I cannot help but also contemplate the nature of history and truth. Why do we assume that the past is ultimately any more knowable than the future, or the present, for that matter? It is easy enough to prove that this is not true. All you have to do is ask three people who shared the same experience ten years ago to tell the story. Chances are you will get three different stories.

When I was younger I did not even consider the possibility that there were parts of the past that could never be known for sure, that some pieces of knowledge, once lost, would never be found. I carried with me a picture of the past as a solid territory of absolute truth. It was as if the past were a place, one that you could travel to like a tourist with trusty guidebook in hand. Once there you would happily discover that everything really was just the way the book had said it would be. Surely the past was the place, probably the *only* place, where you would be forever safe from surprises, lies, and disappointment.

Now I know better. I would not go so far as to say that *nothing* is true, but I wonder if what we take to be the *facts* of history are as necessarily true as we would like them to be. Are they provable, permanent, are they even possible? Do you swear to tell the truth, the whole truth, and nothing but the truth, so help you God?

Our Lady of Prompt Succor

In 1727, a small group of French nuns founds an Ursuline Monastery in New Orleans, Louisiana, which is still a French territory. Financed by King Louis XV, their permanent building is erected in 1734 in what is now known as the French Quarter on the corner of Chartres and Ursulines Streets. It is now considered to be the oldest building still standing in the Mississippi Valley. Although the Ursulines are impressed by the town with its broad straight streets and its large elegant homes, they are scandalized by the decadent and corrupt behavior of its citizens. The good nuns have their work cut out for them.

—The Ursulines, whose main goal is the proper education of young women, were founded in Italy by Saint Angela Merici in 1535, Mary said. The order is named after Saint Ursula who lived in the fourth century, a beautiful British princess, a serious Christian betrothed against her wishes to a pagan prince. In an attempt to postpone the wedding, preserve her virginity, and further dedicate herself to Christ, she made a long and complicated pilgrimage to Rome by boat. She was accompanied by eleven thousand other virgins. On the return journey, they traveled up the Rhine River and docked at Cologne, which had recently been conquered by the Huns.

Overjoyed at the prospect of setting their feet down on solid ground again, if only for a few days, Ursula and the eleven thousand virgins gladly disembark. They are promptly slaughtered by the Huns. For seven centuries, the truth of this tragic tale is doubted. But in 1155, a huge cache of bones is discovered on the site of the Cologne massacre.

—The bones are now on display in the Golden Chamber of the Basilica of Saint Ursula in Cologne, Mary said. Vertebrae, shoulder blades, femurs, and ribs are bolted to the ceiling and walls. Some are arranged to spell out her name. There are rows of shelves filled with skulls, some wearing caps, others wrapped in red brocade with holes cut out for the eyes. In the basilica itself, eleven large stained glass windows each represent a thousand virgins. The whole story is told in a series of paintings done in 1456 by a Cologne artist. They span three walls. The last painting shows the massacre. There are headless corpses wearing frilly pastel gowns, amputated hands and feet oozing blood, a man in brown tights hacking down virgins with a hoe as if they were stalks of corn. Above the banks of the Rhine, the souls of the virgins float.

The New Orleans Ursulines dedicate themselves to nursing the sick and teaching the children of local colonists, Indians, and blacks. In 1763, France gives Louisiana to Spain and many Spanish nuns emigrate and join the Ursulines to carry on their good work. But in 1800, Louisiana comes again under French control and many of the nuns flee, fearing that a replay of the recent

French Revolution will occur here in the New World. In 1803, the Louisiana Purchase takes place by which the American president, Thomas Jefferson, buys over 825,000 square miles of territory from Napoleon Bonaparte, who has lost interest in taking over the New World. This effectively doubles the area of the United States. By this time, there are only seven Ursulines left in New Orleans. In 1808, exhausted and overwhelmed, they appeal to France for help.

—The woman they wanted to come and lead them was Mother Saint Michel, a well-known Ursuline educator, Mary said. She very much wanted to go to New Orleans, but her bishop, who did not want to lose her, made it virtually impossible by saying that only the pope himself could give her the necessary permission. But at the moment, Pope Pius VII was being held incommunicado by Napoleon in Rome.

Mother Saint Michel writes her letter to the pope anyway and then begs Mary for help. She promises that if Mary will see that the letter is delivered safely and that it receives a prompt and positive reply, she will have her honored in New Orleans as Our Lady of Prompt Succor. She sends the letter on March 19, 1809. Six weeks later she receives an answer: yes, she may go to New Orleans.

Keeping her promise, Mother Saint Michel has a small statue of Mary carved in Paris and carries it with her to New Orleans. She arrives on December 31, 1810, and the statue is immediately installed in the chapel of the convent. Miracles soon follow.

In 1812, Louisiana becomes an American state; the United States declares war on Britain; and back in France, with which the Ursulines continue to maintain close ties, Pope Pius VII, along with the rest of Europe, is still in the grip of Napoleon Bonaparte's megalomaniacal ambition to control the world. His invasion of Russia that same year, however, proves unsuccessful and Napoleon returns defeated to Paris. Only 20,000 of his original army of 550,000 have survived the disastrous campaign.

Also in 1812, the French astronomer Pierre Simon de Laplace proposes a mechanistic model of the universe. According to his theory, the entire history of the universe can be determined by knowing the position, velocity, and mass of every particle. This theory of determinism, which reduces the universe to a system of equations, implies that both history and the future are ultimately and absolutely knowable. This theory, which effectively changes world thought for the next hundred years, apparently escapes the notice of the Ursulines who, it seems safe to assume, simply carry on teaching, worshipping, and praying just as they always have.

—Obviously this theory, Mary said, left no room and no need for God, miracles, mystery, or faith.

Also in 1812, part of New Orleans is ravaged by fire. Whipped into a virtual conflagration by high winds, the fire advances rapidly and soon threatens the Ursuline convent. Terrified, the nuns prepare to abandon the building. As they are about to leave, a lay sister places the statue of Mary on a windowsill facing the approaching flames. Mother Saint Michel prays: Our Lady of Prompt Succor, we are lost unless you hasten to our aid.

In an instant, the wind changes direction and the convent is saved.

Three years later, in 1815, the Battle of New Orleans takes place, the final conflict of the War of 1812. Although the war between the British and the Americans officially ended two weeks earlier with the signing of the Treaty of Ghent in Belgium, this news, lamentably, has not yet reached New Orleans. On Sunday, January 8, 1815, British troops attack the city. The American general, Andrew Jackson, gamely confronts them with his ragged band of volunteers. As the battle rages on the swampy plains of Chalmette just south of the city, women and children gather in the convent to pray with the nuns. They beg Mary to provide assistance to Jackson's men. The statue of Our Lady of Prompt Succor is placed above the main altar in the chapel and the nuns promise to have a Mass of Thanksgiving said every year if only Mary will see to it that the Americans win the battle.

At the exact moment of Communion, a courier runs into the chapel with news of the overwhelming American victory.

—In historical accounts of the battle, Mary said, the numbers vary. Some said there were two thousand British casualties with only eight Americans killed and thirteen wounded. Or there were twenty-five hundred British casualties and seventy-one Americans killed. Or there were thirteen Americans killed and thirty-nine wounded, as opposed to 858 British deaths and 2,468 injuries. One cannot help but wonder who counted the bodies. Anyway, afterwards, General Jackson himself went to the convent to thank the nuns. He then made public acknowledgment of divine intervention in the outcome of the battle.

Fourteen years later, in 1829, Andrew Jackson becomes the seventh president of the United States and sixty-six years after that, in 1895, by decree of Pope Leo XIII, Our Lady of Prompt Succor is officially crowned in the first such ceremony to be held in North America. She remains to this day the beloved patroness of the city of New Orleans and the state of Louisiana. Each year on January 8, as the Ursulines promised, the archbishop of New Orleans celebrates a Mass of Thanksgiving at the convent.

This story, like most of the stories Mary told me, left me with more questions than answers.

I thought about Saint Ursula and the eleven thousand virgins:

all that untouched skin, all those graceful necks, slender shoulders, dainty little hands and feet, all twenty-two thousand of those luminous eyes. I imagined all those unkissed lips: full, moist, ripe for the picking. I wondered why we automatically think of all virgins as beautiful, timid, and slim, carrying their virginity always with them like some precious possession: a necklace, a tiara, a purse. Virginity is not a thing but a state (state of body, state of mind), one that women have traditionally and historically gone to great lengths either to keep or give away. I was puzzled but not unduly dismayed by this paradox.

Being neither virgin nor martyr, I contemplated virginity and martyrdom anyway and came to no conclusions. I, like most women of my generation, lost my virginity more than two decades ago ("lost" it, we say, as if it were a mitten, an earring, that extra ten pounds gained over the winter). At the time, I did not think of myself as bravely sacrificing or magnanimously giving *away* something precious but rather as gratefully (and none too soon) giving *up* something burdensome and unnecessary. At the time, I thought of my hymen as being much like my appendix: a dead-end body part that might have been important once but now served no known purpose or function. My appendix, useless though it might be, remains intact, but my hymen is long gone. I loved the man I gave it to and, although we did not stay together, I have never regretted this.

I pictured the bodies of Ursula and the eleven thousand virgins, hymens and all, hacked apart by the Huns, all that unresisting flesh butchered, all those fine bones scattered, all that red blood spurting into the sunlight, dripping, gushing, oozing onto the banks of the Rhine.

I thought about New Orleans, where I have never been. Considering my aversion to travel, this is hardly surprising. But I found that I carried a vivid, if rather stereotypical, picture of it anyway. The very name of the city brought to mind impressions of voluptuous sensuality and extravagant decadence, of antebellum buildings, sprawling plantations, and swampy bayous, of a sinister underworld of voodoo priestesses, alligator wrestlers, and preening drag queens. The air there, I imagined, was always hot, hazy, and humid, perpetually sultry with the sounds of jazz music and the odors of Cajun cooking.

What I knew of the city I knew in some subliminal way from television and newspaper stories I'd seen, from an article about Mardi Gras I'd read once in a travel magazine in my dentist's waiting room. I remembered from the article that Mardi Gras, which means Fat Tuesday in French, is the raucous, flamboyant, unbridled culmination of Carnival which is actually a religious celebration that begins on the sixth of January, Twelfth Night, and ends on Shrove Tuesday, the day before Ash Wednesday, the beginning of Lent. In this part of the world, many people call Shrove Tuesday Pancake Day, the day when thousands of church halls and basements fill up with people gorging themselves on stacks of pancakes slathered in butter and maple syrup before moving into Lent, those forty days before Easter which is supposed to be a time of giving things up, including food and fun.

I thought about human nature and its inherent tendency to go to extremes: from feasting to fasting, from love to hate, from wild hope to abject despair.

Sometime later, after Mary had left, I, being neither astronomer nor physicist, thought about Laplace's 1812 mechanistic model of the universe as best I could and then I looked it up. According to this theory, nothing would be uncertain and everything about both the future and the past of the entire universe could be absolutely known for sure. I have trouble enough thinking about the universe as it is at this very moment, never mind its future or its past.

What am I supposed to think when I read that the volume of the sun is 1.3 million times that of the earth? What picture can I possibly have in my mind when I read that, much as the earth is 93 million miles away from the sun, the planet Pluto is 3.7 *billion* miles away and takes 248 years to complete a single orbit? Bear in mind that in Laplace's time, the known universe was smaller: these measurements had not been derived and Pluto had not even been discovered yet. Imagine living in a time when people still believed they could know everything there was to know.

I read somewhere once that the mass of the observable universe is 2×10^{51} pounds. That is twenty followed by fifty-one zeros: 20,000,000,000,000,000,000,000,000,000,000,000,000,000, 000,000,000,000. I have neither room in my head nor a name for a number this big. According to the same book, 10^{51} is also the number of years it would take for a mile-high stone of a substance a million times harder than a diamond to be worn away by a holy man touching it just once every one million years.

I have also read that if the DNA contained in a single human being could be stretched out in one strand, it would be long enough to reach from the earth to the sun and back again. Even more mind-boggling is the fact that the capacity of the human brain has been expressed as the number one followed by 6.5 million miles of zeros—a number so large that it would stretch from the earth to the moon and back again more than thirteen times.

What manner of miracles are these?

Clearly there are many kinds of knowledge that can only be taken on faith. I wonder why so many people find these outlandish and unimaginable pieces of information more plausible and easier to believe in than God.

Laplace's model of the universe was supplanted in 1927 by Werner Heisenberg's proposal of the uncertainty principle. This twenty-six-year-old German physicist proved that it is impossible to know both the momentum and the position of a subatomic particle with complete accuracy. Heisenberg showed that in obtaining an accurate measurement of a particle's position, the scientist necessarily alters its momentum, and vice versa.

Also known as the principle of indeterminism, this discovery, coming close on the heels of Einstein's Special Theory of Relativity, had far-reaching implications for all areas of human thought, from physics to philosophy. Like Ockham's razor six centuries earlier, it, too, resulted in an epistemological paradigm shift. It was a revelation of sorts, a whole new way of thinking about the world that produced new symbols, new metaphors, and vast new possibilities. Simply stated, Heisenberg's principle means that when any system is observed, the observer necessarily exchanges energy with that system and thereby changes its original properties.

I do not recall ever studying the uncertainty principle in either high school or university. I remember, though, a description of it in a novel called *The Theory of Everything* by Lisa Grunwald, which I read two or three years ago. One character tries to explain Heisenberg's principle to another by means of an analogy. He says it is like trying to figure out if the refrigerator light stays on when the door is closed. If you open the door to look, the experiment is ruined.

I am no scientist but I can see how the uncertainty principle effectively made the idea of complete objectivity impossible and how the irrefutability of facts has been cast into question ever since.

Consider an anthropologist who has traveled to a foreign country to observe a primitive ritual. Imagine that the anthropologist is from North America, the foreign country is in Africa, and the ritual is one of female genital mutilation, also known as FGM.

The anthropologist, having done the required research, knows that this practice takes one of three forms. Sunna circumcision is the removal of the prepuce and/or the tip of the clitoris. Clitoridectomy, the most common form, is the removal of the entire clitoris, the labia minora, and some or most of the external genitals. Infibulation or pharaonic circumcision, the most extreme form, begins with the removal of the clitoris and the labia minora. Then the two sides of the labia majora are sliced off or scraped raw and sewn together with catgut. The entrance to the vagina is thus closed except for a small opening at the back to allow for the passage of menstrual blood. This opening is created by the insertion of a splinter of wood or bamboo. In some countries, acacia thorns are inserted to hold the two sides of the vulva together. The girl's legs are then bound from the waist to the knees with strips of goat skin which are left in place and not changed for at least two weeks.

The anthropologist, having studied the history of FGM, knows that it likely originated in Egypt more than two thousand years ago. The purpose of FGM, obviously, is to preserve the girl's virginity, and it is most frequently performed on girls between the ages of six and eleven. It is also believed that the mutilation makes a girl more attractive and prevents her from disgracing her family by running wild sexually. Once she is married, she must be cut open again to allow for sexual intercourse and for the delivery of each child.

The anthropologist knows that although FGM is usually thought of (if it is thought of at all) as a primitive ritual once performed in certain barbaric Third World countries, it is none of these things. It is still a current practice in twenty-six African countries, as well as in parts of Asia and the Middle East. Recent estimates put the number of girls and women mutilated in Africa at 127.33 million. Think again about large numbers, virginity, martyrdom.

The anthropologist knows that the procedure is not accompanied by any ritual or ceremony and is most often performed without anesthetic in the girl's own home by a midwife, a doctor, or a barber using an unsterilized razor.

The anthropologist knows that in 1859 clitoridectomy was advocated by British gynecologist Isaac Baker Brown for relief of hysteria, nervousness, catalepsy, dementia, nymphomania, and masturbation. The anthropologist has read an 1894 article called "Sexual Perversion in the Female" by New Orleans physician A. J. Block, in which he reported having successfully cured a fourteen-year-old girl of nervousness and pallor by excising her clitoris.

The anthropologist has also read that the last recorded clitoridectomy performed in the United States took place in 1948. It was performed on a five-year-old girl as a cure for excessive masturbation. The anthropologist has not found this fact in any of the standard history textbooks written by men. It appears only in a book of women's history, as if it were just another one of those marginal topics gathered under the umbrella of the phrase "Women's Issues." You know, all those little things that women worry their pretty little heads about: cellulite, stretch marks, wrinkles, facial hair, housework, child care, equality, breast cancer, rape.

According to the uncertainty principle, the system being observed will be changed by the presence of the observer. Owing to the presence of the anthropologist as witness, the performance of the procedure will be altered in any number of ways. The mother of the girl being operated on will sweep the floor beforehand and put on a clean dress. The midwife who performs the procedure will sharpen the razor this time. The naked girl, depending on her nature, will scream more or less loudly. The female neighbors and relatives who attend the procedure will hold the girl down more or less firmly. They will wipe up the squirting blood more or less carefully. Afterwards, they will smile shyly or boldly at the anthropologist as they take turns plunging their fingers into the girl's bloody hole to be sure the removal of her organs is complete.

Maybe they will offer the anthropologist a turn. While politely declining their offer, the anthropologist will think about Doubting Thomas. Popular piety holds that he did not believe in the Resurrection of Jesus until he had touched the nail holes in Jesus' hands and feet and thrust his fingers into the gaping wound in his right side where one of the Roman soldiers had sliced him open with his spear.

Maybe the anthropologist will remember Caravaggio's painting, *The Incredulity of Saint Thomas*. Three unkempt apostles cluster around Jesus. Jesus: dead, bare-chested, holding back his plain white robe, steadying the hand of Thomas. Thomas: alive, brow furrowed, shirt torn, fingernails filthy, index finger stuck up to the knuckle into the hole.

The anthropologist will also contemplate the fact that the wood used to build the Ark of the Covenant, in which the stone tablets bearing the Ten Commandments were carried, came from the acacia tree just like the thorns used to hold the sides of the girl's vulva together.

Now apply the uncertainty principle in the other direction: the observer of the system will also be changed by having thus observed it. It seems safe to assume that the anthropologist, having once observed the ritual of clitoridectomy, will never be the same.

I spent many days thinking my way through (also over,

under, around, and beyond) the uncertainty principle. I had not thought so long and hard about abstract concepts since university. I was relieved to discover that, with much concerted effort, I could still do it. Much as contemplation of the uncertainty principle often left me feeling uncertain, I was also occasionally dazzled by a sense of everything falling into place. I had a glimpse at least of the strings that connect one cornerstone of human thought and endeavour to another.

History, like science, is limited by its own methodologies.

Consider a historian writing about the Battle of New Orleans. The historian must consider the irony of the fact that this battle, now regarded as the dramatic climax of the War of 1812, was actually fought two weeks after the war was officially ended. Depending on how fond the historian is of irony and on which side the historian's allegiance falls, the Battle of New Orleans can be cast as either a glorious victory or a gratuitous slaughter. Reading the story in a standard American history textbook and then in a British one would no doubt yield two very different stories. Neither one of them is likely to mention the Ursulines and Our Lady of Prompt Succor.

Even the so-called facts are uncertain. In various accounts, the British troops are said to have numbered anywhere from eight thousand to fifteen thousand and the Americans from fifteen hundred to five thousand. As Mary pointed out, the casualty counts are similarly contradictory. And yet in each history book the numbers are put forth without admission of doubt. How can we ever know for sure? We cannot go back and count the bodies again. Perhaps history, then, is simply a matter of choosing a story and sticking to it. You might argue that the numbers don't really matter, that in war it's not how you play the game that counts but only who wins and who loses. Remember that while it was a victory for the Americans, for the British it was a defeat.

Remember that, at the time, the numbers *did* matter, both to those who died and those who didn't. Remember that, at the time, while some citizens of Louisiana hailed Andrew Jackson as a conquering hero and honored him with parties and parades, others called him the Butcher of New Orleans.

Following the uncertainty principle, it is not only beauty that lies in the eye of the beholder. But also victory, integrity, honor, truth, blood.

I have recently found a picture of a painting of the Battle of New Orleans by an American artist named Eugene Louis Lami. It is a poor reproduction and the details are unclear. Against a gray foggy sky the American flag stands proudly erect. Smoke billows at the base of the flagpole. I can see the American troops to the right of the flag and the British to the left. I can see one British soldier in his red coat falling backward off a white horse. I can see another American flag and a warship in the harbor. I cannot see the blood.

Months after Mary had left, on the evening of one of those days when I was obsessing over the uncertainty principle and all its ramifications, there happened to be a Physics category in the second round of *Jeopardy!* When the middle contestant, an exuberant young lawyer from Rhode Island named Dan, selected the $600 question in that category, it said something like: *According to the uncertainty principle the position and this of a subatomic particle cannot be accurately measured at the same time.*

—Momentum! I cried, leaping off the couch in my excitement.

But not one of the three contestants would even hazard a guess. The allotted time for an answer passed in pregnant silence, the buzzer rang, and Alex Trebek revealed the correct response.

—Momentum, he said sadly. His disappointment was palpable.

I felt momentarily smug, superior, somehow confirmed in my own brilliant grasp of the universe.

Young Dan won the game anyway, having amassed $11,800 in half an hour. He was the only contestant to correctly answer the Final Jeopardy question, which said: *1 of 2 women to appear most often on the cover of* Time *magazine, they are separated by 2000 years.* His correct answer was the Virgin Mary. The other woman, Alex Trebek said, was Princess Diana and they have both appeared eight times.

For the whole rest of the evening, I felt inordinately pleased with myself for knowing the answers to both these questions. Obviously, whether we ever get to be on *Jeopardy!* or not, we can all live quite happily without knowing how many times Mary has appeared on the cover of *Time* and without knowing the exact measurements of the momentum and position of subatomic particles.

Still it is worth trying to understand how the uncertainty principle applies to all areas of thought, life, longing, and faith. It all depends, I suppose, on how comfortable you are with uncertainty, how fond you are of mystery, how willing you are to make the quantum leap that faith requires.

Doubt

—When I was younger, Lucian said: and so much more confident,
I was entranced by praying. I soared upwards on wings. But now
I'm older, I find God through doubt as much as through belief. We
search for him in the darkness. I'm full of doubts. That's what
faith means.

—Michèle Roberts, *Impossible Saints*

*E*ach evening after dinner Mary and I sat together in the
living room and she told me her stories. Then at ten o'clock we
sat silently in our overstuffed armchairs in my comfortable house
and watched the news, witnessing that day's anthology of hor-
rendous but familiar stories of murder and mayhem. Each evening, the anchorwoman, dressed in a series of brightly colored
stylish outfits, brought us details and images of various crimes,
accidents, scandals, famines, disasters, and wars, adjusting her
facial expression and tone of voice according to the magnitude of
each horror being reported.

Each evening somewhere in the world a natural disaster was
occurring, a multiple murder had been discovered, a revolution
was taking place, a plane crash was being investigated, a genoci-

dal massacre was in progress, a child had been neglected, abandoned, abused, abducted, raped, murdered, or starved to death. Each evening somewhere in the world a war was breaking out or continuing and hundreds of thousands of refugees were fleeing their homelands.

Each evening I was distressed, disgusted, outraged, and frightened by all that was going on in the world.

After the news we took turns making our ablutions in the bathroom and then we went to bed. I knew from past experience that watching the news right before bed is seldom conducive to falling quickly and smoothly into a deep and peaceful sleep. But still, it was a hard habit to break, a habit that had become a compulsion, fostered perhaps by my growing sense of a moral obligation to pay attention, for better or worse.

If I had expected Mary to explain to me why these atrocities keep happening day after day after day, I was wrong. During the newscast, she would occasionally sigh and cross herself. But she said nothing. And I went to bed each night no more able to make sense of things than I had ever been.

On the first afternoon of her visit, Mary had said she probably had more faith in me than I had in myself, more faith in me than I had in her.

She was right. The truth was that no matter how much I might long to become one of the faithful, still I had not managed it. I believed in God but I had no faith.

Much as I understood, at least theoretically, the difference between belief and faith, still I did not understand the difference between faith and *blind* faith. I could not think about faith without also entering into the labyrinth of doubt and uncertainty. If your eyes are open, I wondered, how can you possibly have faith? If there is such a thing as blind faith, for most people, it is no longer a tenable position. We know too much, see too clearly, watch the news and shake our heads. Thanks to the wonders of modern technology, we have all been faced too many times with too many wars and too many crimes. Day after day, we have seen the slaughter of the innocents. Night after night, we have seen the bodies and the blood. We have seen with our own two eyes the perpetrators of such evils and we have seen the victims and the survivors too.

On Thursday evening, Mary and I watched an interview with the parents of a twelve-year-old girl who had been missing for twenty-seven days and then her body was found in a junkyard on the outskirts of their small, sleepy town. She had been raped, stabbed, and then hacked to pieces. Her body parts had been stuffed inside an abandoned refrigerator.

Why do I remember that the pretty mother was wearing a pale yellow sweater and the handsome father, a crisp blue dress shirt? They were sitting in their living room, holding hands and crying. Why do I remember that their couch, like mine, was green?

The mother said it was their faith in God that would help them through this tragedy.

—God is good, she said through her tears. He comforts us and gives us strength.

—But why then, I wondered with angry indignation, as we have all wondered, why then did God let such a thing happen in the first place?

And what about the forces of nature turned malignant and murderous? What about earthquakes, hurricanes, tornadoes, fires, and floods? We have all watched the survivors of these various disasters weeping in front of the wreckage of their homes, their villages, their cities, their lives. Such events are commonly called "acts of God." In theological circles, they are referred to as acts of "physical evil" or "natural evil," meaning evil that is nobody's fault, evil that just happens. In my head, I know this means that the suffering caused by such events is evil, while the events themselves are "natural," simply a part of nature. But this phrase strikes me as an oxymoron: How can evil be natural? Sometimes I try to leave God out of it and blame Mother Nature instead. But if God is all-powerful, then he must be in charge of Mother Nature too. So in my heart, the question I have to ask is still the same: Why did God let this happen?

What about illness, so many people cut down in their prime by disease; so many children in cancer wards, hairless and brave with big eyes and trembling smiles; so many old people in nursing homes losing their minds to the ravages of Alzheimer's, unable to feed themselves, dress themselves, or remember their grandchildren's names? What about AIDS? What about birth defects, babies born without arms, legs, eyes, brains? These diseases and afflictions are also considered to be events of "natural evil." But I cannot see how there is anything natural about them.

What about plane crashes, car wrecks, train derailments, sinking ships? These are called acts of "accidental evil." This and natural evil are distinguished from "moral evil," those acts intentionally committed by one human being upon another. Examples of moral evil are apparently unlimited. Some of them are unthinkable. What about terrorism and torture? What about twelve students and one teacher massacred at Columbine High School in Littleton, Colorado, on April 20, 1999?

What about the Holocaust?

We have all found ourselves grieving for strangers, past and present, living and long dead, grieving and wondering why God saw fit to put them through this. We have all heard the platitude that God does not give us more than we can handle. But how are we supposed to believe this? Study history, watch the news, look at the suicide statistics, visit your local mental institution and stare into the faces of all those people who could not handle what God gave them.

At one time and another, we have all had our doubts. We have all found ourselves furious with God, on our own or someone else's behalf.

I think I have lost my way in the conundrum of theodicy: If God is all-good, all-powerful, all-knowing, then why do such things happen? Why, for that matter, is there evil in the world at all? Since the beginning of recorded history and probably before, these questions have preoccupied philosophers and theologians of every culture—not to mention less cerebral people who make their livings not as thinkers but as farmers, doctors, hairdressers, engineers, mechanics, musicians, and fiction writers.

Far greater minds than mine have not been able to answer these questions.

Maybe the question of evil is the central mystery of existence, even more fundamental and pervasive than that other ubiquitous question: What is the meaning of life? Maybe these two questions are so inherently entwined as to be inseparable. If it weren't for the undeniable presence of evil in the world, then maybe the question of meaning would not come up, at least not so often. If everything and everybody was good, then maybe the meaning of life would be self-evident. It could be our futile efforts to make sense of evil that lead us to ask what it all means. They are both essentially religious questions. When we ask, What is the meaning of life?, maybe what we are really asking is, Why does evil exist? I am not suggesting that evil is what gives life meaning. I am suggesting that it is evil that throws the meaning of life into question.

Perhaps our persistent need to ask these questions about evil and meaning is the best evidence of the fact that faith, while often apparently absurd, is also unavoidable. Faith, along with food, water, and shelter, is one of the basic needs of humanity. Faith is an instinct for self-preservation just like the others. We all want and need to think about evil. We all want and need to believe that our lives have purpose and meaning. We all want and need to believe in something greater than ourselves.

Some philosophers have said that since God created everything in the universe, he must also have created evil. Since God himself is all-good and everything he created is also all-good, then, these thinkers say, evil must be a necessary part of the good. I cannot follow this argument very far.

Others have suggested that God cannot be held responsible for evil because he did not create it. But in the Bible, he says he did just that: *I form the light, and create darkness: I make peace, and create evil: I the LORD do all these things.* This quote is from the King James Version. In some later versions, the wording has been changed, its implication softened or hedged somewhat. In the New Revised Standard Version, it says: *I make weal and create woe,* and in the New International Version: *I bring prosperity and create disaster.* Call it what you will, in these words God would seem to be saying that he *is* responsible.

With Mary sound asleep (I presumed) in the next room, I lay in bed and thought about evil. I did not know what I thought. I think about evil now and I still do not know what I think. I do believe that there have been (and still are) people in the world who could be considered the embodiment of pure evil. Adolf Hitler, Pol Pot, Charles Manson, Jeffrey Dahmer, Clifford Olson, Paul Bernardo and Karla Homolka: these are the names that come immediately to mind. The list goes on.

I am no Pollyanna, but still I cannot bring myself to believe that we all have evil, or the capacity for it, lurking within us. I use the word *evil* here carefully, as distinguished from a multitude of lesser sins: greed, lust, envy, unkindness, indifference, selfishness, anger, stupidity, and the making of mistakes. I know that I am as capable of committing any or all of these sins as the next person.

I imagine evil existing not within us but lurking somewhere out there in the universe, gathering in putrid pockets like a noxious gas just waiting to be released.

I imagine evil as being something like a black hole in space. The renowned physicist Stephen Hawking has estimated that there may be more than 100 billion black holes in our galaxy. By definition, a black hole begins as a massive celestial body, a gigantic star that contracts to a very small size with enormous density. The star is crushed and swallowed by the sheer force of its own gravitational field. The star then disappears, but the gravitational field remains, sucking in anything and everything that comes near, including light. Anything consumed by the abyss of a black hole is gone forever, sucked irretrievably into this celestial heart of darkness.

I imagine evil as operating in much the same way, sucking in anyone who comes near and then devouring them. The person disappears but the force of evil remains. Like a ship lost in the Bermuda Triangle, anyone consumed by evil is lost forever.

Every night I watch the news and I realize that in comparison to other people's tragedies, mine are small. But still they are mine. And so sometimes I hold them close to my heart, feed them, foster them, and let them grow big enough to get the better of me. By that point, I am fairly dripping with self-pity. It oozes from my pores like oil, spreading like a slick over everything so that nothing is immune to its amorous thrall.

Sometimes I feel depressed for no good reason. Sometimes I feel sorry for myself more on principle, it seems, than anything else. I know full well that if you look hard enough at your own life, you can always find something wrong with it. There are times when it seems that the quickest way to be sure I *don't* get what I want is to pray for it. If it is true that God always has my best interests at heart and that he knows what I need before I even ask, then why, I have often wondered, are what *I* think I need and what *he* thinks I need always two completely different things? I am not the only person who has noticed this. As the prophet Jeremiah put it in the seventh century B.C.: *When you look for light, he turns it into gloom, and makes it deep darkness.*

I sometimes get more than a little tired of what strikes me as God's overly developed sense of irony.

But then I watch one of those television documentaries, one of those twenty-minute true stories on a newsmagazine about people surviving terrible tragedies, overcoming seemingly insurmountable odds, enduring unspeakable torment, and emerging triumphant.

Mary and I watched a few of these programs together. One of them was about an extremely successful athlete who had been left a paraplegic after a car accident. He was struck by a drunk driver two blocks from his home while jogging to the corner store to buy milk. The drunk was not injured.

The athlete in his wheelchair also said that it was his faith in God that gave him the strength to carry on. The interviewer asked him if he ever wondered why God had let such a terrible thing happen to him.

—Before the accident my life was perfect, this man said. I had a tremendously successful career, a wonderful wife, three lovely children, a beautiful home filled with trophies, a garage filled with sports cars, and lots of money in the bank. I had all that and I never once asked: God, why me? So how can I ask it now?

Often I am cured of my own malaise by watching these programs. I am uplifted and moved to joyful tears by these demonstrations of the triumph of the human spirit. My depression lifts, my problems put themselves back into perspective, and I feel, if not invincible, at least strong enough to carry on.

But sometimes these stories just make me feel guilty for being so miserable about my own minor problems. I was not emotionally, verbally, physically, or sexually abused as a child. I have never been raped. I do not have a terminal illness. I have never been in a serious car accident, a war, a plane crash, a tornado, an earthquake, a flood, or a hurricane. No one I know has ever been murdered, kidnapped, tortured, or forced to flee their homeland. The only dead body I have ever seen was that of my maternal grandfather at his funeral and he looked very nice in his coffin in his navy blue suit with all that ruched white satin around him.

The worst thing that has ever happened to me does not even register on the same seismic scale of tragedy as the things these people have lived through. When all is said and done, I have to admit that I hardly know the meaning of the word *suffering.* I am well aware of (and whole-heartedly thankful for) the fact that I have only an arm's-length acquaintance with evil, that all of what I know (or think I know) about it has come to me from secondary sources, from television, books, history, and the news. I know full well that I have only ever looked at evil through the safe filter of stories told with images on a screen or words on a page.

So what right do I have to feel sad, even a little bit? What right do I have to indulge my own sadness and press it close to my heart?

When the list of deadly sins was first drawn up in the late fourth century by Evagrios of Pontus, it included eight sins, not seven, and one of them was sadness. In the late sixth century, the list was reduced to seven by Pope Gregory the Great and still sadness remained. It was not until the seventeenth century that the intangible sin of sadness was replaced by the more specific sin of sloth.

In addition to sloth, the list now includes pride, avarice, lust, anger, gluttony, and envy. Who among us has not been guilty of practicing each and every one of these sins at some point in our lives?

Contrast the seven deadly sins with the seven virtues: faith, hope, love, prudence, fortitude, temperance, and justice. Who among us has not also practiced each and every one of these at some point, however fleeting, in our lives?

For hours on that Thursday night I tossed and turned in my bed in my white room. Obviously I was nowhere near falling asleep. Neither the potpourri nor my interior decorating strategies were working. These thoughts about evil, faith, doubt, and sin went round and round and round in my head just as they had on many other nights before. I was thinking and thinking and getting nowhere, as has so often happened in the never-ending conversation I've been having with myself for all these years.

That night my thoughts continued to spin like the two neighborhood tomcats that sometimes fight in my yard in the middle of the night and when I go outside in my nightgown to chase them away, they are rolling up and down my driveway in a ferocious ball of teeth and claws, oblivious and screaming. I have to turn the hose on them to break it up, and in the morning I find chunks of fur all over the asphalt: black, white, orange, some with the skin still attached.

Sometimes I feel fed up with all the irony and injustice in the world, utterly exhausted by the Sisyphean effort of trying to make sense of things: of myself, of my life, of the world (which both is and is not mine), of other people (who both are and are not like me). On October 12, 1999, the population of the world reached 6 billion: another large number of which I cannot truly conceive. Of the 370,000 babies born that day, the designated six billionth baby was a boy born at two minutes after midnight to twenty-nine-year-old Fatima Nevic in a Sarajevo hospital. With so many people in the world, how can I possibly know any-thing for sure about any one of them?

Sometimes I feel completely defeated by the daily struggle of trying to understand, of trying to be mature, responsible, happy, and good. Sometimes I long to throw off the yoke of reason, to crawl out from under what Cervantes called "the melancholy burden of sanity." Sometimes I want to get out of the way, stop trying so hard, and just let things happen.

Sometimes all I want is for someone to tell me that every-thing is going to be all right. I want someone to tell me this over and over again in a sweet but firm voice, the way you would tell it to a child sobbing in the dark after a nightmare about a hairy green monster under the bed. I want someone to tell me this often enough to banish my doubts and make me believe it.

For all these years, I had thought of doubt and faith as mutu-ally exclusive opposites. Also faith and reason, faith and despair, faith and fear. I had thought that as long as I still had doubt, I could not have faith. For all these years, I had assumed that God did not want to hear from me until I had resolved my doubts and vanquished my uncertainty.

But that Thursday night in April with the Virgin Mary sleeping in the room next door, it suddenly occurred to me that I was wrong. Maybe this endless internal monologue need not be a monologue at all. Maybe it was meant to be a dialogue. Perhaps, for all these years, I had not needed to be talking to myself. Perhaps, for all these years, I could have been talking to God. Perhaps that night, when I thought I was thinking, really I was praying. Maybe I had been praying all along.

Perhaps it was more important to ask these questions than to have all the answers. Perhaps God was just as interested in hearing about my doubts as anything else. I finally understood that just as, according to Heisenberg's uncertainty principle, a system is changed by the observer, so I, too, was being changed forever by asking the questions in the first place. I finally understood that my uncertainty and my doubt were gifts that made me the perfect candidate for faith.

More than anything, I wanted to master the state of being that John Keats called "Negative Capability." I, too, wanted to be "capable of being in uncertainties, Mysteries, doubts, without any irritable reaching after fact and reason." I wanted to have my doubts and my faith, too, both of them at once, without having to lose one for the sake of finding the other. When faced with all these mysteries and questions, I wanted to be able to admit that I did not know how to make sense of it all and that, in the end, my not knowing did not matter.

—I don't know, I wanted to say in answer to these questions, and I wanted to say it with utter confidence, without discomfort, regret, or apology. I wanted to surrender.

—I don't know, I whispered then, trying it out in my white room in the middle of the night.

At that moment, just for a moment, I had the distinct sense of a small window opening, of all my spinning thoughts lining themselves up and slipping single-file through the crack. And then they were gone.

I was not naive enough to believe that they were gone forever. Maybe they weren't even gone for long, but for the moment, they were indeed gone and that, in itself, was a great relief. That, for the time being, was enough.

History (7)

... the philosophical artist, at his or her best, possesses the ability to link the foreground action of particular characters and settings to the deep currents flowing beneath the surface of a culture. ... Transformation is what faith and imagination have in common: they take the stuff of ordinary life and place it in the light of the ultimate questions of sin and redemption.

—Gregory Wolfe, "The Christian Writer in a Fragmented Culture," in *The New Religious Humanists: A Reader*

In the act of looking back, the past is inevitably colored by everything that has happened between then and now. The further back you travel in time, the more the coloring builds up. It is a kind of camouflage, like thin layers of paint applied to a canvas, one color on top of another. Blue plus yellow equals green. Or does it?

If I were a visual artist, I might call it "pentimento." Named from the word *repentance,* this is when the painter, having "repented," has covered over the original image with a new one. This could happen several times on one canvas, the original being buried ever deeper and deeper. But with the passage of time, parts of the top layers wear off or grow transparent with age. What is revealed are portions of the earlier paintings showing through like vague ghosts, misplaced memories, half-remembered dream images: two crows perched on top of the gallows with two dead men dangling beneath them; a profusion of Castilian roses blooming and bathed with summery dew in the desert in December; a battered statue standing in flood waters up to her chest and still the rain continues to fall.

The observer is thus granted fleeting glimpses of the past like seeing out of the corner of your eye a person sliding by an open doorway. If only all those lost pieces could be found and put together again, then you might be able to see the true picture, what was there in the first place before time ran on ahead and changed everything.

Our Lady of La Salette

On September 19, 1846, in the French Alps, a boy and a girl are tending a small herd of cattle on the slopes of Mont Planteau some distance above the remote hamlet of La Salette. The children are from the town of Corps near Grenoble. The girl, Mélanie Calvat (also known as Mélanie Mathieu), is almost fifteen, and the boy, Maximin Giraud, is eleven. They have been sent out to work as herders to help support their large poor families. Mélanie has been working since she was seven years old. She is the fourth of ten children and, since early childhood, has been rejected and mistreated by her mother, who is known to have locked her out of the house for days at a time. Maximin also comes from a troubled family. His father is a wheelwright who drinks most of his wages away. Maximin's mother died when he was only eighteen months old, and his father was remarried four months later to a woman who turned out to be a stereotypical wicked stepmother. Neither Mélanie nor Maximin know how to read and they have never been to school.

—Mélanie, Mary said, was described by her family and her employer as lazy, disobedient, irresponsible, unreliable, sullen, moody, and morose. At the time, these characteristics were considered personality problems and earned her relentless criticism and condemnation. Today, she would likely be seen as just another teenage girl overwhelmed by a deluge of hormones and a large dose of adolescent angst. Maximin, like most eleven-year-old boys, both then and now, was high-spirited and reckless, innocent and impulsive, lacking in both malice and foresight. Back then, his family was always trying to knock the spirit out of him. Now they would just shake their heads and murmur, Boys will be boys, while waiting more or less stoically for him to grow out of it. Now both their families would be called dysfunctional and they would all end up in therapy. Times change, Mary said. Or should I say: Time changes how we look at things.

After the noon Angelus has sounded, the children take the cattle to drink from a spring in a small ravine on the southern slope of the mountain. Then they have a drink themselves, eat their meager lunches of bread and cheese, and stretch out on the grass for a nap.

—The Angelus, Mary explained, is a devotion that originally came from that moment when the angel Gabriel appeared to me back in Nazareth and told me I would give birth to the Son of God. Churches toll their bells three times a day, morning, noon, and evening, to signal that it is time to pray. In Mélanie and Maximin's time, the people in that part of France, having survived the Revolution, more or less, had not returned to their

former faith. Few attended mass, and the other Catholic obser-
vances were seldom practiced. The Angelus had become more of
a time clock or a meal bell than a call to prayer.

When Mélanie and Maximin awake an hour later, they find
that the cattle have wandered away. The children climb to the
top of a nearby knoll from where they can see their cows a little
ways off, quietly grazing, safe and sound, happily chewing their
cuds. Relieved, the children go back to the ravine to retrieve
their knapsacks.

In the ravine, they see a blazing ball of light hovering just
above the ground. As they shrink back in fear, the light whirls
and turns in upon itself, growing to the size of a person. Mélanie
begins to make out the shapes of a face and hands. Terrified, she
drops her herder's stick. Maximin clutches his ever more tightly,
assuring Mélanie that if the thing tries to hurt them, he'll give it
a good whack.

Inside the globe of light, the figure of a woman gradually
becomes clear. She is seated on a rock with her elbows on her
knees and her face in her hands. She is weeping.

When the woman stands up, Mélanie and Maximin can see
that she is tall and very beautiful, dressed in a peasant woman's
typical garb. She is wearing a long white dress and a yellow
apron, a small shawl around her shoulders, and a close-fitting
white bonnet on her head. At first, the children think she must
be just another poor local woman who has been abused by her
family.

But as they watch, astonished, a crown appears on the
woman's head, edged with multicolored roses and emitting rays
of light. Her dress, too, is sprinkled with bursts of light like
stars and her apron glitters like pure gold. Her white slippers are
decorated with pearls, gold buckles, and tiny roses. A large crucifix hangs from her neck on a golden chain. To the left of the

body of Christ on the cross is a hammer and to the right, a pair
of pliers. As the woman moves closer, the children are enveloped
in her light. The woman speaks.

—At first I spoke to them in French, Mary said. I warned
them that unless the people of the region returned to the faith,
they would soon suffer unbearable hardships. I told them that
babies would be seized by convulsions and die in their parents'
arms, that another great famine was coming, even worse than the
last one with the potatoes. When I said the French word for potatoes, *pommes de terre,* they frowned, and I realized they weren't
understanding me very well, so I switched to their local dialect.
I warned them that this time the grapes and the walnuts would
rot too.

The mysterious woman continues to speak warnings, complaints, secrets, and stern admonitions to pray often and spread
the word. Then, with her feet not touching the ground, she steps
across a streambed, walks down the ravine and up the side of the
mountain. With her face turned heavenward, she rises up and
disappears.

Although Mélanie has her suspicions that this woman they
have seen might be a great saint or something, in fact it is the
mother of her employer who first suggests that it is Mary.

—Don't forget, Mary said, that the events at La Salette took
place twelve years before I appeared to Bernadette at Lourdes.
People were less inclined then to jump to conclusions. It was
Bernadette's experience that really set the precedent in that part of
the world. Unfortunately, what happened to Mélanie and Maximin afterward was also very much like what happened to poor
Bernadette. They, too, were interrogated relentlessly even as word
of my visit quickly spread and pilgrims began to make their way
to La Salette. They expected miracles and they got them.

In late October, a group of military recruits passes through the town of Corps. The two lieutenants with them have heard about the apparition. They are very curious and, upon encountering Maximin in a local café, ask him to get them a souvenir from the site. Maximin leaves the café and quickly returns with a rock half the size of a man's hand. The lieutenants both want a piece of the rock so they split it in half with a hammer. On one surface of the broken rock there is an image of the face of Jesus.

In the following weeks, many miraculous healings occur to those who partake of the water from the spring at La Salette. Among them is a woman from Corps named Marie Laurent who has been disabled by rheumatism for twenty-three years. For the last sixteen years she has been on crutches. This woman makes a big pot of soup from the spring water and eats it every day while praying. She begins this on November 17, a day on which seven hundred people have gathered at the site. By November 24, Marie Laurent is virtually cured. On November 28, the number of pilgrims has increased to one thousand.

The healings continue, the pilgrims keep coming. On September 19, 1847, the first anniversary of Mary's meeting with Mélanie and Maximin, fifty thousand people crowd together on the mountainside to worship. In 1851, on the fifth anniversary of the apparition, papal approval is given, and in 1879, a church is built on the site and consecrated by the cardinal archbishop of Paris to Our Lady of La Salette.

—This story does not have a happy ending, Mary warned.

Maximin does not live to see the church built. He dies in 1875 at the age of forty, having led an utterly aimless and occasionally scandalous life. Mélanie, too, leads a troubled life in various convents in France, England, and Italy. She writes a questionable book about her vision that is eventually banned by Pope Pius XI. She dies alone in 1904 at the age of seventy-two, a miserable, stubborn, obnoxious old woman at odds with the church and everyone who knew her.

—Obviously Mélanie and Maximin were not saints, Mary said. They were all too human: flawed, foolish, and weak. By any worldly standards, they were disappointing failures. And yet, they did what I asked them to do: they spread the word and this drew thousands of people back to the faith. Being called to perform a special duty does not necessarily come with a guarantee of special sanctity. What Mélanie and Maximin did with their lives afterwards was up to them. Remember what I said to Bernadette: I cannot promise to make you happy in this world, but only in the next.

It was George Orwell who said that all history is a palimpsest, scraped clean and reinscribed as often as necessary. In the days before the invention of paper, writing materials were scarce and often reused. Vellum could be rubbed clean, papyrus could be washed, then written on again. But sometimes the earlier work was not completely erased and it would eventually begin to show through the later manuscript. As with pentimento, in a palimpsest, history can be found beneath the present work.

The example I like best involves a Syriac text of the writings of Saint John Chrysostom. Once an anchorite in the mountains near Antioch, and eventually the archbishop of Constantinople at the end of the fourth century, Chrysostom was renowned for his eloquence and his name, given posthumously, means Golden Mouth. The discovered manuscript had apparently been written by someone else long after his death, probably in the tenth century. It was found to be superimposed on a Latin grammar text written in the sixth century. This, in turn, was found to be written over a set of fifth-century Latin records.

I do not know the details of the various texts of this palimpsest, but I like to imagine the vaunting sweetness of John Chrysostom's sermons, the top layer covering page after page of the conjugation of Latin verbs: *veni, vidi, vici.* These, in turn, cover table after table on the bottom layer, census records perhaps, lists of births, deaths, debts, and crimes.

Each layer of the palimpsest is a piece of the past, true in its own way. Taken together, what they reveal is, like any good story, more than the sum of its parts.

Think of those bald records as the facts. Think of the grammar text as an explanation of the medium by which they may be transformed. Think of the eloquent prayers of John Chrysostom as both the language and the narrative of history brought to life. Think of those thin places where the past shows through as the truth itself seeking to be transparent.

Our Lady of Hope

On January 17, 1871, in the village of Pontmain in the district of Mayenne in northwestern France, twelve-year-old Eugène Barbedette and his ten-year-old brother Joseph are in the barn helping their father prepare the horses' evening feed. It has been an ordinary day for the Barbedette family, insofar as such a thing is possible during wartime.

The family rose early on this Tuesday morning. They went to mass where Father Guérain, the parish priest, led the congregation in prayers for divine intervention to end the Franco-Prussian War which has been raging around them for almost a year. Paris is under siege and weakening daily, inching toward surrender to the Prussians. Having just won the battle for LeMans, the enemy is now intent upon overrunning the nearby town of

Laval. The congregation prays every day for the safe return of the thirty-eight men from Pontmain who have been conscripted. One of them is the Barbedettes' oldest son, Auguste.

—It had been an exceptionally hard winter, Mary said, and it wasn't only the Prussians that threatened Pontmain. Hungry wolves were slinking into farmyards in search of food, and deadly epidemics of smallpox and typhoid were breaking out in the area. Still the citizens of Pontmain refused to abandon hope. They prayed every day for God to take pity upon them. They prayed every day that his mercy would come to them through me.

After mass, the two younger Barbedette boys went on to school. After school, they headed straight home to get started on their chores. Preparing the horses' feed is a laborious and unpleasant process. Grain won't grow around Pontmain, so branches of gorse bushes must be gathered and pounded in a mortar to make them edible. Young Eugène is tired and hungry. The branches are prickly and his hands are sore and scratched all over. He hates this job. Sometimes he hates these stupid horses too. He wanders to the open barn door when his father isn't looking.

It is almost six o'clock by now and the evening is clear and cold. Both the snow and the stars are sparkling. Looking up toward the gable of a neighboring house, Eugène sees a beautiful young lady in the indigo sky.

—The night was so still, Mary said. I could hear cannon fire in the distance and two wolves howling at each other or the moon.

The lady is wearing a dark blue dress dotted with golden stars and a pair of blue silk slippers decorated with golden ribbons. She is also wearing a black veil and a golden crown trimmed with a red ribbon. Around her head there are three bright stars. She spreads her hands in greeting. She smiles.

—The slippers were a mistake, Mary said. My feet were very

cold. And although I was smiling, the boy was frightened at first. He thought my black veil was a sign that his brother Auguste had been killed in the war.

Eugène cries out and his father and brother rush to join him in the doorway. Joseph can see the lady but their father cannot. Eugène runs to the house and gets his mother. But even after she goes back inside to get her glasses, still she cannot see the lady in the sky. She is very angry and accuses her mischievous boys of lying. She will have none of this foolishness and makes them go inside for supper.

—Supper, Mary said, was a pot of beans, some old carrots, and a heel of stale bread shared among the four of them. I could hear their stomachs growling. They drank pitchers of water until they felt full.

After supper, the lady is still out there, waiting patiently in the evening sky. Word of her presence has already spread. Sister Vitaline, a nun from the village school, has come to the Barbedette barnyard with two young girls. Both the girls can see the lady but the nun cannot. The six-year-old grandson of a neighbor sees her too. A two-year-old held in his mother's arms points and squeals the name of Jesus several times.

—Soon the whole village was gathered in the barnyard, Mary said, almost eighty people staring up at the sky. None of the adults could see me, not even the priest and the nuns. They could see only the three bright stars around my head. Nevertheless, they were all weeping and praying the rosary, singing hymns while kneeling in the barn and the snow.

As the people praise her, the lady begins to grow larger and larger until she has doubled in size. An oval frame forms around her and a sentence is spelled out letter by letter in French in the white space below her feet: *Mais priez mes enfants. But pray my children.* Eugène Barbedette and the other young seers relay the message to the eager adults. This sentence is followed by a second: *Dieu vous exaucera en peu de temps. God will hear you in a little while.* And then by a third: *Mon fils se laisse toucher. My son permits himself to be moved.*

A red crucifix and a banner bearing the name of Jesus appears, also two small white crosses on her shoulders and four candles lit by the stars. She offers the crucifix to the children. The crowd continues to pray fervently. After three hours, a large white veil begins to swirl like a cloud around the lady's feet. Slowly she is lifted and enshrouded and then she disappears.

—I had done everything I could, Mary said.

Later that night the Prussian army stops its advance through the French countryside. Nine days later, on January 26, more than five hundred pilgrims fill the Barbedette barnyard, offering their prayers all day long to Our Lady of Hope. The following day a full armistice is signed and the war is ended. All of the Pontmain men who had gone to fight the Prussians return to the village unharmed. Among them is Auguste Barbedette, handsome, hungry, and proud, without a single scratch on him.

Now I understand that the past is not necessarily any more knowable than the future, that facts are not necessarily any more true than fiction. Fact and fiction. What is the difference, how can you tell, and who decides?

I used to think that much as fact and fiction might originally arise from the same source (from some metaphysical desire to understand the world, the soul, or the meaning of life), from there they must run in opposite directions like rivers on either side of a watershed.

Now I see that the dividing line between fact and fiction becomes increasingly unclear the harder you search for it. The same, I must note, has been said of searching for faith, searching for God.

Now I see that fact and fiction are the inseparable Siamese twins of reality and everything we think we know for sure.

Although the Marian apparition narratives have all of the ingredients of factual accounts, all the scholarly research and necessary documentation, still many people dismiss them as pure fiction. Some have gone to great lengths to disprove the apparitions and their accompanying phenomena, declaring them to be nothing more than elaborate hoaxes designed to exploit the gullibility, ignorance, and desperation of the faithful. According to these skeptics, the inexplicable light effects and the images of Mary appearing on windows, billboards, and the like are really just natural reflections or shadows, optical illusions, tricks of the light. They say the phenomenon of silver rosaries turning to gold that is frequently observed during apparitions is really the result of oxidation or erosion. As for the reports of the sun spinning, dancing, and radiating colors, the skeptics say all this is the product of a combination of local meteorological and atmospheric conditions, mass hysteria, and retinal damage.

And yet the apparitions continue to occur, the stories of them continue to be passed on, and the faith of all those who believe continues to grow: undaunted, shining, and true.

It was John Berger who said that poems are "nearer to prayers than to stories." It seems to me now that the stories of the Marian apparitions are in fact prayers, precious gifts, innocent truths that are, as Werner Heisenberg said of the probability wave, "standing in the middle between possibility and reality." It is in that still point, that *point vierge,* between fact and fiction that faith not only survives but thrives.

Our Lady of the Cape

In the middle of the seventeenth century, the settlement of Cap-de-la-Madeleine consists of a fort and a handful of houses on the north shore of the Saint Lawrence River in Lower Canada, which will become the province of Quebec.

—The river was named, Mary said, in honor of the third-century martyr who, while being roasted on a large iron grill over a slow fire, said, with a cheerful smile: Turn me over now, I'm done on this side. Lawrence became, among other things, the patron saint of cooks and a jar of his melted fat is preserved in the Escorial palace in Spain.

The village lies between Montreal and Quebec City near the fur trading post of Trois Rivières. In 1662, a chapel dedicated to Mary is built by the Jesuits in Cap-de-la-Madeleine and in 1694, Canada's first Confraternity of the Holy Rosary is established there. A generous parishioner donates a large statue of Mary to the church. As in the image on the Miraculous Medal, Mary stands atop a star-studded globe. Her bare feet crush the serpent beneath them. She is wearing a white veil and a golden crown. On her chest there is a large gold heart circled with roses and bursting with flames.

Religiously speaking, things start off well enough. Because the tiny settlement is very vulnerable to attack by hostile Iroquois natives, its residents turn to Mary for protection. They erect shrines in their homes and attend mass daily. But as the years pass, the settlement grows larger and the danger recedes. Human nature being what it is, the parishioners become complacent. As their fear wanes, so does their devotion, and church attendance falls off steadily.

In 1867, the four provinces of Quebec, Ontario, New Brunswick, and Nova Scotia are united by the British North America Act to become one sovereign nation, the new Confederation of Canada. That same year, Father Luc Désilets is dispatched by the bishop to Cap-de-la-Madeleine. His mission is to revitalize the religious devotion of the parish. Other priests before him have tried and failed. At first Father Désilets does not do very well either.

—It was on the eve of the feast of the Ascension, Mary said, that Father Désilets finally understood how far the parish had fallen. He waited and waited in the confessional that evening but nobody came. When he ventured out and surveyed the nave, he saw that not one person had shown up. Instead there was a large pink pig wandering down the aisle, snuffling and grunting, poking its hairy snout under the empty pews. By the time it reached the altar, the pig had a rosary in its mouth and was munching happily. Finally the pig swallowed it, beads, cross, and all, with a slobbering, satisfied gulp.

The next day Father Désilets's sermon is called "The Pig and the Rosary." The negligent parishioners hang their heads in shame. Set back on track now, they resume their former religious enthusiasm, and the size of the congregation grows well beyond its former numbers. A new church is needed to hold them.

In 1877, work begins. Stone is cut in the quarry across the river from Cap-de-la-Madeleine. The cutting takes two years. The plan is then to haul the rock across the mile-wide river when it freezes over.

—Although winters there are notoriously long and cold, Mary said, the winter of 1879 proved to be unusually mild. On the river there was still open water. The thin crust of ice that had formed on some stretches was not solid enough to hold a child, let alone a block of stone weighing several tons. So Father Désilets prayed. He promised that if I would make him an ice bridge, then he would leave the original 1662 chapel alone instead of dismantling it as he had planned.

Father Désilets prays for a bridge on March 14, 1879. The next day gale-force winds begin to blow over the Saint Lawrence. Ice floes begin to accumulate. By the following morning, Sunday, March 16, the ice that spans the river is strong enough to bear the weight of forty men. By the next day the river is solid ice between the quarry and Cap-de-la-Madeleine. The formation of this miraculous bridge is front-page news in newspapers throughout the province. It takes one week for more than 150 horse-drawn sledges to haul the stone across. Then a thaw sets in and the ice bridge melts completely away.

The new church is opened a year and a half later on October 3, 1880. Then the original chapel is restored and reopened. It is consecrated to Mary on June 22, 1888.

—A promise is a promise, Mary said. I kept mine and Father Désilets kept his. I took a few moments that evening to show him my thanks after the official ceremony was over.

Around seven o'clock that evening, Father Désilets enters the newly consecrated chapel with Father Frédéric, a new priest who has recently joined the parish. With them is a sick man from Trois Rivières, Pierre Lacroix, who needs their support to make it to the altar. Father Désilets is an old man, and he groans as he kneels at the altar rail. Getting down there is a struggle these days, and he always wonders if he will be able to get up again. Father Frédéric, who is young, kneels effortlessly. Pierre Lacroix, who cannot kneel at all because of his affliction, sits on a chair between them.

All three men gaze up at the statue of Mary as they pray, thanking her for their various blessings, asking for her continued guidance and protection. The usually downcast eyes of the statue open and lift so that she is looking over the heads of the men into the far distance, maybe all the way to Trois Rivières. All three men blink hard and go pale. Each is hugely relieved to discover that the other two have seen it too. This makes it easier to believe, easier to spread the news.

Eight weeks later Father Désilets dies peacefully in his sleep.

The miracle is thoroughly investigated and documented. Father Frédéric and Pierre Lacroix do not waver in their faith. They both sign written declarations as to the details of the event. The news spreads quickly and the shrine becomes the most popular Marian pilgrimage destination in Canada.

In 1904, Pope Saint Pius X orders the official coronation of Our Lady of the Cape, and in 1954 she is crowned again by order of Pope Pius XII. She remains the only Madonna in Canada to be so honored.

Now I see that the opposite of fact may not be fiction at all, but something else again, something hidden under layers of color or conscience or meaning. If I were a visual artist, I might call it pentimento. If I were a historian, I might call it a palimpsest. But I am a writer and I call it the place where literature comes from.

It is a place akin to those known as "thin places" in Celtic mythology. Like the thin places in both palimpsest and pentimento, these are threshold bridges at the border between the real world and the other world, still points where the barrier between the human and the divine is stretched thin as a membrane that may finally be permeated and transcended.

Now I see that the opposite of knowledge may not be ignorance but mystery; that the opposite of truth may not be lies but something else again: a revelation so deeply imbedded in the

thin places of reality that we cannot see it for looking: a rever-
ence so clear and quiet and perfect that we have not yet begun to
fathom it.

Thanks be unto God for his unspeakable gift.

Our Lady of Knock

On the evening of Thursday, August 21, 1879, in the hamlet
of Cnoc Mhuire in County Mayo, Ireland, Mary McLoughlin,
housekeeper to the local priest, Archdeacon Cavanagh, is on her
way to visit her friend, Margaret Beirne. It is about seven o'clock,
raining heavily, and the streets of Knock are deserted. As Mary
McLoughlin passes the small village church, she sees three white
figures standing near the south gable. She assumes they are new
holy statues purchased by the archdeacon. She clucks her tongue:
more dusting for her and more money to be squeezed out of the
parishioners, no doubt. It is too wet to linger and she hurries on
her way.

—The two women passed a pleasant hour drinking tea and
gossiping, Mary said. The tea was laced with whiskey, the gossip
peppered with ribald laughter and bawdy innuendo. Knock was
a very small village then, little more than fifteen or so houses
clustered around the church. Everybody minded everybody else's
business and, when facts were in short supply, the two women
felt free to fill in the gaps with their own lascivious speculations.

The women enjoy themselves immensely and then Mary
McLoughlin heads home. She is now accompanied by Margaret
Beirne's sixteen-year-old daughter, also named Mary.

—There are too many Marys in this story, Mary said.

When the two Marys reach the church, they see that the
three statues are still there. Mary McLoughlin wonders why the

archdeacon has been so careless and left them standing out in the rain. It is Mary Beirne who first realizes that they are not statues at all.

The divine trio is floating two feet above the ground. Mary is in the middle with Saint Joseph on her right, looking up at her with his head slightly bowed. On her left is Saint John the Evangelist in the white robes of a bishop with a book in his left hand and his right raised in a gesture of benediction or admonition. Mary is wearing a flowing white cloak tightly fastened at her throat. Suspended from her large yellow crown is a single red rose dangling in the middle of her forehead. The three figures are silent. To their left is an altar with a cross on top and a small white lamb curled up at its base.

—After staring at us for a few minutes, Mary said, Mary Beirne ran home to get her family. Mary McLoughlin ran to fetch Archdeacon Cavanagh but he was not impressed. He said it was probably just a reflection in the stained glass windows and he did not even come outside to have a look. Mary McLoughlin had a fanciful mind and was a little too fond, he thought, of those old Celtic stories about the wee folk, faeries, leprechauns and the like. Besides, she had a reputation for overindulging in alcohol, and he could smell it on her breath.

But no matter what the archdeacon thinks, fourteen people have already gathered at the church. Everyone in the group can see Mary and the two saints, who move around a little but do not speak. When thirteen-year-old Patrick Hill boldly approaches them, the figures step back. When seventy-five-year-old Bridget French drops to her knees and tries to kiss Mary's feet, she finds that she is kissing air even though the feet are visible right there at her lips. And the ground all around the figures is dry despite the day's heavy rain. At his farm half a mile away, sixty-five-year-old Patrick Walsh fears the church is on fire when he sees a large glowing light in its vicinity.

The apparition lasts for about two hours and then the figures vanish, still without having said a single word.

Soon miraculous healings are taking place regularly at the little church, especially for those who have scraped bits of concrete from the wall and eaten them. Pilgrims come by the thousands and the church wall becomes so weakened by people chipping away at it that it must be reinforced and covered with wood.

Today, Knock is still a small town but it has its own airport, built to accommodate the annual onslaught of more than a million pilgrims. Housed now in a basilica large enough to hold two thousand people at a time, the sacred wall of the old church is displayed behind a sheet of unbreakable glass to protect what is left of it from the unflagging enthusiasm of the faithful.

Truth

When you are in the middle of a story it isn't a story at all, but only a confusion; a dark roaring, a blindness, a wreckage of shattered glass and splintered wood; like a house in a whirlwind, or else a boat crushed by the icebergs or swept over the rapids, and all aboard powerless to stop it. It's only afterwards that it becomes anything like a story at all. When you are telling it, to yourself or to someone else.

—Margaret Atwood, *Alias Grace*

On Friday it rained all day. In the morning we followed our usual routine. After breakfast and coffee, we got dressed and retired to our respective rooms.

—Now this is my idea of the perfect vacation, Mary said with satisfaction. At last I have a chance to catch up on my reading. So many books, so little time.

She shook her head regretfully and went into her room, quietly closing the door behind her.

I went into my study. I settled in at my computer, checked my e-mail, and sent the necessary replies. I wrote several letters to be dispatched later in the regular, nonelectronic way. I took out the red spiral-bound notebook in which I had been jotting down ideas and images for my next novel. I read over what I had written the day before:

I went to the gallery early in the morning. I rode my bicycle through the fog. I have always been partial to fog. I like the way it hides a multitude of sins. I like the way it makes me feel invisible and safe. I like the picture of myself emerging from the fog with shreds of it still hanging off me like skin.

I made spaghetti and salad for dinner. By the time the food was ready, I could not eat.

—I have never understood the nature of coincidence, I said. It was Sunday evening. I was washing the dishes and he stood beside me, drying and putting away.
—You will, he said, smiling in a superior way and moving the dish towel in slow circles around the face of a blue and white plate.

I had begun to notice how lately all of my sentences started with "I." I was always thinking or talking about my problems, preoccupied with the shortages of money, love, and peace of mind that seemed to chronically plague me. I was always describing, explaining, and justifying myself, both to myself and to others.

I said I did not love him anymore.
He said he did not love me anymore.
What it all boils down to is this: Who said it first? Therein lies the story.

Imagine this sentence is a secret: tell nothing, tell no one: tonight.

Although I had written these lines just twenty-four hours earlier, they now made no sense to me at all. I remembered writing them. I remembered liking them. I distinctly remembered being excited by them. But now I could not remember where I had imagined they might be leading, what I had thought they might eventually amount to.

This was akin to having one of those earthshaking, life-altering epiphanies just as you are falling asleep and then in the morning it is lost, gone, forgotten, the earth is not shaken, your life is not altered, and you have no choice but to go on without knowing whatever miraculous truth it was that you knew for that one precipitous moment in the luminous darkness of the revelatory night before.

Without making a conscious decision to do so, I put aside the red notebook and took a new blue one from my stationery cabinet. Centered on its first page, I printed in large block letters: *OUR LADY OF THE LOST AND FOUND.* In smaller letters below I printed: *This is a work of fiction.*

I sat and stared at these words for a long time.

For lunch we had cheese and mushroom omelettes with fruit salad for dessert. After we had finished eating, neither of us was especially inclined to get up from the table. Outside it was still raining. Inside, all the lights were on, glowing yellow and warm, inviting laziness, a leisurely afternoon, another pot of coffee, a long conversation filled with confidences and confessions.

During the earlier days of her visit, Mary had been more than generous in telling me the stories of her life. On Friday, it seemed only natural that now it was my turn, that now I should tell her the story of mine.

Mine, of course, is a much shorter story. And if there are miracles in it, they are much harder to see.

I have already told you the facts. Now I will tell you the truth. In one way or another.

Over the centuries, a great many things have been said and written about truth. Some of them might even be true.

It is an inherent and inevitable characteristic of human nature, I think, to go looking for the truth. We use the word *truth* in the same ways we use the word *history*: both with and without a capital letter. We seek both the truth about ourselves as individuals and the Truth about the universe at large. Deeply ingrained in each of us is the expectation that someday we will indeed figure it out. We share the belief that finding the truth will ultimately bring the seeker only and all good things: peace, love, justice, joy, safety, and salvation.

To our way of thinking, the words *true* and *good* are synonyms.

We envision Truth as a magical set of laws by which the universe and all things and creatures in it are governed. It is as if Truth were a sophisticated and invisible system of checks and balances operating behind the scenes of daily life, a system that keeps us (well, most of us anyway) from running completely amok.

To our way of thinking, the words *true* and *evil* are antonyms.

But much as we may sometimes ponder Truth with a capital *T,* mostly when we talk about truth, we talk about it with a small *t.* We talk about the many varieties of truth. We qualify and modify the word with circumstantial adjectives and strategic disclaimers. We talk about poetic truth, human truth, scientific truth, metaphysical truth, half-truth, whole truth, plain truth, simple truth, hard truth, gospel truth, the absolute truth. But mostly when we talk about truth, we talk about ourselves. We say:

—I believe in God. I do not believe in God.

—I am lonely. I am not lonely.

—I am afraid. I am not afraid.

—I am patient and impatient, responsible and irresponsible, rational and irrational, certain and uncertain, faithful and unfaithful, innocent and guilty, lost and found. I am truthful. I am a liar. On any given day, I am any or all of the above.

—I have brown eyes and short brown hair that is just beginning to go gray. I am of average height and weight. I have worn glasses since I was nine years old. I am the middle child of three. I like coffee. I like Bach and Beethoven. I like a quiet rain.

When in doubt (as we so often are), our inherent inclination is to stick to the facts. We are so easily led astray by our collective tendency to equate facts and truth, logic and reality. But when all is said and done, human nature is not logical and the truth is more than the sum of the facts.

Just as we can live quite happily without knowing the momentum and position of subatomic particles, so we can also probably live quite well without knowing the Truth about the general workings of the universe. But can we also live well without knowing the truth about ourselves?

We have been led to believe, by pop psychology, self-help books, and daytime TV talk shows, that it is our failure to know the truth about ourselves that allows room in our lives for all unhappiness, doubt, pain, and fear. We have been led to believe that once we are wise enough to find our truth and know it, then all doubt and fear will vanish and everything will be all right.

Remember that Jesus said: *And ye shall know the truth, and the truth shall make you free.*

But also remember Emily Dickinson: *Tell all the truth but tell it slant . . . / The Truth must dazzle gradually / Or every man be blind.*

And then there was Friedrich Nietzsche: *We have art in order not to die of the truth.*

I have never been to confession in the formal, ritualized manner. My true confessions have not taken place in a darkened booth in a cavernous, possibly chilly, church. I have never sat there, contrite, with my head bowed, my face hidden, and my hands clasped. I have never said: *Bless me, Father, for I have sinned,* addressing myself humbly to a shadowy, benevolent priest, who then listens patiently to my whispered recitation of heinous, mundane, or pathetic little transgressions.

I have never said: *O my God, I am heartily sorry for having offended thee; and I detest all my sins because of thy just punishments. But most of all, because they offend thee, my God, who art all-good and deserving of all my love. I firmly resolve, with the help of thy grace, to sin no more and to avoid the near occasion of sin.*

I have never had a priest bestow absolution upon me and send me on my way with some expiatory homework: Say twelve Hail Marys. Say ten Our Fathers. Get down on your knees and promise you will never do it again. Cross your heart and hope to die.

I have never been to confession, but still I am no stranger to trying to tell the truth about myself to myself or someone else. I am no stranger to putting my own life into words. But my true confessions have always taken place in less ecclesiastical settings, often with little or no premeditation.

Often it happens at my computer in my study when I think I'm writing about a wholly fictional character, but the next thing you know she is wearing my clothes, cleaning out my fridge, watering my plants, thinking my thoughts, remembering my memories, and making my mistakes.

Equally often, I have confessed to all manner of high crimes and misdemeanors while drinking many cups of coffee at a cluttered table in a warm, cozy kitchen and outside it is gloomy and raining and the streetlights have come on though it's only two o'clock in the afternoon, and I am sure that if only I can tell my story accurately and often enough, I will eventually come upon the truth, either on purpose or by accident.

I have always thought of myself as an honest person, as a person who is not afraid to look myself in the eye. It is hardly surprising that being a writer, I tend to assume that truth resides in story. But still, it is easy enough to forget that story, like language itself, can both reveal and obscure the truth.

My penchant for story (and all that it involves: structure, form, order, plot, cause and effect, metaphor, allegory, theme, conflict, crisis, and resolution) has led me to seek and find patterns in my own life where perhaps there are none. When I was younger, I dreamed of starring in my own dramatic narrative. I imagined it would be a romantic story, an inspiring parable of love filled with passion, wisdom, and tenderness. It would have a happy ending, of course, the inevitable ending beside which all other endings would look wrong.

Much to my surprise, things did not turn out that way.

Of course there is more than one way to tell this story. I know there are other ways of telling it by which I could make myself look better or worse. But this is the way I most often tell it to myself. This is the way I told it to Mary that Friday afternoon in my warm, cozy kitchen. I talked and she listened patiently, dispensing sympathetic smiles, encouraging comments, and frequent coffee refills. She did not judge, ridicule, or rush me. I kept talking and outside it kept raining and the streetlights came on at only two in the afternoon.

This is the story I can live with.

When I taught writing, I was always telling my students that they must hone their powers of observation, that they must never underestimate the importance of concrete details in a story. I would often emphasize how precision in the details helps create atmosphere, character, and verisimilitude; how the color of a bedroom wall, the dirt on a third-floor window, the drape of a black silk skirt can all be used to draw the reader deeper into the fictional world, a world that should be, as John Gardner advised, a "vivid and continuous dream" in the reader's mind.

I have scrupulously followed this advice in my own writing. I have become addicted to details. I can never get enough of them and if, as they say, God is in the details, then surely he should have shown up by now. I have put my faith in the transformative power of the telling detail, however small and apparently insignificant. I have never doubted the omnipotence of objects, innocent or otherwise, and yet I cannot explain how or why the most ordinary object becomes extraordinary in the process of observing it and putting it into words. Bearing in mind Heisenberg's uncertainty principle, the writer is the observer and all of reality is the system. Both are forever altered in the process of their exchange.

I can always see what Italo Calvino described as the "web radiating out from every object." I absolutely believe his theory that any object—a table, a suitcase, a statue—can serve as the starting point, the seed of a story, just like the famous mustard seed of faith. And, if the writer pursues the ever-multiplying network of details, digressions, and meditations to which it gives rise, the result may in the end encompass the entire universe.

Many of the details I have used in my fiction were drawn from my own life, bits and pieces of autobiography transplanted into or grafted onto the lives of my fictional characters. I discovered early on that I could not write the stories of *their* lives without also writing something of my own. But I am not writing about myself. Paradoxically, putting some part of myself in the story draws me out of myself, toward something greater, deeper, and very far away.

I have also discovered that writing about an incident from my own life and calling it fiction often seems to make it more true. Sometimes I have piled detail upon detail until I can no longer remember what is real and what I have embroidered, exaggerated, or invented altogether. Now I have to wonder how much of my own history has been revised and rewritten, amended and appended, misremembered and misrepresented, by accident or on purpose. Now I have to wonder about the difference between honesty and truth.

I am either the victim or the villain of this story.

Contrary to John Gardner's advice and my own practice, in this part of my story, the details don't much matter now. Dates, times, places. Weather, wardrobe, food. The color of shirts, rooms, eyes. The look on a man's face or mine, somebody always saying goodbye, the sound of another door closing (softly, sadly, or with a resounding and immensely satisfying slam). Promises, lies, disappointments, and betrayals.

In this part of my story, all the chapters end up the same, never mind about the details along the way. When I taught writing, I also always told my students that what you leave out can be just as important as what you put in.

When I was in my twenties, I put my faith in love. I was a product of my place and time, a middle-class girl who had been led to believe that romantic love was the most important thing in the world. I saw no reason to question this received wisdom, no reason to doubt that I would eventually find it. When I was in my twenties, I thought I had all the time in the world to get it right.

I had several relationships in those years, each of them short, exciting, and doomed. I was an old hand at obsession. I always had to have some man's name in my head like a chant, an incantation, a constant tintinnabulation, the subtext beneath everything I said and did, a one- or two-note song I sang silently to myself in bed at night even when the man in question was right there beside me, sweaty and snoring and hogging the blankets. It is only in retrospect that I understand that obsession has nothing to do with love and everything to do with anxiety, insecurity, uncertainty, and fear.

At first I was most often attracted to men with the names the Ouija board had spelled out to me the summer I turned fourteen: Andrew, Robert, David, John. But I didn't stop there. I was attracted to men who were married, gay, or chronically afraid of commitment. I was often attracted to men who were not attracted to me. I was attracted to men who were bad for me, men who were dangerous, men who were not very smart, men with whom I had absolutely nothing in common.

I was a devoted proponent of the idea that opposites attract. I had first encountered this theory back in Grade Nine Science class when we studied the law of electrical charges: while like charges always repel, unlike charges always attract. I do not remember why learning that this is a law of science led me to believe that it must also be a law of love. Nor do I remember my Science teacher ever warning us that, much as this law is a *true* thing, that does not necessarily make it a *good* thing.

I did not see any of these men for who they really were. I saw them only for who I wanted them to be and for how they might play into my desire to live out my own romantic story. I always thought I was in love and then it always turned out that I wasn't. I hurt them or they hurt me. I betrayed them or they betrayed me. I left them or they left me.

It may well be true what Tolstoy said, that all happy families are alike but each unhappy family is unhappy in its own way. But as far as love and romance go, I would beg to differ. It has been my experience that the opposite is true: the happiness I felt at the beginning of each new relationship was different, and I was always certain that, finally, this time I was feeling feelings I had never felt before. But the pain at the end was the same every time.

When I was in my twenties, I gave so much of myself away that eventually there was nothing left for me or anybody else.

As soon as I started liking a man, I started disliking myself. Whenever I became interested in a new man, I began to rewrite myself. I can see this only now, in retrospect, thanks to the miracle of twenty-twenty hindsight. At the time I looked with scorn at women I knew who changed themselves to try and catch or keep a man: women who suddenly found an interest in hockey, fishing, or fast cars; women who suddenly lost twenty pounds, quit smoking, or bought a whole new wardrobe because the man had once mentioned that he thought skirts were much sexier than jeans. At the time, I could see the deception and the danger of this in other women's lives, but I could never see it in my own.

Looking back at the machinations I went through then, now I think of the whole process as a further demonstration of Heisenberg's uncertainty principle at work. Granted, falling in love might not at first glance seem to have much to do with quantum physics or subatomic particles, but it does necessarily have a lot to do with momentum, position, chemistry, history, and uncertainty. Not to mention exhilaration, expectation, and doubt.

Consider the case of two people who have recently become romantically involved. Call them Lovers A and B. At this early stage of their relationship, Lovers A and B are just getting to know one another, each trying to take the accurate measure of the other. Following the uncertainty principle, this is technically impossible. Both will change and be changed by the advent of the other in their lives.

Observe:

Lover A gets her hair cut, begins wearing leg makeup to cover up those unsightly spider veins, buys new underwear and perfume, starts reading self-help books, and stops schlepping around the house in her sweats in case Lover B decides to drop by.

Lover B has his teeth cleaned, buys season's tickets to the symphony, gives up greasy burgers for Lent, starts renting romantic comedies instead of sci-fi thrillers, stops making (and laughing at) politically incorrect jokes about women, and cleans up his filthy apartment in case Lover A decides to drop by.

Both Lovers A and B soon become kinder, cleaner, friendlier people. They are more talkative, more attractive, and more patient in their dealings with the rest of the world. They take to smiling at strangers in the street. Both Lovers A and B are, for the time being, better people all around.

Consider the possibility that, according to the uncertainty principle, by the time Lovers A and B actually do believe they have fallen in love, they will bear little or no resemblance to the people they were before they met. When I was in my twenties, I did not understand why this could be a dangerous thing. I did not understand how you are changed, a little or a lot, for better or worse, by each new person you choose to let into your life.

I also did not understand that although you cannot do anything to make somebody fall in love with you, there are any number of things you can do to make sure they don't.

I am neither the victim nor the villain of this story.

I wish I could look back over my own history and put my finger on one single event and say, unequivocally:

—There! That was when everything changed.

This is how it happens in books. The conventional plot structure of a novel is often diagrammed as an inverted checkmark. The long side represents the rising action of the conflict and its complications. The point of the checkmark is the crisis or the climax, the central event of the story. It is followed by the shorter side of the checkmark, the falling action, which then ends in the resolution or *dénouement*.

It was the crisis, the climax, the turning point for which I yearned, the moment from which I would go forward forever changed. I wish I could tell you the story of some great conflagration, a climactic cataclysm, an eyebrow-singeing lightning bolt, a pivotal precipice off which I leapt, defying death, waving my arms and shrieking:

—Eureka!

But that is not how it happened in real life.

In real life, it was more a matter of accretion or erosion or both. All around me, my friends and family were getting on with their lives: getting married, having babies, buying houses, moving forward. But there I was: stuck.

I was a slow learner. It took me a long time to understand that any relationship could end at any time for any number of reasons, some obvious, others obscure. Coming to know this was not especially comforting, but it was, at times, in a certain reckless frame of mind, strengthening—in the manner of Nietzsche's aphorism: *What does not kill me makes me stronger.*

It took me even longer to understand that, once you have reached a certain age, you can no longer suffer one loss at a time, that loss is cumulative and, with each new experience of it, all your old losses will join forces and come back *en masse* to haunt you again.

So here's the trouble with love: perhaps it is only in retrospect that you can know for sure it was love, only after twenty or thirty years that you can look back and say, with surprise and satisfaction and absolute certainty:

—Yes, I loved him. And yes, he loved me too.

And here's the trouble with truth: it is disorganized, plotless, unsatisfying, often unbelievable, apparently pointless, sometimes boring, and it frequently amounts to much ado about nothing.

Thinking about truth too long and too hard leads me into a metaphysical labyrinth where I experience a kind of panicky paralysis, where I realize that every single thought I have ever had or pushed away, every single word I have ever whispered or shouted, every single sentence I have ever written or deleted, could just as well be false and that, if the truth were known, I might be, after all, the consummate unreliable narrator.

History (8)

History is a story chafing against the bonds of documentary fact.

—Janet Malcolm, *The Crime of Sheila McGough*

There are many ways to divide up the world. One of those divisions is between those who make lists and those who do not. To my way of thinking, this distinction has been sadly neglected in favor of the more usual demographic categories such as male and female, young and old, black and white, have and have-not. I am sure that a detailed investigation of the propensity to list or not to list would yield remarkable new insights into the deepest psychological crevices (or crevasses) of human nature.

I am a veteran and inveterate member of the list-making faction and can hardly imagine how a person without a list ever gets anything done. But those who don't make lists are frequently amused by those of us who do. Back in university I had a boyfriend who liked to annotate my lists when I wasn't looking. To my to-do list he would add items like *Eat, Breathe, Have sex, Sleep.* On my shopping list he would draw funny pictures: a little cow beside *hamburger,* a chicken beside *eggs,* or a penis (his, presumably) beside *condoms.*

Checking off the items on my lists one by one as the day goes by gives me a sense of accomplishment and makes me feel that I'm in control of my life. Of course I know this is an illusion, and yet the lists satisfy my need to make order out of the potential chaos of any given day. In a larger sense, I realize that my writing itself is born out of the same desire.

For a list-maker looking into history, chronology, the listing of events in order of their occurrence, would seem, at first glance, to present the past in its simplest, most reductive and seductive form. A chronology is so orderly, so clean, so self-contained. For a list-maker like myself, with decidedly architectonic leanings, it is extremely appealing to imagine that the unruly tumult of the past can be thus distilled and neatly poured into the jar of time, that all those events have apparently followed one after another naturally enough, the way Monday follows Sunday, May follows April, one year follows another, requiring absolutely no intervention on the part of humanity.

I suspect that Mr. Skinner, my Grade Ten History teacher, with his insistence on the facts and nothing but the facts, must have loved chronologies as much as I do. But Dr. Sloan of Ancient History 101 would no doubt have dismissed them as nothing more than an elaborate exercise in *reductio ad absurdum.*

I own several fat chronologies of world history and consult them often when doing research for my books. I invariably find them reassuring and comforting. They make history look so manageable. Imagine the chronologist training the long lens of a telescope upon the past. Imagine the facts piling up like stars. Or imagine the chronologist taking aim at the past with the serpentine hose of a vacuum cleaner, sucking all the facts into its gigantic bag. Imagine all the chronologists making their lists and checking them twice. Imagine every single thing that has ever happened falling into place and staying there.

When I began to read about Mary after she left, I turned naturally enough to these chronologies. I already knew that she was reported to have made more than twenty thousand appearances in the past two thousand years. But I found that in these books she made few or no appearances at all. In a chronology of women's history, she was listed only five times, as having given birth to Jesus in 1 A.D., as having given rise to a cult-following by 1100, as having appeared to Juan Diego in Mexico in 1531, to Catherine Labouré in Paris in 1830, and to Bernadette Soubirous at Lourdes in 1858. She was not mentioned at all in any of the other books.

How can this omission be explained in light of the fact that Marian veneration has flourished around the world ever since her death in the first century? How is it that the most influential, inspirational, and significant woman in the history of the world is not accorded a single mention in most standard history books?

Despite having been thus rendered virtually invisible by most secular historians, Mary has not become a quaint and feeble anachronism. She has remained an important and ongoing part of history. Like most people, she has continued to exist as both a part of and apart from history.

In the twentieth century, an age generally considered the most secular and least religious age ever, the number of recorded Marian apparitions has escalated well beyond those documented in any previous age. How is it that none of these modern apparitions which have affected the lives of millions and millions of people are included in the standard histories?

1917 On May 13, Mary appears to three children tending sheep in a valley called Cova da Iria at Fatima, Portugal. Lucia dos Santos and Jacinta and Francisco Marto see Mary on the thirteenth of each month for six months. On October 13, the day of the last apparition, the miracle of the sun is witnessed by seventy thousand people gathered at the site. It has been raining all day, but suddenly the clouds part and the sun begins to dance and spin, scattering red flames through the sky. It then plunges in a zigzag toward the terrified crowd before returning to its usual place overhead. Within three years, Jacinta and Francisco die of pneumonia. Lucia becomes a cloistered nun in 1929. She eventually reveals two of the secrets Mary told them in 1917. These involve a terrifying vision of hell, and predictions of the end of World War I, the horrors of World War II, and the rise and fall of Soviet Communism. She writes down the third secret and puts it in a sealed envelope, which is kept in a locked vault in the Vatican. It is widely believed that the third secret is an apocalyptic doomsday prophecy too frightening to be publicly revealed. When Pope John XXIII reads it in 1960, he faints dead away.

1932 On November 29, five children see Mary near the Sisters of Christian Doctrine Academy in Beauraing, Belgium. By January 3, 1933, Mary has appeared thirty-three times to Gilberte, Fernande, and Albert Voison, and Andrée and Gilberte Degeimbre. In the final apparition, Mary reveals to the children her heart, made entirely of gold and sending off shimmering rays of light. On January 15, 1933, Mary appears to eleven-year-old Mariette Beco in the garden of her home in another Belgian village, Banneux. Mariette sees Mary another seven times, the last apparition occurring on March 2. Although these events at

Banneux are first dismissed as copycat visions patterned after those at Beauraing, in 1949 they are accepted and approved by the church.

1953 On August 29, in Syracuse, Sicily, a plaster-of-Paris image of Mary hung above the bed of Antonina and Angelo Iannuso begins to weep. Antonina, in the middle of a difficult pregnancy, suffers from toxemia, which causes convulsions that leave her temporarily blinded. As the tears fall from the plaque, Antonina's sight is restored. The image continues to weep for four days.

1953 On a September evening, five young girls watching a football game see Mary in a privet hedge in Fairmont Park, Philadelphia, Pennsylvania. The next night Mary appears again to the girls and two more friends in the same spot. On October 25, fifty thousand people gather in the park because it is rumored that another vision will occur, three miracles will be performed, and one of the girls will be taken up to heaven. Mary does not show up.

1961 On June 2, Mary appears to four young girls in San Sebastián de Garabandal, Spain. Her first appearance to Conchita González, María Dolores, and Jacinta and María Cruz is preceded by several apparitions of Saint Michael the Archangel. Between 1961 and 1965, Mary appears to the four girls more than two thousand times in and around the village. During these visions, the girls are frequently transported into states of ecstasy in which they feel no pain, even when stuck with needles, and their bodies become so heavy they cannot be lifted. In July 1962, many people observe the miraculous appearance of a Communion wafer on Conchita's tongue. Mary warns that eventually the girls will deny the reality of their visions and by 1966 they have all, in three separate periods of doubt, retracted their miraculous claims. This does little to discourage people's belief in the apparition.

1968 On April 2, two Muslim mechanics see Mary atop the dome of the Coptic Church of the Holy Virgin in Zeitoun, Egypt, fifteen miles north of Cairo. Between 1968 and 1973, hundreds of thousands of people, Egyptians and foreigners, Christians and Muslims, see Mary in an ongoing series of apparitions in Zeitoun.

1970 On April 7, Mary appears for the first time to Veronica Lueken, wife of a construction worker and mother of five, at her home in Bayside, Queens, a borough of New York City. On June 18, Mary appears again to Veronica at nearby Saint Robert Bellarmine Church and asks that a shrine be erected there. The shrine, dedicated to Our Lady of Roses, Mary, Help of Mothers, gives rise to a following known as the Bayside Movement. Until her death in 1995, Veronica continues to see Mary during vigils held at the shrine.

1973 On June 28, a painful cross-shaped wound appears on the left palm of Sister Agnes Katsuko Sasagawa, a forty-two-year-old deaf nun at the Institute of the Handmaids of the Holy Eucharist in Akita, Japan. A week later the wound begins to bleed. On July 6, a small wooden statue of Mary speaks to Sister Agnes and assures her that her deafness will be cured. The next day blood is found flowing from an identical cross-shaped wound on the statue's left hand. On July 27, Sister Agnes's wound disappears and on September 29, so does the wound on the statue. On October 13, the anniversary of the sun miracle at

Fatima, Mary speaks to Sister Agnes for the last time. But on January 4, 1975, the statue weeps. Between that day and September 15, 1981, the statue cries 101 times. On May 30, 1982, Sister Agnes's hearing is permanently restored.

1981 On June 24, Mary begins appearing to six young Croatians on a mountainside near the village of Medjugorje, Herzegovina, in the former Yugoslavia. What follows is an unprecedented, complicated, and well-documented series of daily apparitions and messages from Mary to all six visionaries that continues to the present day. This has transformed Medjugorje into a major international center of Marian devotion filled with hotels, shops, and restaurants. Despite the bloody civil war that begins in the area in 1992, Medjugorje remains miraculously undamaged by the conflict, and millions of people continue to make the pilgrimage to the site every year.

1981 On November 28, Mary, with dark skin and long dark hair, appears to sixteen-year-old Alphonsine Mumureka while she is serving dinner at the Benebikira Sisters' School in Kibeho, Rwanda. During the following year, Mary also begins appearing to six other Rwandans, five girls and one boy. Five of the girls are Catholic, one is a Muslim, and the boy is illiterate. With no religious upbringing whatsoever, he has not ever even heard the names of Jesus Christ and Mary. In one of the apparitions, Mary shows the young people a river of blood in which Rwandans are killing each other, a prophecy of the coming war between the Hutus and the Tutsis in which millions will die.

1982 On November 22, in Damascus, Syria, the palms of eighteen-year-old Maria Nazzour begin to ooze oil. Maria, known as Myrna, then places her hands upon Layla, her husband's seriously ill sister, and Layla is instantly healed. On November 27, a three-inch statue of Mary and the baby Jesus in Myrna's bedroom also begins to ooze oil, enough to fill four saucers in one hour. Mary tells Myrna not to be afraid. On December 15, while a large group of people is praying before the statue, Myrna sees Mary, shining as if she is covered with diamonds. For years, the oil continues to pour from Myrna's hands and many miraculous healings occur. On Good Friday 1987, Myrna experiences the stigmata, including the bloodied outline of a crown of thorns across her forehead. Myrna continues to receive the stigmata regularly. She cries and writhes in pain while her wounds bleed for several hours.

1988 In July, while attending a Greek Orthodox Church Camp in Mercer, Pennsylvania, fourteen-year-old Sam Boumis of Lorain, Ohio, buys a large laminated portrait of Mary and the baby Jesus at the camp gift shop. The painting has been blessed with holy water and tears from the weeping icon at Saint Nicholas Albanian Orthodox Church in Chicago. When Sam takes the painting back to his cabin, it begins to exude oily tears and the fragrance of myrrh. Eighteen other pictures of Mary at the camp, some on paperback book covers, are also found to be crying.

1988 In late summer and early fall, Mary begins speaking to a prayer group of nine young adults meeting every Thursday evening at Saint Maria Goretti Church in Scottsdale, Arizona. During the next year, Mary begins to appear to various members of the group, first and most frequently to Gianna Talone, former model, television actress, now a divorced pharmacologist. Gianna is also regularly assaulted by the devil at night in violent episodes which leave her bruised and scarred. In November 1993, about to marry a physician named Michael Sullivan, Gianna has a vision in which Mary tells her to leave Scottsdale and move to Emmitsburg, Maryland. Michael and Gianna do as they are told. Since then Mary has continued to appear and give messages to Gianna once a week in the Thursday evening prayer service at Saint Joseph Church on North Seton Avenue in Emmitsburg.

1990 On December 3, Ray Trevino sees a large image of Our Lady of Guadalupe on the concrete floor near the shower stall in the restroom of his auto parts store in Progreso, Texas. Soon more than fourteen thousand people are coming to the store every week, leaving flowers, candles, milagros, and holy cards around the image on the floor.

1992 On January 8, Mary Jo Kalchthaler and a small prayer group are saying the rosary before a statue of Our Lady of Fatima at Saint James Church in Totowa, New Jersey. The statue is a traveling Mary, purchased from the Vatican, which tours different churches and homes in the parish. When Mary Jo asks the white statue for a sign of Mary's divine presence, it begins to glow blue, then red, green, yellow, and pink. Once permanently installed at Our Lady of Pompeii Church in Paterson, the statue continues to go through its rainbow permutations and is credited with healing physical and mental problems, broken marriages, and fractured souls.

1993 In September, Santiago Quintero, operator of an auto-body business out of his home in Elsa, Texas, sees the image of Our Lady of Guadalupe on the bumper of a late-model Camaro he is repairing. That day a local man is shot in the head and the doctors say he will not survive. His wife comes to see the car and the man recovers. Quintero builds a small shack for the Holy Camaro of Elsa and thousands come to worship.

1995 On two separate occasions in late May, Mary is seen by ten thousand people gathered at a Catholic church in Dong Lu, China. This pilgrimage site was built following the 1900 invasion of Dong Lu during the Boxer Rebellion. In the midst of firing upon seven hundred Christian residents, the soldiers suddenly turned and fled, having seen Mary and Saint Michael the Archangel in the sky above them. Those who witness Mary's two appearances in 1995 have gathered to worship in defiance of communist government edicts. May is Mary's special month and they must honor her. As the sound of Gregorian chant and the fragrance of incense waft over the rice fields, the Chinese seers are transported and transformed by her presence.

1996 On December 17, a gigantic image of Mary appears in four tinted glass panels covering the first and second stories of the Seminole Finance Corporation building in Clearwater, Florida. By January 18, 1997, more than 450,000 people have come to see the iridescent hooded figure with head inclined and no facial features. In addition to filling up the parking lot with votive candles, bouquets of flowers, and baskets of fruit, the faithful have also left $14,000 at the site. Because the image is clearly visible day and night from the nearby coastal highway, it is dubbed Our Lady of the I-19.

I might not go so far as to suggest a conspiracy theory among world historians to suppress and marginalize Mary, but I do wonder how and why they have so consistently managed to ignore her.

The conflict between science and religion has occupied

thinkers of every century. With the advent of the theory of relativity, the uncertainty principle, wave-particle duality, and quantum physics, science has begun to ask some of the same questions as religion: questions of faith, meaning, and God.

Science can no longer be regarded as the method by which all the mysteries of the universe will eventually be dispelled. Now it seems that each new mind-boggling scientific discovery serves rather to increase both our awe in the face of these mysteries and our awareness of the fact that reality far exceeds our ability to understand it. Some would say that because we are living in an age when things like heart transplants, cloning, computers, walking on the moon, and taking pictures of Mars are no longer the province of science fiction, people are less likely to believe in miracles, apparitions, visions, and the like. But, seen from another angle, such scientific discoveries actually make it easier to be open to the possibility of the miraculous. Until Dr. Christiaan Barnard transplanted that first human heart in a hospital in Cape Town, South Africa, that December day in 1967, few people would have dreamed that such a thing could ever happen. In an age where heart transplants have become a frequent procedure, perhaps anything can be believed.

Although the apparitions of Mary would seem at first glance to suspend all known laws of physics, in fact, in recent years, some of the quantum discoveries have made them all that much more plausible, adding to the vocabulary of the scientific world a renewed sense of wonder, creativity, and surprise. To paraphrase Saint Augustine, miracles are not contrary to nature or science or history. They are only contrary to what we know (or think we know) of nature, science, and history.

The languages of faith and science are becoming remarkably similar, but as the physicists and the faithful put their heads together more and more closely over the big questions, the historians are still sitting on the sidelines. They remain obstinately oblivious to what has been going on around them for the past two thousand years, studiously avoiding what Susan Sontag has called "Moments of slippage, when anything seems possible and not everything makes sense." History is still dodging the questions, still slipping around miraculous Mary, still refusing to acknowledge her presence and her power. What are the historians afraid of? Do they think that by expunging Mary from the annals they will never have to think about her, never have to hazard an opinion as to whether the stories about her are fact or fiction, true or false?

I have since taken another look at those fat chronologies and I must admit that I have been awfully naive. I have had to revise my picture of the chronologists with their telescopes and vacuum cleaners. I have had instead to picture them picking and choosing from the vast garden of facts. I have had to recognize that the chronologists and other historians are faced with the same decisions that any writer must face: what to leave out and what to put in. These decisions are made on the basis of a conscious or unconscious sense of what matters and what doesn't. For a long time, I thought those chronologies had avoided this problem by putting everything in, by embracing all multiplicity, and so had in the end served up a look at the world which was the apparent opposite: absolute and complete simplicity. Now I know otherwise. Now I know they can be no more complete, no more absolute, than any other story.

I took another look at the events that various chronologists have chosen to include in their listings for the year of Mary's now legendary appearance at Fatima, Portugal. Picking and choosing from what they have already picked and chosen, here is some of what I found.

In 1917, World War I was in full swing. Many countries

declared war on many other countries. There were advances and retreats, victories and defeats, casualties and survivors, more casualties, fewer survivors. The Russian Revolution began. Tsar Nicholas II abdicated. The United States officially entered the conflict. The first bombing of London by German planes took place. Canadian forces captured Vimy Ridge and later, Passchendaele.

In 1917, John Fitzgerald Kennedy was born. As were Indira Gandhi, Ferdinand Marcos, Dizzy Gillespie, Andrew Wyeth, Heinrich Böll, Thelonious Monk, John Lee Hooker, Lena Horne, Nat King Cole, and Robert Mitchum.

In 1917, the Trans-Siberian railroad was completed. It had been under construction for twenty-six years. In the world's worst railway disaster so far, a troop train was derailed in the French Alps and 543 people were killed. In the harbor of Halifax, Canada, the French munitions ship *Mont Blanc* and the Belgian steamer *Imo* collided. Sixteen hundred people died in the ensuing explosion which leveled the city's north end, leaving at least six thousand homeless.

Also in Canada, the National Hockey League was formed in Montreal, Quebec. In baseball, Ernie Shore of the Boston Red Sox pitched a perfect game against the Washington Senators. The Chicago White Sox defeated the New York Giants to win the World Series.

In 1917, Auguste Rodin died. As did Edgar Degas, Scott Joplin, Tom Thomson, Ferdinand von Zeppelin, and Buffalo Bill Cody. Dutch-born dancer Mata Hari was convicted of spying for the Germans. More than fifty thousand Allied casualties were determined to have been the direct result of her treachery. She was executed by firing squad.

In 1917, Sigmund Freud published *Introduction to Psychoanalysis*, Carl Jung published *Psychology of the Unconscious*, and T. S. Eliot published "The Love Song of J. Alfred Prufrock." The annual salary of silent-film star Charlie Chaplin reached one million dollars.

Using equations derived from Einstein's general theory of relativity, German astronomer Karl Schwarzchild predicted the existence of black holes. The proposal first suggesting their existence was put forth in 1798 by Pierre Simon de Laplace, the same French astronomer whose 1812 mechanistic model of the universe would be displaced in 1927 by Werner Heisenberg's uncertainty principle, for which Heisenberg would receive the Nobel Prize in Physics in 1932.

Seven years later, in 1939, World War II began. Heisenberg played a leading role in German nuclear research. Heated controversy continues to surround Heisenberg's activities during the war, thus making the interpretation of his own life a matter of great uncertainty.

But in 1917, none of this was history yet: it was still the future, which is, by its very nature, always uncertain.

In the midst of all the history of 1917, there is no sign anywhere of Mary and three children in a valley called Cova da Iria near Fatima, Portugal. There is no mention made of secrets or the original sun miracle witnessed by seventy thousand people. No mention made of all those lives forever changed.

With or without the historians' acknowledgment, the story of Fatima continues. On May 13, 1981, the sixty-fourth anniversary of the first apparition, Pope John Paul II is shot by a Turkish terrorist in Saint Peter's Square in Rome. The assassination attempt occurs just as the pope is bending down to look at a medallion of Mary around the neck of a young girl. The shooter is Mehmet Ali Agca, a trained killer who is arrested minutes later. At his trial, Agca claims to be Jesus Christ and insists that the third secret be revealed. He is given a life sentence in an Italian prison. John Paul II credits Mary with saving his life and, as a gift of thanksgiving, the bullet removed from his body is embedded in the crown of her statue at Fatima.

A year later, on May 13, 1982, when John Paul II visits Fatima to thank Mary personally, another attempt is made on his life. A Spanish fanatic named Juan Fernandez Krohn, wearing a priest's black robes and carrying a bayonet, tries to break through the security cordon as the pope mounts the steps to the altar of the shrine. This time the pope is unharmed.

On May 13, 2000, John Paul II again visits Fatima, despite widespread fears that he is putting himself in danger by doing so. To the statue of Our Lady of Fatima he presents a second gift, a golden ring given to him at the beginning of his pontificate by his mentor, the late Polish Cardinal Stefan Wyszynski, and inscribed with his motto, *Totus tuus*, which means "All yours." He has come to beatify the two dead children, Jacinta and Francisco. Beatification is the last step before full sainthood and can be performed only after death. The ceremony is attended by over 700,000 people including the one surviving visionary, Sister Lucia, who is now ninety-three years old.

After performing the beatification mass, John Paul surprises everyone by revealing the third secret, which he had first read days after his election as pontiff in 1978. In addition to predicting the mass suffering of people throughout the twentieth century, Mary had also warned of the 1981 assassination attempt, describing "a bishop clothed in white" who "falls to the ground, apparently dead, under a burst of gunfire."

From his prison cell in Italy, Mehmet Ali Agca says that he was indeed compelled by a supernatural force to pull the trigger and that if his petition for early release is successful, he will travel to the shrine at Fatima and kneel before Mary for ten days in prayer.

Five days later, on May 18, 2000, the eightieth birthday of

John Paul II is marked in the largest concelebration in the history of the world.

The pope had requested clemency for his would-be assassin many times in the years since the shooting, and on June 13, 2000, Mehmet Ali Agca is pardoned by the Italian government and extradited to Turkey where he will serve eight years in prison for the murder of newspaper editor Abdi Ipekci in 1978.

With or without Mary, it seems to me that history itself, the actual unfolding of events through time, takes no prisoners: everybody dies in the end.

But the writing of history takes them by the thousands: prisoners of interpretation every one; prisoners of revisionism, positivism, determinism, deconstruction, reconstruction, skepticism, subjectivity, twenty-twenty hindsight, tunnel vision, cause and effect; prisoners of the paradox of being stuck in their own place in time.

Faith

In terms of faith, what brings meaning and integration to one's experience, the facts are quite secondary. It's the story (and not the facts) that grips the imagination, impregnates the heart, and animates the spirit within. . . .

—Diarmuid O'Murchu, *Quantum Theology*

On Saturday morning I stayed in bed until eight o'clock. It was the weekend after all and, although I work at home, I too tend to observe many of its time-honored traditions. I awoke to familiar sounds coming from the kitchen. I could hear the water running, the coffeemaker gurgling, and then the doors of the refrigerator and the cupboards being opened and closed several times. Still groggy, I was transported back to a time when I was a sleepy teenager still balled up in my blankets while my mother made a big Saturday morning breakfast for the family. In her efforts to roust me out of bed, she usually made as much noise as possible in the process. Any minute now she was likely to fire up the blender or even the vacuum cleaner just to get me moving.

But, of course, it was not my mother. It was Mary.

By the time I came fully awake and got out there, she was

setting the table and there was an open cookbook and a big bowl
on the counter beside the waffle iron which she had managed to
dig out from its usual hiding spot in the bottom cupboard. The
radio was on but it was no longer tuned to my regular station,
which would have been broadcasting news at this hour. Instead
she was listening to a program of Gregorian chant.

—Good morning, she said cheerfully. I hope you're hungry. I
wanted to surprise you.

Usually I eat a small breakfast of yogurt and fruit because I
know I *should*, not because I really want to. I am seldom ever
hungry first thing in the morning. But suddenly I was.

—How wonderful, I said. I'm starving.

She poured me a cup of coffee and handed me the newspaper.

—You sit down and relax, she said. I'll do the rest. I warned
you before that I'm not much of a cook, but I figured, with a little luck and the help of this cookbook, even I could manage to
whip up an acceptable batch of waffles.

I could not remember the last time anybody had made
breakfast for me and I was touched all out of proportion by her
simple gesture. My eyes filled foolishly with tickling tears.

She patted me on the shoulder and turned back to the counter,
measuring flour and cracking eggs into the bowl. I wanted nothing more than to lay my head down on the table and weep. With
gratitude, self-pity, and relief. But I did not.

I sipped my coffee and read the Books section instead. Soon
Mary was plopping two fat Belgian waffles onto our plates and
passing me the butter.

This time there was no talk of nutritional self-improvement
and the chronic quest for healthier habits. We slathered on the
butter and the maple syrup with shameless abandon, admiring
the way each perfect square filled up with the sweet melting
mixture.

—These are definitely the best waffles I have ever eaten, I said with my mouth full.

—Thank you, she said, obviously pleased. They *are* pretty good, even if I do say so myself.

We cleaned our plates with enthusiasm and then I poured us each another cup of coffee. We passed portions of the newspaper back and forth between us and read quietly for a while.

There were the usual front-section stories of catastrophic weather events, further dangerous developments in the world's current and/or chronic hot spots, political upheavals and shenanigans at home and abroad, as well as news of another gigantic corporate merger, another celebrity scandal, and another missing child.

The German philosopher Hegel once described the ritual reading of the daily paper as the secular equivalent to morning prayer. What manner of prayers are these, I wondered, and to whom should I address them?

I skimmed over all of these stories, unwilling at that pleasant moment in my comfortable kitchen with Mary beside me and more coffee brewing, to contemplate or even acknowledge the massive amount of misery in progress beyond the pretty walls of my home and the tranquil Saturday morning streets of my peaceful neighborhood. Habitually hungry for information though I may be, there are times when I just want to keep my head in the sand for another hour or two.

—The world is too much with us, I muttered with a nod to Wordsworth and turned to the potentially more palatable section called Life.

—Amen, Mary said, taking up the Books section that I had set aside earlier.

My attention was caught by the full-page story of a woman

named Ellen Sanderson who had been killed in a house fire in the large city to the west where I used to live. The top third of the page was filled by a photograph of this woman hamming it up in a jolly pose in front of a brick wall with frilly white curtains at the window and a pot of geraniums hanging beside the door. She looked to be about my age, of average height and weight, with tidy dark curly hair and glasses. She was wearing a stylish, knee-length summer dress and woven, low-heeled shoes. The story of her death was actually the story of her double life.

Ellen Sanderson had been employed as a secretary at a large insurance firm for the last ten years. Her coworkers knew her as a friendly, outgoing woman: busy mother of two teenagers, Sarah and Michael; happy wife of Bob, owner of a plumbing company; active member of a book club, a bowling team, and the church choir. Ellen kept photos of her family on her desk, changing them annually as the children grew. There was also a charming picture of their dog, Comet, a grinning yellow Lab. Ellen was well liked at work, especially known for the stories of family life that she told during lunch and coffee breaks with a flair for entertainment and humor just like Erma Bombeck.

She was very proud of their large home in the suburbs and liked to always have a new decorating project on the go. Sometimes she brought in paint chips, fabric swatches, and wallpaper samples to show what she was working on. None of her coworkers had ever been to Ellen's home, but once she had everything finished just right, she told them, she was going to throw a party and everybody would be invited. She was proud of her garden, too, and said she had once received honorable mention in a contest held by the local Horticultural Society. Sometimes she brought in flowers and shared them around the office. Sometimes she went out for drinks after work with the other secretaries, but not often because, although Bob was a wonderful man, she said, he was a lousy cook and, if she didn't get home and make supper, the kids would be dining on potato chips and chocolate ice cream.

But her death told a different story.

Shocked enough in the first place by this tragedy, her friends at work were puzzled by an obituary that made no mention of Sarah, Michael, or Bob. At the funeral, they were even more shocked to discover from Ellen's neighbors and her only surviving relative, a cousin from California, that she had, in fact, been a reclusive, never-married, childless woman who lived in a small apartment near the train station. There was no family, no house, no garden, no book club, no bowling team, no choir. There was no dog. The photos on her desk, as it turned out, were of her cousin's husband and children and the picture of the dog was the one that came with the frame. Apparently the flowers she brought to the office had been purchased at a nearby shop.

When interviewed by the journalist, the cousin admitted that she had suspected for years that Ellen was creating a fictional life for herself. She speculated that it had all started when Ellen was around thirty.

—Maybe she was tired, the cousin said. Tired of people always asking when she was going to settle down, get married, have children. Maybe she was tired of asking herself the same questions. Maybe she just wanted to feel normal.

The cousin told the reporter that she'd said nothing about it to anyone because she figured Ellen had a right to reinvent herself any way she wanted to. She wasn't hurting anyone, she wasn't committing any crimes in either of her incarnations, and she was happy enough in both.

—Maybe one life story is as good and as true as any other, the cousin said. Ellen had the best of both worlds. And besides, how many of us would not want to rewrite at least some part of our lives, if only we had the chance or the nerve?

I read parts of Ellen Sanderson's story aloud to Mary, who had started to clean up the kitchen.

—Not one of us is exactly who we appear to be, she said when I was finished.

—True enough, I agreed.

—And what about you? she asked over her shoulder as she headed down the hallway to get dressed.

It was a leading and/or loaded question, one I could have answered in any number of ways.

After we were both dressed, we set about doing the regular Saturday chores, and I chose then to answer Mary's question by picking up the story of my life where I had left off the day before. While we did the housework together, she encouraged me to go on with my story, and again she listened quietly, without judgment or impatience.

I am both the victim and the villain of this story.

I was about to turn thirty when I moved to this city. I was tired. I was still alone. I found myself slipping into the ever-seductive slough of despair. This was hardly unpredictable, considering that I had reached an age at which most people begin to have some reservations—about themselves, their lives, the past, and the future. This swamp of self-doubt led, also not unpredictably, to an obsessive spasm of self-examination. I desperately wanted to figure out what was wrong with me. I spent an inordinate amount of time studying pop psychology paperbacks and doing quizzes in women's magazines. I gave serious thought to questions like:

1. Would you rather be a dead hero or a live coward?
2. When you get up in the morning, do you check the color of your tongue?
3. If your best friend sleeps with your boyfriend, do you blame the man?
4. When somebody's dog licks your face, are you disgusted?
5. Have you ever thought you would be happier living alone on a desert island?
6. Do you frequently pray for favors or forgiveness?

My answers to these and other equally metaphysical questions would, the authors assured me, reveal my true personality. Using an intricate numerical scoring system, I would find out once and for all if I was pessimistic, optimistic, passive, aggressive (or passive-aggressive), impulsive, reliable, anxious, depressed, tender, or tough-minded. My score would also determine if I had leadership qualities.

Everybody knows these quizzes are stupid and I knew it, too, but I could hardly help myself. I felt compelled to seek them out and complete them, just in case everybody was wrong, just in case there really was one quiz somewhere that would explain my self to myself, a catechism of self-help that would open the door to the happiness to which I felt I was entitled but which stubbornly continued to elude me.

The trouble was that these quizzes allowed no room for uncertainty, no room for explanations, contradictions, exceptions, or extenuating circumstances. And so, given the choice of answering Yes, No, or Sometimes, I always chose Sometimes.

1. Sometimes I take my left sock off first.
2. Sometimes I wash my hands when they're not dirty.

3. Sometimes I watch sad movies in the middle of the night while crying and eating chocolate ice cream.

4. Sometimes I pray for favors and forgiveness.

The trouble was that Sometimes always scored zero. So no matter how carefully I calculated my score at the end of the quiz, I always ended up with nothing.

Finally I had to admit that I was getting nowhere and I made an appointment to see a therapist. After three sessions, she said there was nothing wrong with me. This was nice to hear but I was not convinced. I still believed that if only I tried hard enough and poked deep enough, I would wake up one morning utterly changed. As in my relationship with time, in my relationship with change I was chronically ambivalent. While mostly dreading change, at the same time I was also always longing for it.

After moving to this city, I stopped looking for love and ostensibly put all my time and energy into writing instead. Unlike love, literature, I figured, was something I understood at least partially, something for which I had already demonstrated an aptitude, a measure of talent, what some had called a gift. But still I thought of my singleness as a temporary condition and, although I was no longer actively seeking love, secretly I was practicing a kind of reverse psychology: secretly I was just waiting for love to find me instead. While thus biding my time, I kept thinking that if I told myself often enough that I did not want or need a man, then surely, in keeping with the irony that seemed to be the driving force of my life, the right one was bound to come along.

As far as love and romance went, my theoretical goal became

finding (or being found by) the one man with whom I could truly be myself, the *same* self that I was when I was alone. This man, while also being his same self with me as he was when he was alone, would proceed to love me *for* (rather than *in spite of*) my own true self, including the unsightly spider veins in my legs, the crepey skin around my eyes, the cellulite dimples in my thighs, my rather dismal history with men, and my tendency to think too much. The longer you contemplate it, the more complicated this theory becomes. According to both the uncertainty principle and practical experience, this theory, appealing and idyllic though it may be, is perhaps neither a reasonable nor an attainable goal. I dated a handful of men during those years but not one of them was the right one.

When I was in my thirties, I sat astride the spiky fence of time, living my life as if the present had little value in itself, as if it were merely a way station: a coda to the past and a preamble to the future.

During those years, I existed in a constant state of regret and anticipation. Regret: for all the mistakes I had made, all the years I had wasted, all the times I had made a fool of myself (mostly for love, *always* for love). Anticipation: believing that just around the corner lay happiness, peace of mind, the perfect life, and that someday I would indeed reach that mythical promised land if only I could get through *now* and make my way to *then*. But the ever-present underbelly of all this anticipation was sheer dread: my sometimes paralyzing fear that just around the *other* corner lay calamity, disaster, tragedy, and death—a sudden, random, gruesome death or a painful, prolonged, also gruesome death—either way, an early death, by which my future would, of course, be rendered utterly null and void. Happiness around one corner and tragedy around the other—that left two corners still unaccounted for. I did not know what to think about them.

I tried to hold these two opposing pictures of my future in my head simultaneously. I tried to figure out how I could live each day as if it might be my last, while at the same time fully expecting that I would indeed live forever—and happily at that.

When I was not thinking that my life was going to end before I got to the good part, I was still thinking, in my heart of hearts (which may be where such thoughts are located—if a thought can be said to have a location—thoughts of the heart rather than of the mind, maybe then not what I should call thoughts at all, but do, for want of a better word, thus giving testament to the all-pervasive struggle of trying to put into words that which resists language—perhaps not thoughts at all then, but something else again: hopes, wishes, dreams, delusions, or rumors of faith) that everything I had lost along the way would someday be returned to me a hundredfold and more, that all my trials and tribulations would be rewarded and revealed to have been worth it in the end, that I would indeed eventually find that proverbial pot of gold at the end of the proverbial rainbow, never questioning where I, like most people, had acquired the idea that God does indeed have a happy ending in store for each and every one of us, never doubting that "happily ever after" was exactly what I deserved.

(Fond as I am of long looping sentences cantilevered with clauses and stitched together with commas as intricately as lace, the preceding is arguably the most complex sentence I have ever written, providing still further evidence of what every writer is bound to discover eventually: that not only is language, that finest of human inventions, inherently inadequate as the tool for the expression of that which we most want and need to say, but that punctuation and grammar have their limitations too.)

Despite occasional lapses into pessimism, cynicism, and downright despair, still we cling, by and large, to the prospect of a happy ending, a fortuitous *dénouement* that we perceive as a promise, a covenant, a God-given birthright: *All things shall come to he who will but wait.* Perhaps I should not generalize or presume to speak for everyone but who, after all, hopes for an unhappy ending?

Perhaps our dogged devotion (practiced with varying measures of patience and impatience) to the pursuit of our own happiness is the ultimate manifestation of what Coleridge called "that willing suspension of disbelief . . . which constitutes poetic faith." His call for faith has as much to do with life as with literature, with reality as with poetry, with truth as with fiction. We are holding out for a happy ending but take a look around: how many people do you know who are actually having one?

Our persistent belief in our own future happiness is perhaps the better part of faith in our ordinary everyday lives: *Now faith is the substance of things hoped for, the evidence of things not seen.*

Against all odds and despite all evidence to the contrary, still we trust that there will indeed be a light at the end of the tunnel, of our own personal tunnel anyway. But what if there isn't? What if there is only the back wall of the tunnel, a concrete wall four feet thick and covered with spiderwebs, mold, graffiti, and bats?

I am both the victim and the villain of this story.

Grace

As for myself, I have come to think of Mary as the patron saint of "both/and" passion over "either/or" reasoning, and as such, she delights my poetic soul. Ever since I first encountered Mary . . . I have learned never to discount her ability to confront and disarm the polarities that so often bring human endeavours to impasse: the subjective and objective, the expansive and the parochial, the affective and the intellectual.

—Kathleen Norris, *Amazing Grace*

This is not irony so much as grace, that in learning to be faithful to his vow of celibacy, the monk developed his talent for relationship.

—Kathleen Norris, *The Cloister Walk*

By mid-afternoon on Saturday, Mary and I had vacuumed the whole house including under the beds, dusted everything including the books and the pots and pans hanging on the cast-iron rack, cleaned the bathroom from top to bottom, and washed the kitchen floor. We had also stripped and remade the beds, changed the towels, and carried all the dirty clothes down to the laundry room in the basement.

As we sorted it into appropriate piles, I could not help but notice that her clothes were no more unusual than mine and that, as far as our laundry went anyway, neither of us came close to matching the mystery of my neighbor's shirts that I had been trying to decipher the day she arrived.

I put in the first load and then launched into a detailed lecture on how to work the washing machine. As I droned on, Mary reached past me, twirled the several dials, and closed the lid with a laugh.

—I think I've got it, she said. You know, it's been centuries now since I had to do laundry on a rock in the river.

Back upstairs, she proceeded, without comment, to pull the refrigerator away from the wall and vacuum all the furry dust off the exposed coils on the back, while I fussed around her with embarrassment, muttering about sloth and sin and how I'd meant to do that weeks ago. She waved away my apologies and promised not to look in the oven.

As I have already said, I am a perfunctory housekeeper, tending to approach the whole enterprise with ambivalence at best and with seething resentment at worst. I have always thought of these tasks as being somehow separate from and at odds with my real life. And, while performing them, I am frequently bogged down by the knowledge that no matter what I do accomplish, it is essentially a futile exercise because it will not stay done for long. Whether this is part of my nature or simply a matter of long habit, I cannot say for sure. Maybe it's nothing more than a case of protracted adolescent rebellion against my mother, who was always cleaning something and seemed to derive inordinate amounts of satisfaction, pleasure, and pride from the never-ending eradication of dirt, dust, and all forms of untidiness.

Mary, too, tackled each new chore with fresh vigor. She actually seemed to be enjoying herself. But how often did she have to do housework anyway? I wondered. Perhaps even cleaning the toilet could be an amusing novelty if you only had to do it every twenty years or so.

Despite these rather unkind thoughts, still I suspected there was something important to be learned here. Mary seemed to approach housekeeping as an action, rather than a reaction. As she worked, it was clear that she was involved not in a process of negation (of dirt, dust, and the inevitable debris spawned by every activity of daily life) but of creation (of order, shiny surfaces, perfectly aligned towels, floors to which your feet did not stick). She seemed to have no doubt that what she was doing was important. She had faith, obviously, in the restorative power of domesticity.

But I decided to leave the contemplation of the possible joys of good housekeeping for later. Mostly, by mid-afternoon, I was just glad to have accomplished as much as we had. I was not willing to even consider the possibility that the Virgin Mary had come to me to teach me a lesson about keeping a cleaner house and enhancing my spirituality in the process.

For now, it was time to make my weekly pilgrimage to the grocery store. Mary said that, if I didn't mind, she thought she would just stay home. She had a few things she needed to do, she said. I did not question what those things might be. I headed off alone, reflecting yet again on the fact that, since I work at home and set my own hours, I could conceivably get my groceries anytime, so why do I always end up shopping on Saturday afternoon with seven million other people?

I returned an hour later, with an empty wallet and a car full of food. As I carried three or four bags at a time in through the back door, I noticed that Mary's runners were not there in the porch where they had been. Her brown cardigan was not hanging from the wooden rack on the wall. In fact, there was no sign of her at all.

I went into the kitchen. The radio was still playing softly into the now very clean but very empty room. I called her name. There was no answer. I went back into the porch and called down the stairs, thinking she might be in the laundry room finishing up the last couple of loads. There was still no answer.

Fearing the worst, I was just heading for the front closet to see if her trench coat was still there, when suddenly she materialized at the end of the hallway, having apparently just stepped out of her room.

—Oh good, you're back, she said, sounding rather flustered. I was . . . I was . . . I was just outside having a look around, she added, by way of explanation, I supposed, for the fact that she was wearing both her runners and her cardigan.

If I hadn't known better, I would have thought she had a guilty conscience or at least that she was bent on keeping something from me and practicing the fine art of mental reservation in the process.

She hung up her sweater and took off her shoes which, I noticed, looked a little wet. Then she helped me put away the groceries, chatting on about my garden, my flower beds, how it would soon be time to put in the annuals, and how the grass would need mowing before you knew it. She kept up a steady stream of conversation that did not require much in the way of response from me and that also did not allow room for any questions. Then she gave what struck me as an exaggerated stretch and a forced yawn.

—It's been a busy day, she said. I think I'll just have a little nap before dinner.

She went to her room and closed the door. I went to the basement and took the last load of laundry out of the dryer. Then I, too, had a nap, nodding off quickly in my white bedroom that was, I noted, even more soothing and attractive for having been thoroughly tidied and cleaned. I fell asleep happily, even while appreciating the freshness of the bedding and the orderliness of everything back in its place. I fell asleep quickly, secure in the knowledge that, for the moment anyway, there were no rambunctious dust bunnies gleefully reproducing themselves beneath me.

After dinner that evening, I set up the ironing board in the living room. With Glenn Gould once again on the CD player and Mary curled up with a cup of tea in one of the armchairs, I proceeded to make my way through the pile of clean clothes in the wicker laundry basket.

Ironing, I can honestly say, is one household chore that I do truly enjoy. I find it relaxing and comforting: the smooth pointed glide of the iron, the steamy hot smell of the fabric, the tug of the muscles in my upper arm. I still use a heavy steam iron that must be twenty years old now. I bought a new one once, not because there was anything wrong with the old one but just because I thought it was time. But I found it unsatisfying. It was too light in my hand, altogether lacking the serious and stalwart heft of the old one, so I returned it to the store with a flimsy excuse, got my money back, and carried on happily as before.

While I ironed, Mary and I chatted about nothing special. Somehow, no matter what topic we touched on, the conversation kept coming around again to me. Was she gently steering me back to telling her the rest of the story of my life? Or was it simply that, the floodgates having been opened, I, being as self-absorbed as the next person, could not help but start talking about myself again?

*   *   *

Whether or not I have rewritten the story of my past, now that I am in my forties, I have indeed had to rewrite the story of my future as I told it to my younger self. I have come now to the place in my life where I have to admit that it is not going to turn out the way I had assumed it would. I am not going to get married, have children, and live happily ever after in all the traditional ways. Now that I am in my forties, I can see that certain kinds of change are no longer likely, perhaps no longer possible. It is as if, while certain doors were opening before me, others were falling shut behind, closing silently, so silently that I never even noticed. It is as if for a long time my life was all potential but then, having made a series of choices, decisions, and mistakes, the other options became no longer available.

I believe that sometimes you just have to decide: decide to stop feeling badly about yourself, decide to stop wanting what you do not (and apparently cannot) have. You must decide to stop believing that your real life (the life you were *supposed* to have, as opposed to the one you *do* have, this one in which you have been feeling unfulfilled, unappreciated, and unloved) is elsewhere.

Having come now to this realization, I like to think that I have accepted it gracefully enough. Neither searching nor waiting brought me to the romantic happy ending I had in mind. I see now that neither regret nor anticipation served me well. Now I tell myself that what I am living is my life and I had best get on with it.

I know I have lost something by coming to this conclusion, and yet it is liberating too. I have stopped hoping for the standard happy ending. I have stopped bracing myself for either the worst or the best. I think I have accepted the fact that, try as I may, there is no way of knowing what will happen next, no way of knowing how my story will end. If there is a trick to life, maybe it lies in being able to experience this uncertainty with detachment, rather than with doubt and fear. Although I do not always understand the difference between acceptance and resignation, still I am no longer holding my breath in the face of the future and this, in itself, is a great relief.

Now I understand that an essential part of becoming happily middle-aged is being able to acknowledge and accept your limitations, to recognize that what you have always thought of as your weaknesses may be, in fact, your strengths, and so also may your strengths prove to be your weaknesses. Now I understand that losing one thing may open the door to finding something even better. The irony of this does not escape me.

I have finally given up feeling sorry for myself about being alone, being alone again on a Saturday night, ironing maybe, as I was that night. Or watching a funny video and making my solitary-laughter smile and sound into the empty room. Or maybe watching a romantic drama and crying at a happy ending even more than at a sad one. It has been years now since I allowed myself the luxury of imagining a man there on the couch beside me, sharing my popcorn, handing me another Kleenex, rubbing my feet, or resting his handsome head in my lap.

I try no longer to think of my singleness as something that has happened to me: something like a car accident, something unfortunate and unfair, something that I have suffered, through no fault of my own. Make no mistake: I am not always successful

in this endeavour. But when I am, I can now think of my singleness as something that I have chosen. Admittedly, I do not yet
know when or why I made this choice.

I do know that my singleness is not some kind of ascetism or
abnegation or martyrdom. Nor is it a punishment, a condemnation, an abomination, an embarrassment, an inversion of the natural order, or a cruel joke played upon me by God.

Having been alone for all these years, I know a lot more
about relationships now than I did when I was actually having
them. Again, the irony of this does not escape me. Now I understand that finding a man is not the answer, whatever you think
you have lost, whatever the question may be.

That Saturday night, as I unplugged the iron and folded up
the board (which emitted its customary earsplitting, metal-on-
metal shriek in the process), I said:

—Irony has been the hallmark of my life.

Even to me, this pronouncement sounded more than a little
pretentious.

Mary looked puzzled for a moment and then she laughed.

—Oh, irony! she cried. I thought you said "ironing."

—That too, I said, joining in her laughter.

I admitted that I have been known, in times of great stress,
to take half a dozen perfectly pressed shirts from my closet and
iron them again, just for the sake of it, just to calm myself down.
But for now I was finished and it was time to put the iron and
the board away.

Becoming serious again, Mary said:

—Sometimes what looks like irony turns out to be in fact
grace.

* * *

Having abandoned my quest for love, now I have put my faith in books instead. The joy and satisfaction I take from them (from reading them, writing them, buying them, owning them) never diminishes and, unlike most things, is never diluted by repetition.

On a good day, when I am writing and it is going well, this is the only time that I am truly happy. This is the feeling I love the most. This is enough. This is better than winning the lottery. This is better than hearing the words "I love you" at long last fall from those much-desired lips that are at long last clamped onto yours. I might even go so far as to say that this is better than sex. (Or at least this is better than my memory of sex. I read somewhere once that it is because we can never remember exactly what sex feels like, that we are compelled to keep having it over and over again. I wish I could remember who said this. I also wish I could figure out exactly how this idea is connected to the theory that those who cannot remember the past are doomed to repeat it.)

Of course there are bad days, too, days when the words won't come and the possibility of my ever writing another good sentence again seems unlikely and I cannot imagine why I ever wanted to be a writer in the first place. On those days I am plunged into a pit of despair, crippled by a crisis of faith, engulfed by a mushroom cloud of misery unlike anything known, I presume, to the average accountant, beautician, bank teller, pharmacist, auto mechanic, or anybody else who has been smart enough *not* to become a writer and has pursued instead some saner, more reasonable, less capricious career.

Much as I have convinced myself that books are enough, still there are times when I think of a book that was given to me twenty years ago by an old boyfriend, a slim volume called *Books Are Not Life, But Then, What Is?* I have never actually read this book, but I haven't had the heart to give it away either, if only because someday I might or maybe because the man had signed it to me with all his love and that makes me feel guilty for having been unkind to him in the end.

Much as I have convinced myself that what I have is enough, still there are dangerous moments in the day when my energy and my enthusiasm can abruptly leak away, when I lose faith and cannot get it back. I find myself then in the grip of what the early desert fathers called the "noonday demon" or "acedia," one of the original seven deadly sins. This demon convinces me that my whole life is utterly devoid of meaning, nothing more than an apparently endless series of useless days that must somehow be endured.

This seldom happens at those moments when you would most expect it. It seldom happens when I sit down to dinner alone (again), or when I climb into bed alone (again), or when I wake up in the morning alone (again). More often than not it happens at less predictable moments when suddenly and for no good reason, I feel bereft and unequal to the task at hand, be it making the bed, doing the dishes, going to the bank, washing my hair, or writing another book. Sometimes it happens when I walk into the kitchen and am confronted by the telephone poised there on its stand beside the fridge, mute but always harboring the potential of ringing at exactly the wrong moment or of not ringing ever again (either way announcing, after all, that it is not enough).

I would like to know if other people have these moments too.

These intermittent losses of faith (or confidence or courage or strength or nerve or heart or all of the above, each being a constituent of faith) would seem to have little to do with love or loneliness. Rather, they seem to be about something less tangible, something to do with purpose or meaning or a sudden visceral suspicion of the lack thereof. At my age, maybe they are intimations of mortality or maybe they are simply a reaction to the drudgery of dailiness, a mute reiteration of the age-old question, Is that all there is?

Sometimes such a moment is brought on by a memory, a fleeting but vivid image from the past that springs to mind for no apparent reason. These memories take the form of pictures as clear and potent as photographs. I see myself sitting on the green wooden bench in the far corner of the playground where, as a child, I once ate three blue popsicles in a row, and where, as a teenager, I once kissed a boy for an hour straight. I see myself in a green dress in a dimly lit restaurant where I once put forkful after forkful of jambalaya into my mouth while my date ordered another bottle of wine and asked the waitress for her phone number. I see myself in a red plaid shirt waiting for the phone to ring. I see myself in a black wool coat shrugging my shoulders and walking away. I see myself in a white cotton nightgown crying.

Mostly I bat away these memories and these moments like a horse batting away flies with its tail.

—I'm okay, I say to myself when they catch me.

—I'm fine, I say out loud into the empty house.

Sometimes I say this a hundred times in a day. I would like to know if other people do this too.

It was not until I told my story to Mary that I understood how much I am missing, how much I have lost, how hard I have worked to convince myself that I am happy with my life as it is. But I also began to understand how much I have learned, how much I have indeed changed. For all those years before, I was always dreading and hoping and waiting for change, imagining that when it finally happened it would be sudden and unmistakable, like turning on a lightbulb, like night and day, black and white, then and now. It was only in the telling of my story that I could recognize how change has been happening all along. Now I understand that change (like time, history, and words) is both quick and slow. Too quick. Too slow. Now I understand that it is time I stopped telling the story of my life only in terms of the men I have loved, lost or found or both.

It was not until I told my story to Mary that I understood that the hardest person in the world to forgive is yourself. And that the hardest person in the world to have faith in is also yourself. I am still trying to reconcile who I am *now* with who I was *then*. I know my former self is still there, waving to me through time just like a phantom limb. I am still trying to figure out how I both am and am not the person I was then, the person I appear to be now, the person that I think I am; how I both am and am not the person that I will eventually become. If who I am now is the "real" me, then who was the person I used to be: an impostor, a fugitive in disguise, the out-of-focus shadow of my future self? If who I am now is the "real" me, then who is the person I will be twenty or thirty years from now?

My own penchant for order and clarity does not happily or easily admit the contradictions and the opposites within me. I have problems with paradox. If I am *this*, then how can I be *that*? When I was younger, I thought I could be only one or the other. I did not understand how I could be both.

From a very early age, we are indoctrinated into seeing the world in pairs of opposites. Think of all those children's books in which the world is so clearly and cleverly laid out two by two: big and little, boy and girl, stop and go, up and down, happy and sad. Perhaps it is some unconscious atavistic longing for the simplicity of the old mechanistic universe (where there were no contradictions and all mysteries could be solved) that keeps us clinging to these tidy constructs: yes and no, weak and strong, give and take, love and hate, heaven and earth. Perhaps it is some subliminal collective nostalgia for the good old days of Plato and Heraclitus (before Einstein and relativity, Heisenberg and uncertainty, quantum physics and chaos theory) that keeps us stuck in the resolute land of opposites: body and soul, lost and found, life and death, good and evil, truth and lies.

Fact and fiction.

Victim and villain.

Alpha and omega.

Beginning and ending.

Virgin and mother.

Human and divine.

It is time now to venture out of the comforting land of either/or opposites and travel into the uncertain territory of both/and. Time to realize that irony is not cynicism, paradox is not chaos, and prayer is not wishful thinking. Time to accept the possibility that these, irony, paradox, and prayer, are the still points, the thin places, the perfect quantum qualities. It is time now to admit that reality is not as simple as we would like it to be and that, given half a chance, it will indeed expand to fill the space available.

Gifts

And though I still make mistakes, I am less inclined to delude myself about their cost. I no longer expect things to make sense. I know there is no safety. But that does not mean there is no magic. It does not mean there is no hope. It simply means that each of us has reason to be wishful and frightened, aspiring and flawed. And it means that to the degree that we are lost, it is on the same ocean, in the same night.

—Elizabeth Kaye, *Mid-Life: Notes from the Halfway Mark*

*W*hen I awoke on Sunday morning, I knew she was already gone. The very air in the house was altered by her absence.

I got up slowly. I put on my glasses. I took my house-coat from its hook on the back of the door and wrapped it tightly around my waist. Even through my slippers the floor felt cold.

I peeked into the kitchen. It was empty. I went down the hallway to her room. It was empty too. Everything in it was exactly as it had been before she arrived. The room, which had been somehow enlarged by her presence, had shrunk back now to its former size. It was once again a small, ordinary bedroom furnished with odds and ends. The bed, the night table, the bookcase, the armchair, and the trunk had all returned to their former simple selves. Reflected in the mirror on the dresser, they were nothing more than pieces of furniture with their subatomic particles invisible and their feet planted firmly on the floor, bearing little or no resemblance, I presumed, to that perfect furniture which graced Plato's higher plane of reality.

The closet door was open and I could see the few rejected items of clothing I had hung there a week before. The rest of the hangers on the rod were empty and swaying slightly in the still air as if in the wake of someone having passed by just a moment before.

The curtains were closed and, in the shadowy half-light, I didn't notice at first that there was something sitting on the folded afghan at the foot of the neatly made bed.

I switched on the lamp and then I saw what she had left me. It was the carved wooden box into which we had put the milagros on the first night of her visit. Having still not completely shaken off my expectation of some flashy pyrotechnics, I lifted the lid cautiously. Again, no music, no light, no butterflies, no angels, no doves. And again, a frisson of disappointment on my part. But there were the milagros: an eclectic assortment of prayers and promises, a catholic collection of questions and answers, all the holy relics of the lost and found.

Tucked beneath the box, with just one corner showing, was a small white envelope. On the front was my name, written in black ink in a fine calligraphic hand. I realized that I had not seen any samples of her handwriting during the past week, but of course it was hers. I would have known it anywhere.

Inside was a single folded piece of paper, heavy, creamy, edged with gold. Her note was brief:

It's time for me to go now. It will soon be May and I am needed else-where. Thank you for everything. Keep in touch. I am with you always.
   Love, Mary.

I sat on the bed for a length of time that could have been sec-onds or hours. I held her note in my hand and the box on my lap. Over and over again I slipped my other hand deep into the box, lifting the milagros and letting them fall. Winking in the light of the bedside lamp, they slid through my fingers like sand or pearls.

I could not immediately think of what to do next. I could not imagine how I was going to pass the rest of this day or any other.

Finally I put the note into the box and carried it to my bed-room. I opened the top drawer of my dresser and took out my charm bracelet. I put the bracelet into the wooden box on top of the milagros and the note. I put the box on top of the dresser beside the white candles.

Then I went into the kitchen and made coffee, just as I did every morning. I turned on the radio. The weather report prom-ised clouds, wind, and rain for the morning, clearing later in the afternoon.

I went to the back porch and brought in the newspaper. The wind pulled the open door from my hand. It banged against the side of the house before I could grab it and pull it closed again.

I stood and looked out the kitchen window while the coffee brewed. The sky was more like autumn than spring. The clouds were moving in the opposite direction to what they usually do on a windy day. I thought about how many ways there are to describe dark gray clouds passing quickly across a colorless sky. It began to rain. A robin flitted around in the lower branches of the fir tree. A red car passed in the street going too fast, its driver

intent upon his destination, whatever it might be, and oblivious
to me, the observer there at the window, alone and invisible.

When the coffee was ready, I poured myself a cup and opened
the fridge to get out the milk. There in the middle of the top
shelf sat a plain white bowl with three plums in it. Purple, perfect, out of season. I ate them and then licked the sweet juice
from my fingers one by one.

I opened the newspaper. I was not really reading. I was just
turning the pages and skimming the headlines out of habit.
Toward the back of the section called Life, on a page filled
mostly with stories about fashion, food, and a new treatment for
depression, with ads for luxury cars, laptop computers, and diamond jewelry, my eyes fell upon a small headline in the lower
lefthand corner. It said: MOTHER MARY TO THE RESCUE.

The item below was short, not more than four column
inches. It told the story of two young brothers who lived on a
farm twelve hundred miles west of here. It seemed that, on the
previous afternoon, despite their mother's repeated warnings,
they had been playing near a creek at the far edge of their property. Although normally shallow and innocuous, the creek was
now swollen with the spring run-off. The younger boy, who was
only five, slipped and fell into the deep, fast-flowing water. Neither of the boys knew how to swim. The other brother, who was
eight, ran back to the farmhouse for help. By the time he returned
with his frantic mother in tow, the younger boy was sitting on a
tree stump beside the creek, perfectly safe and dry and eating a
chocolate bar.

He said that a pretty lady in a long black dress, a brown
sweater, and white Nikes had come swooping out of the sky like
a giant bird and plucked him from the water. He, of course, was
terrified. But the lady, he told them, said:

—Fear not. It's me, Mary, Mother of God.

Then, the little boy explained, she set him down on the tree stump and gave him a chocolate bar and a stern lecture about the importance of listening to his mother.

Just as the boy finished telling his story, the pretty lady stepped out from behind a large tree. Her feet were not touching the ground and there was a circle of stars around her head. She smiled and waved and then she disappeared.

Upon witnessing this, the boys' mother, a devout Catholic, fell immediately to her knees, sobbing and praising God. She had no doubt, she said, that the Virgin Mary herself had come down from heaven and saved her young son's life.

I had no doubt either.

And now I knew where Mary had been the afternoon before while I was at the grocery store.

I continued to go through the motions of morning. I went into the bathroom, brushed my teeth, washed my face, and fixed my hair. I went into my bedroom, got dressed, put away my nightgown, and made the bed. I went back into the kitchen. I put the plum pits in the compost bucket, set the white bowl in the sink, and poured myself yet another cup of coffee. Just as the grandfather clock was striking ten, I went into the living room to open the drapes.

There was a statue standing in front of the fig tree.

She was about three feet tall, wearing a long white gown trimmed with gold at the neck and the hem. Over her dress there was a blue cape also edged with gold and, over her hair, a white shawl. There was a gold cincture at her waist. Her hands were raised to her breasts and between them there was a painted red heart with pink rosebuds encircling it and yellow flames shooting from the top. The heart was pierced by a golden sword. Her head was slightly bowed and her brown eyes were downcast. Her pale plaster skin was flawless and her pink lips were caught in a gentle half-smile. Her bare feet, perched on the top half of a blue globe, were very small.

Taking a step closer, I could see there was a silver chain around her neck. Hanging from it was a simple gold cross and one silver milagro. It was a miniature book, opened flat to reveal two blank pages.

I made my solitary-laughter smile and sound into the empty room. Then I carefully picked up the statue. She was much heavier than she looked. Cradling her in my arms, I went down the hallway to my study.

I set the statue down in the corner between my computer desk and my work table. I lifted the necklace from her neck and placed it around my own. The cross and the book were cold against my skin.

I opened the blue notebook. I began to write:

Looking back on it now, I can see there were signs. In the week before it happened, there was a string of unusual events that I noticed but did not recognize. Seemingly trivial, apparently unconnected, they were not even events really, so much as odd occurrences, whimsical coincidences, amusing quirks of nature or fate. It is only now, in retrospect, that I can see them for what they were: eclectic clues, humble omens, whispered heralds of the approach of the miraculous.

Her skin was very smooth, golden brown as if she had been spending time in the southern sun. Her eyes were deep brown and the skin below them was a little crepey and thin-looking. There were fine friendly lines around her mouth.

Tell me no secrets, I'll tell you no lies.

I knew that I was already in over my head. She was already here. She had already talked to me, eaten with me, used my bathroom. I knew there could be no turning back now. I knew there was nothing else I could do.
    —Yes, I said. Yes, of course you can stay.

I could hardly write fast enough to keep up with the sentences that were coming fully formed into my mind.

Over and over again, they whispered their prayers of petition. Sometimes their prayers were answered.

And sometimes, sweating and sleepless in the middle of a long hot night, I, too, with the humid darkness pressing down upon my mouth like a hand, had whispered:
    —Forgive me, God. Please forgive me.

I already know how stories are made.

Ideas were sparking off each other like flint, tumbling one after another through my brain like autumn leaves in a windstorm. I felt a little feverish, breathless, shaky. My heart was beating too fast. I was talking aloud to myself or to the statue as I wrote.

Everything they have ever said about me has become true.
In one way or another.

Years have passed since that day. It is another spring now, an unreliable one this time, balmy one day and frigid again the

next. Easter was late this year, falling near the end of April. That
weekend there was an overnight storm, and in the morning the
budding tulips were buried under six inches of snow. By the next
morning it had melted and all around the neighborhood the
flowers had cheerfully reemerged, undaunted by their ordeal.

The neighborhood itself has both changed and stayed the
same. It is still quiet, comfortable, respectable, and safe. But
there have been a few more paint jobs, two new front decks, one
new garage, and a major addition to the house across the street
occasioned by the birth of their fourth child, a girl this time.
Bulldog, ferocious guardian of his front yard, is older but no
wiser. For reasons unknown to the rest of us, Peter and his
family, the people with five striped shirts and Jesus' face on their
clothesline, did not stay long. Their house is now occupied by a
young childless couple who are never home and who apparently
dry their clothes in the dryer.

There have been a few changes at my house, too, both inside
and out. I have had my driveway resurfaced and my roof reshin-
gled. I have painted the bathroom green. I have hung new ivory-
colored drapes in the living room and, of course, new calendars
throughout the house each January first.

My kitchen calendar this year features twelve paintings by
Salvador Dalí. The picture for last month, April, was *The Persis-
tence of Memory* with its familiar melting watches and a distorted
face with long eyelashes lowered, sleeping, we presume, or dead
or otherwise lost in some metaphysical limbo where time and
space do not exist. It is May now and this month's image is *The
Madonna of Port Lligat.*

Against a background of deep blue sky and slightly deeper
blue water, Mary sits with the baby Jesus on her lap. They are
framed by six unconnected blocks of masonry floating above the
water, two of them cracked and worn to reveal layers of rock

inside. Mary and Jesus, too, are floating unanchored in space. Directly above Mary's head hangs an egg suspended by a string from a large, bowl-shaped seashell. There are other shells in the picture, too, also a gold-embroidered square of cloth, two somewhat battered lemons, and a fish on a broken plate, all of these laid before her like gifts. She is wearing a voluminous gown with red shoulders, blue sleeves, lilac and brown layers of satin draped over her legs and feet. Her head is bowed, her eyes are closed, her hands are raised in an incomplete gesture of prayer.

But whole parts of her body are missing: her upper arms, her throat, a wedge-shaped piece in the middle of her head. Her torso is an open rectangle in which Jesus sits, floating above a green cushion. His head, too, is bowed and he is naked. In the middle of his chest there is a small rectangle like the opening for a lightswitch. In his right thigh there is a circular hole with a cross at the bottom, forming the traditional scientific symbol for woman.

When I began to write this book, I had no idea how it would end. I had to put my faith in the process of writing it. I had to believe that in the time it would take to tell this story, the ending would sort itself out and come clear to me. I have always known that writing is an act of faith, the one which has always been my own salvation. I imagined that, given time, I would find the perfect ending after all, the ending which would unlock the beginning and, when I looked back over the story I had written, everything that came before would be changed and it would all make sense.

I have come now to the end. The statue stands beside me as I write. I wear the silver necklace while I work, often rubbing the little book milagro between my fingers like a worry stone. By the time I'm finished for the day, it is warm when I hang it back around her neck. I like to imagine it filling up again with stories while I sleep.

When I am expecting visitors (family or friends, the plumber, the electrician, or the refrigerator repairman), I hide the statue in my bedroom closet.

—Sorry, sorry, sorry, I say as I tuck her carefully in among the tail ends of my clothes and they fall softly over her face.

She doesn't seem to mind. When I return later to rescue her and carry her back to my study, she is smiling just the same. But she has never moved around the house on her own. She has never changed position or color. She has never wept tears, oil, milk, or blood.

Sometimes I talk to her. Sometimes I tell her what I've been doing lately, how the book is going, when I hope and/or expect to have it finished. I suspect she already knows all this, but I tell her anyway. Sometimes I ask her the questions I should have asked when she was here but didn't, out of diffidence, discretion, or imagining that I had all the time in the world to find the answers and get it right.

Sometimes I pray and sometimes my prayers are answered.

But I still have my questions. I still have my doubts. I still often feel fed up with all the irony and injustice and suffering in the world. I still watch the ten o'clock news every night and frequently find myself furious with God. I am still alone and sometimes I am still afraid. I still don't understand about evil.

—I don't know, I say to the statue and she remains silent.

She, in fact, has never said a single word. The irony of this does not escape me.

But sometimes, early in the morning, when the light is just

right, her brown eyes are shining, her silver-streaked curls are sneaking out around the edges of her white shawl, and I can see the fine friendly lines around her mouth.

I have come now to the end and all I know for certain is that I both am and am not the same person I was when I began. I know that I have barely begun to fathom the gifts that Mary gave me.

I know now that her story will continue whether I am writing it or not. Now I understand that there is no way of knowing how the story will end: her story, my story, yours.

And that, for the time being, is a great relief. That, in itself, is an unspeakable gift.

Author's Notes and Acknowledgments

One evening in the spring of 1996 I happened by chance to watch a television documentary called *Miracles and Visions: Fact or Fiction?*, broadcast on the Fox network. Of all the miraculous events it included, I was especially intrigued by the stories of those who claimed to have seen the Virgin Mary. This, of course, was something I had heard about but not something to which I had ever given much serious thought.

Fascinated, I began reading about Marian apparitions and, like the narrator of this novel, I soon discovered that the body of material available was truly enormous and that my research was leading me in all kinds of unusual directions. As I began to formulate my own thoughts about the Marian apparitions, the uncertainty principle, quantum physics, irony, narrative, fact, fiction, and both/and possibility over either/or opposites, I was increasingly excited to discover repeatedly in my reading that others had made these connections too. Also like the narrator, I was actually in the early stages of writing another novel at that time but soon I put that book aside and began to write this one.

Although the story of Mary's visit to the narrator is fictional, all but one of the historical apparitions included in this book are based on actual documented accounts. The exception is the one in the last chapter, which is wholly invented. For the others, I have remained faithful to the records of these events. Although, as described in "History (7)," skeptics take the whole notion of apparitions to be pure fiction, I took the opposite approach. In shaping and retelling these stories for the purposes of my narrative, I worked from the basic premise that it was all true. In most cases, several accounts of each apparition were available. Where these differed in the details, I chose to follow what was reported most consistently. For example, in the story of Our Lady of Einsiedeln that appears in "History (1)," one account said Meinrad's pet birds were ravens, but two others said they were crows. So I chose to make them crows. Wanting to honor these visions as they have been recorded, I felt free to invent only minor descriptive details about the visionaries, the settings, the weather, and such. I did not invent any of what they said they saw and heard during these experiences.

As Sara Maitland writes in the Introduction to her book *A Big-Enough God: A Feminist's Search for a Joyful Theology*: "I am not a theologian. I am a Christian . . . and a writer: a fictionalizer, a liar in Plato's definition." I am also not a philosopher, a historian, a scientist, or a Catholic. Any errors of understanding and interpretation in these matters are mine.

Of the many books I used in my research, those that I found the most valuable include:

Answered Prayers: Miracles and Milagros Along the Border by Eileen Oktavec (Tucson, Arizona: University of Arizona Press, 1995).

Brave Souls: Writers and Artists Wrestle With God, Love, Death, and the Things That Matter by Douglas Todd (Toronto: Stoddart Publishing, 1996).

Butler's Lives of the Saints, edited by Michael Walsh. Concise Edition Revised and Updated (San Francisco: HarperCollins, 1991).

Can God Be Trusted? Faith and the Challenge of Evil by John G. Stackhouse, Jr. (New York: Oxford University Press, 1998).

Dictionary of Mary (New York: Catholic Book Publishing Co., 1985).

Goddess of the Americas: La Diosa de las Américas: Writings on the Virgin of Guadalupe, edited by Ana Castillo (New York: Riverhead Books, 1996).

The Good Book: Reading the Bible with Mind and Heart by Peter J. Gomes (New York: Avon Books, 1996).

The HarperCollins Encyclopedia of Catholicism, edited by Richard P. McBrien (San Francisco: HarperCollins, 1995).

In Search of Mary: The Woman and the Symbol by Sally Cunneen (New York: Ballantine Books, 1996).

The Ironic Christian's Companion: Finding the Marks of God's Grace in the World by Patrick Henry (New York: Riverhead Books, 1999).

A Litany of Mary by Ann Ball (Huntington, Indiana: Our Sunday Visitor, 1988).

Magnificent Corpses: Searching Through Europe for St. Peter's Head, St. Chiara's Heart, St. Stephen's Hand, and Other Saints' Relics by Anneli Rufus (New York: Marlowe and Company, 1999).

Mary, Queen of Heaven: Miracles, Manifestations, and Meditations on Mary by Peg Streep (New York: Quality Paperback Book Club, 1997).

Meetings with Mary: Visions of the Blessed Mother by Janice T. Connell (New York: Ballantine Books, 1995).

Milagros: Votive Offerings from the Americas by Martha Egan (Santa Fe: Museum of New Mexico Press, 1991).

Miracles of Mary: Apparitions, Legends, and Miraculous Works of the Blessed Virgin Mary by Michael S. Durham (San Francisco: HarperCollins, 1995).

Miraculous Images of Our Lady: 100 Famous Catholic Portraits and Statues by Joan Carroll Cruz (Rockford, Illinois: TAN Books and Publishers, 1993).

Ockham's Razor: A Search for Wonder in an Age of Doubt by Wade Rowland (Toronto: Patrick Crean Editions, Key Porter Books, 1999).

Quantum Theology: Spiritual Implications of the New Physics by Diarmuid O'Murchu (New York: Crossroad Publishing, 1997).

Sacred Origins of Profound Things by Charles Panati (New York: Arkana, Penguin Books, 1996).

Searching for Mary: An Exploration of Marian Apparitions Across the U.S. by Mark Garvey (New York: Plume, 1998).

Shrines of Our Lady: A Guide to Fifty of the World's Most Famous Marian Shrines by Peter Mullen (London: Piatkus, 1998).

Sister Wendy's 1000 Masterpieces by Sister Wendy Beckett (New York: DK Publishing, 1999).

A Tremor of Bliss: Contemporary Writers on the Saints, edited by Paul Elie (New York: Riverhead Books, 1995).

Visions of Mary by Peter Eicher (New York: Avon Books, 1996).

Way Stations to Heaven: 50 Sites All Across America Where You Can Experience the Miraculous by Sandra Gurvis (New York: Macmillan General Reference, 1996).

The essay "Liars and Damned Liars" by Merilyn Simonds in *Brick: A Literary Journal* (Number 56, Spring 1997; Toronto) was essential to the development of this novel. This eloquent and insightful exploration of the fiction/nonfiction continuum helped to clarify my own thoughts on the subject. It started me thinking about Werner Heisenberg's uncertainty principle and all its further implications, which became a central theme of the novel. It suggested the anthropological example that appears in "History (6)." It pointed out how the meaning of the word *history* has changed over time and reminded me about Heraclitus' river and Herodotus' histories, all of which are included in "Knowledge." It also posed the question as to when they took the *story* out of *History,* which I asked again in "History (4)." Much of my theorizing on these topics throughout the novel must be credited directly to this essay.

A number of other books have been important for showing me the many ways to discover the "thin place" between fact and fiction and for helping me to find my own way. These include:

Alias Grace by Margaret Atwood (Toronto: McClelland & Stewart, 1996).

The Convict Lover: A True Story by Merilyn Simonds (Toronto: Macfarlane Walter & Ross, 1996).

Einstein's Dreams by Alan Lightman (Toronto: Alfred A. Knopf, 1993).

The English Patient and *Anil's Ghost* by Michael Ondaatje (Toronto: McClelland & Stewart, 1992 and 2000).

The French Mathematician by Tom Petsinis (New York: Penguin, 1998).

The Hours by Michael Cunningham (New York: Farrar, Straus & Giroux, 1998).

Impossible Saints by Michèle Roberts (London: Little, Brown, 1997).

The Lion in the Room Next Door by Merilyn Simonds (Toronto: McClelland & Stewart, 1999).

The Many Lives and Secret Sorrows of Josephine B; Tales of Passion, Tales of Woe; and *The Last Great Dance on Earth* by Sandra Gulland (Toronto: HarperCollins, 1995, 1998, and 2000).

Mariette in Ecstasy by Ron Hansen (New York: HarperCollins, 1991).

Santa Evita by Tomás Eloy Martínez, translated by Helen Lane (New York: Alfred A. Knopf, 1996).

Various Antidotes by Joanna Scott (New York: Henry Holt, 1994).

The Volcano Lover: A Romance by Susan Sontag (New York: Farrar, Straus & Giroux, 1992).

I believe that a writer is necessarily changed by the writing of a book. This, no doubt, is a further instance of Werner Heisenberg's uncertainty principle at work. It has certainly never been more true for me than in this case. Of paramount importance to the evolution not only of this novel but also of my own faith are the following books by Kathleen Norris:

Amazing Grace: A Vocabulary of Faith (New York: Riverhead Books, 1998).

The Cloister Walk (New York: Riverhead Books, 1996).

Dakota: A Spiritual Geography (Boston: Houghton Mifflin, 1993).

Meditations on Mary (New York: Viking Studio, 1999).

The Quotidian Mysteries: Laundry, Liturgy and "Women's Work," 1998 Madeleva Lecture in Spirituality (New York: Paulist Press, 1998).

The following Internet Web sites were also very useful:

The Catholic Encyclopedia at http://www.newadvent.org/cathen/

Catholic Online Saints and Angels at http://www.catholic.org/saints/
index.html

For All the Saints by Katherine L. Rabenstein at http://www.erols.
com/saintpat/ss/ss-index.htm

Hail Mary! Six Thousand Titles and Praise of Our Lady by Florent E.
Franke, M.D., at http://members.home.net/bob.hitt/Mary/Hail
Mary.html

Internet History Sourcebooks Project by Paul Halsall/Fordham University at http://www.fordham.edu/halsall/

The Mary Page at http://www.udayton.edu/mary/

Our Lady of Guadalupe at http://ng.netgate.net/~norberto/materdei.html

The video footage described in "Sightings" is from that 1996
television documentary and from a later one called *Signs from God:
Science Tests Faith* (Fox Broadcasting Company, 1999). The newspaper and magazine articles described in this chapter were actual
publications in *The Montreal Gazette*, *The Ottawa Citizen*, and *Life*.

The fictional story of Ellen Sanderson in "Faith" was inspired by
the actual story of Shirley Horkey as reported by Christie Blatchford
in *The National Post* on March 13, 1999. The questions listed in this
chapter were suggested by those in *Know Your Personality* by H. J.
Eysenck and Glenn Wilson (London: Penguin Books, 1975).

All the Biblical quotations used in this novel are taken from the
Authorized King James Version except where otherwise indicated.

I am grateful to the Canada Council for the Arts and the Ontario
Arts Council for their generous financial support.

For their many and various contributions to the writing of this
novel I would like to thank:

Margaret Atwood, Michael Durham, Father Andrew M. Greeley,
Genni Gunn, Diarmuid O'Murchu, John G. Stackhouse, Jr., Jane
Urquhart, and Reverend Mark Ward, for answering my questions;

Derek Besant, for the Marian mementos from Mexico and the wonderful descriptions of the veneration of Our Lady of Guadalupe;

the Beth Israel Synagogue Creative Writing Class, for our monthly meetings, which are always thought-provoking and inspiring;

Phyllis Bruce, Molly Stern, and Laurie Walsh, my editors, for their thoroughness, their kindness, their good humor, and their enthusiasm;

Jim Campbell, for remembering the graffiti on a bathroom wall in Guelph, Ontario, which I felt free to paraphrase;

Carla Douglas, for conversations about purses, lottery tickets, and obituaries;

Eric Folsom, for the photograph by Carol Stevenson called *Visitation at the Supermarket*;

Nora Gold, Wayne Grady, Katherine Lakeman, Jim Mountain, and Susan Townsend, for their enduring friendship;

Dr. William Closson James, for inviting me to read at the Queen's University Department of Religious Studies Biweekly Colloquia in October 1998, thus providing me with the perfect opportunity to give my Mary her world premiere;

Karl Mohr, for lending me his milagro cross until I could get one of my own;

Timothy Luke Meyer, for his masterful copyediting and his knowledgeable comments on the manuscript;

Bella Pomer, my agent, for her patience, her faith, and all her hard work on my behalf;

Gini Rosen, for her infectious energy and enthusiasm, and for broadening my knowledge of Werner Heisenberg;

Alexander Schoemperlen, my wonderful son, for being, as ever and always, the light of my life;

and especially to Merilyn Simonds, not only for her inspiring books and her important essay, but also for our conversations about the fiction/nonfiction continuum/conundrum, as well as about poetic justice, punctuation, list-making, ironing, dishes, flowers, spider veins, *les nuits blanches,* Madagascar Hissing Cockroaches, and the trials and jubilations of the writing life. I am privileged to call her my best friend.

PERMISSIONS